MW00560511

What others are saying about *Craft Brewed Jesus*

"A truly fascinating account, written by a self-identified former evangelical Christian, of a study group on a profound spiritual quest. Often meeting in local micro-brew pubs in Seattle, the group sought to understand authentic Christian discipleship in light of the latest historical and biblical scholarship. Even those who disagree with some of the conclusions reached will benefit greatly from the wealth of historical information and from the spiritual insights contained herein. Highly recommended.

—**Thomas Talbott**, Emeritus Professor of Philosophy, Willamette University; Author, *The Inescapable Love of God*

"Never yet has a book about the life and times of first-century Jerusalem and the world of the Jesus saga been written that even comes close to the work you have assembled here. I am completely blown away by this information."

—**Ken Dahl**, Author, *What Is God, And How Does It Work?: A Call for Honesty about Reality and Religion*

"The story of a group on a journey to explore Jesus and second Temple Judaism, *Craft Brewed Jesus* is instructional, poignant and often insightful. It is a beautiful study for anyone who seeks to understand or follow Jesus seriously. An exceptionally craft brewed book!"

—**Michael Hardin**, Executive Director of Preaching Peace; Co-editor of Compassionate Eschatology, Author, *The Jesus Driven Life*

"Have we constructed an entire religion around a vengeful God and forgotten that love keeps no record of wrongs? Michael Camp's book, *Craft Brewed Jesus*, rebuilds a framework for seeing God as love, not just in theory, but in actual practice—with historical reasons why it's not just wishful thinking. Despite its large scope, the book is surprisingly engaging. I read it like a starving person eating at a five-star restaurant. I won't tell you it's comfortable, because no such journey ever is. But the wind blew through my hair and I smelled fresh water on the mountain. Just when you start to squirm, Michael raises a glass and shares how far back in Christian history beer and this refreshing paradigm goes."

—**Wendy Francisco**, Singer; Songwriter; Editor; www.wendyfrancisco.com

"In a conversational style, Camp takes us on a journey through history, exploring the beginnings of faith and development of doctrines which have led to the variety of Christian expressions we see today. *Craft Brewed Jesus* invites the reader to wrestle with sorting out living spiritual truth from stagnant theological tradition. And all this while over a pint or two! My kind of book."

—**Bryan Berghoef**, Author, *Pub Theology: Beer, Conversation, and God*

Craft Brewed Jesus

Craft Brewed Jesus

How History We Never Knew Taps
a Spirituality We Really Need

Michael Camp

RESOURCE *Publications* • Eugene, Oregon

CRAFT BREWED JESUS
How History We Never Knew Taps a Spirituality We Really Need

Resource Publications
An Imprint of Wipf and Stock Publishers
199 W. 8th Ave., Suite 3
Eugene, OR 97401

www.wipfandstock.com

PAPERBACK ISBN: 978-1-4982-3467-2
HARDCOVER ISBN: 978-1-4982-3469-6

Manufactured in the U.S.A.

To Lori,
with love and gratitude

Contents

Author's Note

THIS IS LARGELY A work of creative nonfiction with a dose of my own artistic liberty. It's based on the true story of my friends and me studying Christian history together over the course of a year or so. One of us developed an outline of that history called *The Timeline*. We met in each other's homes to watch documentaries and discuss the readings and our findings. Moreover, we often met at local pubs and restaurants for further discussions. Where the story veers from a precise factual record is when I sometimes create settings, dialogue, and some character's conclusions that carry the story forward but may not reflect exactly how it happened. I trust you will overlook this side track off the nonfiction path and understand the inner journey we all took is a substantially true account.

Acknowledgments

Craft Brewed Jesus would not be possible without the small city of supporters in my life who encouraged me every step along the way to question the status quo, honestly tell the story, write with abandon, and not dwell on what other people think.

To John Paul, thanks for your insatiable curiosity to seek and find the truth and for your meticulous research on *The Timeline*. You inspired this story.

Thanks Nancy Benham and Lang Charters for your commendations about the content and suggestions to improve the manuscript. To Ken Dahl, you blew me away with your initial response and really encouraged me.

To Bryan Tomasovich, thanks for your developmental edits and advice on how to complete this project.

I want to especially thank my pub theology and discussion group. Your questions, insights, experiences, and own research helped forge the *Craft Brewed Jesus* journey. Thanks to Nancy Benham, Tom Benham, Lang Charters, John Paul, Jan Paul, Lori Camp, Tony Alivdrez, Marlyce Wright-Alivdrez, Sonia Lien, Beverly Goodman, Nola Whitsett, Gary Ley, Georgina Loughead, and many others who visited our group from time to time.

Michael Hardin, I am honored you were willing to read a later draft and so grateful for your kind and supportive words.

Bryan Berghoef, ever since we met, I feel a kinship with you as a fellow pub theologian. Thanks for inspiring me to write another "beer-themed" book on faith.

To the folks at Wipf & Stock, Matthew Wimer, Amanda Wehner, Brian Palmer, and James Stock, I'm so grateful for your belief in this book and all the ways you helped it come to fruition.

Finally, a heartfelt acknowledgment goes to my wife, Lori. Thanks for all the love, support, and patience you so graciously extended during the researching and writing process.

Chapter One

Why We Need a New Spirituality

I'M CONVINCED AMERICA NEEDS a new spirituality. Desperately. One rooted in reason, love, and a worldview grounded in sound, historical evidence, not in religious fundamentalism or pseudo-spiritual wishful thinking. One not at odds with reality. And one that allows you to responsibly enjoy good, craft beer. As we'll learn, after all, this is what the monks of old did.

The premise of this journey you are about to embark on is that modern America is spiritually broken. On one hand, traditional Christian faith is being increasingly questioned from all sides. A Barna Group study reveals a serious image problem for Christianity, most notably for conservatives (about 34 percent of the population), with perceptions of adherents as "hypocritical," "insensitive," "judgmental," and "anti-gay,"[1] undoubtedly fueled by evangelical scandals over the years[2] and a reputation for being anti-intellectual.[3] Young evangelicals David Kinnaman and Gabe Lyons presented the results of this groundbreaking research of sixteen to twenty-nine-year-olds in their book *unChristian: What a New Generation Really Thinks about Christianity . . . and Why It Matters.*

Another 22 percent of Americans are Catholics, 21 percent are mainline or other Protestants, and a small minority are of other religions. It's no

1. Kinnaman and Lyons, *unChristian*, 22–23.

2. Jim Bakker served time in federal prison in the early 90s for fraud and conspiracy charges; Jimmy Swaggert was implicated in sex scandals involving prostitutes in the 90s; in 2006 Ted Haggard, a mega-church pastor and the president of the National Association of Evangelicals, admitted using crystal meth and being involved with a male prostitute, and in 2007, Richard Roberts, son of the late Oral Roberts, was forced to resign as president of Oral Roberts University when he was named as a defendant in a lawsuit alleging improper use of university funds, to name a few.

3. E.g., see Noll, *Scandal of the Evangelical Mind.*

secret that Catholic churches, notwithstanding the rising popularity and refreshing progressive outlook of Pope Francis, as well as mainline Protestant churches, have been declining for years.

On the other hand, nearly 20 percent of Americans are grouped into what sociologists call "nones," that is, people who have no religious affiliation at all. Of these, nearly 6 percent are atheists or agnostics while the remainder is often called "spiritual but not religious." "Nones" are growing at a rapid pace.[4] The atheistic brand are the ones most likely to mock people of faith—think Bill Maher, Sam Harris, and Richard Dawkins. They claim tolerance for well-meaning religious people but preach to their followers to "show contempt for faith."[5] "Nones" who prefer the "spiritual but not religious" label are most likely to be ambiguous about what they believe or hungry for someone to give them a reasoned, more focused spirituality. A subset of Nones are "Dones," people who are done with church but still might believe. A recent Pew Research Center survey confirms all of these trends showing all Christian traditions dropping as a share of the US population while the religiously unaffiliated is rising.[6]

Taken together, most of these groups engage in our modern, American culture war, each taking conservative or liberal positions and accusing the other of either abandoning our religious roots or using faith to legislate morality. Could it be that both positions are misguided?

Consider this claim that sheds light on our society: With some notable exceptions, few of us Americans, whether evangelicals, progressive Christians, or "nones," have a faith or lack of faith that is informed by sound, historical facts and evidence. Or, the history we purport to "know" is only half the story. For example, conservatives largely base their faith on a Christian worldview that ignores swaths of historical and biblical scholarship. When they cite the roots of "Christian" America, they conveniently forget the widespread tradition of universalism among early settlers (e.g., the Moravians and Quakers) and its adherents among famous Americans (e.g., John Murray, George Washington, Benjamin Franklin, John Adams, Abraham Lincoln, Harriet Beecher Stowe, Hannah Whitall Smith, Hannah Hurnard, and many others). They also ignore historical evidence that shows America

4. "'Nones' on the Rise," Pew Research Center, October 9, 2012, http://www.pewforum.org/2012/10/09/nones-on-the-rise.

5. Grossman, "Richard Dawkins to Atheist Rally."

6. "America's Changing Religious Landscape," Pew Research Center, May 12, 2015, http://www.pewforum.org/2015/05/12/americas-changing-religious-landscape.

is really not a Christian nation and never was.[7] Liberals, on the other hand, although perhaps clued in to more good history (e.g., the myth of Christian America), still sometimes base their faith (or lack thereof) on that same warped historical and biblical perspective. They, for instance, seem unaware that Jesus did not found a new religion or institutional church (but a way of life that transcends all religions and philosophies). They either perpetuate a liberal version of institutional Christianity or reject Christianity altogether on the grounds that it is a corrupt institution. Strident atheists like Sam Harris likewise base their evaluation of Christianity on the unhistorical paradigm of modern fundamentalism/evangelicalism.

For these reasons, it's time to take a second look at what really transpired in early Christian history; to learn how the Christian, first-century sacred texts (the New Testament and other writings) were compiled and what they really taught based on linguistic and historical evidence (as far as is possible); to understand how a fresh view of history can change our perception of our world, undercut the foundation of our culture wars, possibly initiate a ceasefire, and finally, offer hope for the future. For believers, a second look can actually strengthen one's faith and passion to follow Jesus, not erode it. It can bolster one's convictions when one discovers a perspective more in line with reason, personal experience, and a comprehensive view of history. For unbelievers, a second look can help one see there's no need or basis to either have contempt for faith or be defensive about skepticism. In other words, learning earliest Christian history can lead to a new spirituality based on reality that respects both faith and doubt.

How to Gain a Fresh Perspective

A fresh approach is needed to take this second look. For many people, it can't be done within the confines of the organized church. As will be reinforced along the way, institutional religion rarely allows people to think for themselves and come to their own conclusions. I call this new perspective on the early Jesus movement and Christian history a *Craft Brewed Jesus*—one mirrored by the craft beer movement in America today. As craft brewers are small, independent, innovative, use ingredients based on historic styles, and tend to be involved in their communities through charitable giving, followers of a craft brewed Jesus are not entrenched in large corporate,

7. See Boyd, *Myth of a Christian Nation*, and Noll et al., *In Search for Christian America*.

institutional religion, they think for themselves, take the historic path to truth, and give back out of love for humanity.

Craft Brewed Jesus is more than the title of a book. It's an approach of spiritual or philosophical wayfarers who no longer entrust themselves to religious or secular dogma. They are free to cross boundaries and go outside institutional barriers. For believers, it's the path that's willing to rethink traditional theology in light of new discoveries. We are no longer confined to a pew where masses listen to one-way preaching, or when discussion is allowed, it is hemmed in by church walls. We can enter into a two-way exchange in a pub, café, or other open setting. We are free to question, explore, and follow where the religious and historical evidence leads.

How Bad It Is

How has ignorance of history and biblical scholarship negatively shaped our world? Before we look at dogmatic brands of liberalism and modern science, let's look more closely at conservative Christianity. Thirty-four percent of Americans consider themselves born again Christians, with most affiliated with evangelical denominations.[8] Most of these are biblical literalists, in that they believe the entire Bible is the authoritative "Word of God" and "our only guide for faith and practice." They rarely question traditional biblical interpretations. They are the ones most likely to be certain about their faith, immersed in our nation's culture war, and accused of pursuing political power in the name of God. Depending on who does the math, they believe two-thirds or more of humankind will wind up in an everlasting hell because they failed to "accept Christ." Although experience tells us most of them are nicer and smarter than their theologies, and that there are many notable exceptions to this among some evangelical churches, there is countless documentation on their dirty little secret: many streams of conservative Christianity border on cults and are guilty of what is called *spiritual abuse*.

In my first book, *Confessions of a Bible Thumper*, I threw a lot of stones at American evangelicalism as a former, committed evangelical missionary and church leader. Progressive evangelicals, people in the "emergent" church, and mainline Christians welcomed my message, even if not in full agreement, while traditionalists had a predictable response. They cried foul and threw stones back. Regardless, my intention was not to bruise believers but to offer loving, constructive criticism of an American religious movement

8. Wright, "How Many Americans."

that, despite being well meaning, is in dire need of a new spiritual paradigm. This book takes steps beyond critique to suggest positive change.

With some exceptions, much of American conservative Christianity is imploding. Let's first look at exceptions so we can see clearly what the issues are. During the 2014 Ebola crisis, most Americans saw and heard Dr. Kent Brantly in some news story on how he contracted Ebola while heroically caring for patients in Liberia early on in the outbreak. What many may not have realized was that Dr. Brantly was serving in an organization called Samaritan's Purse, a conservative Christian aid agency headed by Franklin Graham, son of Billy Graham. Dr. Brantly credited his recovery to his personal faith and the concerned prayers of thousands of like-minded believers. He deserves the hero title and the admiration of all of us. Few would be so courageous.

As evidenced by this example, evangelicalism has always had two noteworthy strengths to which its followers have been attracted. One, encouraging personal connection to God through Jesus, and two, a focus on practical love and assistance for the needy. These are what drew me and many of my friends into the movement back in the 1980s. We were encouraged to seek God personally and had profound spiritual experiences. I served in evangelical aid/mission agencies or churches, that had these values for many years (Food for the Hungry, Wellesley Baptist Church, Mission to Unreached Peoples, World Concern, and World Vision). These commendable values are not the reason for the evangelical/fundamentalist implosion occurring today. Conservative Christianity has an image problem because of its warped theology and the negative impact of that theology on people, not because of its focus on personal spirituality and outreach to the poor and needy. So what is the core problem?

Fifty years after the American Jesus Movement of the sixties and seventies, when youth and hippie culture sought spiritual freedom in Jesus, and when many of us discovered the presence of a personal loving God, scandals continue to rock fundamentalist/evangelical Christianity. The core of the problem is *control* in the guise of submitting to biblical imperatives.

Let's look at some examples. In the seventies, a movement arose in evangelical and charismatic churches called "shepherding." Despite its good intentions to enable church leaders to care for their "flock" (not a bad notion in and of itself), it ultimately adopted abusive techniques to keep church members obedient to God and church authorities.[9] It was exposed

9. "What Is Heavy Shepherding?," http://www.gotquestions.org/heavy-shepherding.

as an idolatrous religious system, in which leaders act as God over followers. Think cults. The problem is, this extreme form of "pastoral care" never really went away. Only the terms and structure changed.[10] I daresay a minor or major form of it exists in most conservative, charismatic, and evangelical churches today. Why? Because there's a foundation of bad theology not informed by earliest Christian history.

Most evangelical churches have an erroneous belief in "church authority" and what some call the need for "spiritual covering." One example is my former church I wrote about in my previous book, Sovereign Grace Ministries (SGM). Myriad ex-members have painstakingly documented spiritual abuse in SGM churches across the nation.[11] It's another form of shepherding that seeks to control people. Examples include: in the name of "discipleship" members are taught only to marry inside the denomination or its associations; to unquestioningly support leadership even when there are glaring dysfunctions; to accept "church discipline" for not following legalistic interpretations of the Bible, and to get leadership approval for personal decisions. People who resist are shunned or told to leave the church because they have "a problem with authority." In 2013, twenty churches left the SGM denomination. A civil lawsuit has been brought against the legal church entity and several leaders (including founder C. J. Mahaney, whom I met, and two others I counted as friends from my involvement in the 1980s) accusing them of covering up sexual abuse in the church in the name of handling matters "biblically." One of my friends in the SGM church my wife and I attended wrote a book about this trend of irresponsible handling of sexual abuse. She was kicked out of the church when she exposed it.[12] Leading evangelical authorities have defended SGM and C. J. Mahaney despite the mounting evidence against them.[13] Because conservative evangelicals tend to think cases like this are isolated, they find superficial solutions to these types of problems. But SGM is not an isolated case.

Another example is Mars Hill Church, a mega-church family of congregations based in my current home of Seattle. One of its founding

html.

10. "Shepherding Movement—Reformed, Revamped, Reee-diculous," *Wartburg Watch*, April 9, 2009, http://thewartburgwatch.com/2009/04/09/the-shepherding-movement-%E2%80%93-reformed-revamped-reee-diculous.

11. See these websites or blogs: "SGM Survivors," "SGM Refuge," "SGM Nation," and "BrentDetwiler."

12. Melancon, *Things I Learned*.

13. John Piper and Albert Mohler of the Gospel Coalition.

pastors, Mark Driscoll, arose in the 1990s as a relevant, fresh leader bringing "the gospel" to one of the most "unchurched" cities in America. His was a hipster veneer—once known as "the cursing pastor"—with a conservative, Calvinistic, theological core. By all accounts, in the beginning, it appeared like a healthy Christian community with a passion for spiritual and practical outreach.

But by the mid-2000s Mars Hill Church was a regular subject on Seattle's KOMO 4 news station with reports by ex-members of obsessive control (a different form of shepherding), spiritual abuse, outright bullying, manipulation, and shunning members put under "church discipline."[14] Later were reports of mishandling ministry funds, plagiarism on the part of Mark Driscoll, mandatory signing for pastors of a "Unity of Mission" clause that amounts to a non-compete agreement for future ministry or else face dismissal, and using church money to hire an agency to help one of Driscoll's books reach the *NY Times* bestseller list. One fellow evangelical, Tullian Tchividjian, pastor of Coral Ridge Presbyterian Church in Florida said, "It was a one-man show, Mark's way or the highway. He was in complete and total control."[15] Paul Tripp, another pastor and former member of the Mars Hill board of advisors and accountability brought in to help mediate the conflict, said, "This [Mars Hill Church] is without a doubt, the most abusive, coercive ministry culture I've ever been involved in."[16]

When I visited one of the downtown Seattle churches in early 2013, I was shocked to see the tightness of Driscoll's grip. All sermons in fourteen branch churches were preached by Driscoll. They were video-streamed from the church headquarters. More than half of the books and DVDs in the church "bookstore" were by Driscoll. When questioned, members saw no potential problems with this. It was a personality cult.

Mars Hill eventually went into free fall as at least nine former elders and another umbrella organization Driscoll helped start called Acts 29 finally called for Driscoll's resignation. Despite a leave of absence and some public apologies from Driscoll, he remained in control. Finally, amid mounting pressure, he resigned in 2014, although the then current church elders still declared him "fit for ministry." This infuriated accusers because it appeared

14. See http://marshillrefuge.blogspot.com; http://joyfulexiles.com; https://www.facebook.com/groups/433217200154935 (We Are Not Anonymous); and http://musingsfromunderthebus.wordpress.com.

15. Bailey, "How the 'Cussin' Pastor' Got into Megatrouble."

16. Throckmorton, "Mark Driscoll," 1.

like neither Driscoll nor the church elders could acknowledge how serious the abuse was. By the end of 2014, the centralized Mars Hill church folded and the local churches either became independent or closed their doors.

The problem is this new reorganization does nothing to address the root problems with Mars Hill. Church organization was not the main problem. The new Mars Hill structure—centralized churches becoming autonomous, self-governing entities—is still susceptible to spiritually abusive practices. Autonomous churches are the model of the highly-abuse-susceptible Calvary Chapel, as we'll see. Even Driscoll was not the main issue. Getting rid of or reforming one bad apple doesn't solve it. The problem is much deeper. The remaining former Mars Hill churches don't get this. Neither does wider evangelicalism, evidenced by mega-church evangelical pastor Rick Warren preaching the last sermon at Mars Hill before the reorganization.

As we'll discover when we examine history, the problem within modern "Bible-believing" churches isn't an occasional autocratic leader or ill-conceived church polity. The root problem has to do with bad theology based on a poor study of history. A theology that leads churches to idolize the Bible, church authority, and charismatic personalities to the point of warping the message of Jesus and spiritually abusing people.

Then there's the fear-based, escapist "rapture" and "end times" paranoia that gained popularity in the seventies and continues to manipulate people today to abandon hope for an earthly future (and conversely, only have hope for a heavenly one). Most notably, is how much this warped end-of-the-world theology is accepted in mainstream Christianity, as evidenced by the widely popular, best-selling *Left Behind* book series by Tim LaHaye and its movie counterpart released in 2014 starring Nicolas Cage. In the worst case study of this belief, members of a Christian church in South Korea, heavily influenced by American evangelicals, committed suicide or abandoned their families when a popular "return of Christ" prediction arose in 1992, and, lo and behold, failed to materialize.[17] Again, we'll see how this is based on bad theology based on a poor reading of history and an irresponsible handling of the New Testament.

Other familiar names come to mind. Bill Gothard, a popular fundamentalist teacher and conference leader starting in the 1980s eventually fell from grace (as a brand new evangelical Christian, I attended his widely popular "Basic Youth Seminar" in 1981, which is known for its extreme

17. Watanabe, "No Doomsday Rapture."

legalism regarding women in submission to men, God's design for authority, biblical obedience, and even rock music). In 2014, he resigned from his organization after allegations of sexually harassing women and failing to report child abuse cases. Ted Haggard, mega-church pastor and former president of the National Association of Evangelicals was ousted for living a double life and toying with homosexuality. Calvary Chapel, a popular evangelical denomination, has had its share of scandals over the years, including allegations of pastoral misconduct, lawsuits,[18] and spiritual abuse.[19] Many other church movements have seen ex-members set up websites that chronicle the authoritarian and abusive techniques of church leaders.[20]

In 2013, the evangelical organization named Exodus, the largest and most influential "ex-gay" ministry in the movement, folded and made the astounding admission that they were wrong in their counseling techniques that tried to "pray away the gay." They apologized to the LGBT community. "Exodus is an institution in the conservative Christian world, but we've ceased to be a living, breathing organism. For quite some time we've been imprisoned in a worldview that's neither honoring toward our fellow human beings, nor biblical," Alan Chambers, the former president, said.[21] Another former Exodus leader, John Paulk, says the "ex-gay" counseling technique known as "reparative therapy" not only doesn't work, but "does great harm to many people."

Other dysfunctions include the evangelical patriarchy movement, where men are taught it's their "biblical" right to control their wives and daughters. Wives are taught to submit to their husbands, not pursue professions outside the home, and sometimes are taught to refrain from the use of birth control. Daughters are expected to live at home under the authority of their fathers until he approves a husband for her who takes over that authority. These are not taught as options, but a lifestyle commanded by God.

For these and other reasons, young evangelicals are leaving the church or abandoning the old theologies.[22] Everywhere I go, I meet restless evangelicals who have either left the movement or are gravitating toward its emergent, progressive arm. As author Barbara Symons attests in her

18. Brodersen, "Case for Big Change."

19. See Calvary Chapel Abuse (blog), http://calvarychapelabuse.com/wordpress.

20. See blogs: marshillrefuge.blogspot.com, sgmsurvivors.com, sgmrefuge.com, calvarychapelabuse.com, and spiritualsoundingboard.com.

21. "Exodus International Shuts Down," *Huffington Post*, June 20, 2013.

22. As documented by Kinnaman and Lyons, *unChristian*.

journey of escape from "Christianity," these issues are by no means isolated. They are rampant.[23] In my experience, whether it's church authoritarianism, biblical literalism, or assessments on homosexuality, the root of these abuses is a Christian worldview that has lost its grounding in history.

Now, let's take a look at secular America. It has its own form of fundamentalism. With some exceptions, it is awash in materialistic dogma that spurns anything spiritual in the name of science. Richard Dawkins says faith is largely dangerous in his book *The God Delusion*. Sam Harris states "faith is a conversation stopper" and "theology is ignorance with wings."[24] He claims, "It is time that we admitted that faith is nothing more than the license religious people give one another to keep believing when reasons fail."[25] Bill Maher, in his 2008 "mockumentary" film, *Religulous*, asserts, "The irony of religion is that because of its power to divert man to destructive courses, the world could actually come to an end. The plain fact is, religion must die for mankind to live."[26]

As Frank Schaeffer argues in in his book *Patience with God*, these "New Atheists" like Dawkins, Harris, and Maher are only a secular version of religious fundamentalists. Both secular and religious fundamentalists insist they own the truth. According to them, any diversion from it means you're either a fallen-away heretic or a dim-witted religious idiot. As conservative Christians claim progressives and liberals are unbiblical at best and apostate or dangerous at worst, and that America must renounce its unfaithful ways or lose the blessings of God, secular religionists claim faith is "ignorant," "unreasoned," and "destructive," and its death is key to our survival. At the end of the day, both sets of claims sound the same. Believe the way we do or else.

What new atheists miss is how much they are engaging in the same form of black-and-white thinking they claim religious people have. They astutely and rightly critique unthinking, literalist, exclusivist, fundamentalist religion. But they rarely imagine that faith in God doesn't require that one stop thinking or using reason, or one never question the Bible, or one must believe in the doctrine of hell. Gaining a new perspective on history actually reveals the opposite. Thinking, reasoning, historically critiquing

23. Symons, *Escaping Christianity*; Escobar, *Faith Shift*; and Evans, *Faith Unraveled*.

24. Harris, "Goodreads Quotes," https://www.goodreads.com/author/quotes/16593.Sam_Harris.

25. Harris, *Letter to a Christian Nation*.

26. "Religulous Quotes," IMDb, http://www.imdb.com/title/tt0815241/quotes.

the Bible (which is not equal to altogether tossing it), and rejecting the traditional view of the afterlife are part of a historically-grounded faith.

What's more is the form of secular thought that often cites science as the solution to all of humankind's problems, as Neil deGrasse Tyson implies in the new 2014 television show, *Cosmos*. Producer Ann Druyan hopes audiences will "take the revelations of science and act accordingly," in terms of saving the planet environmentally. But science in itself has no authority to change someone to "act accordingly" whether to avert global warming or be a more caring person. As important as science is, it is limited. It cannot form our ethics or sense of purpose. It can tell us how our world works but not its meaning. Spirituality can.

Science must be in tandem with spirituality and ethics in order to be effective in making the world a better place. Moreover, science can inspire and spur important questions about our spiritual heritage and origins that an open-minded society should address. A new spirituality can bridge the gap between science and faith (and between rationality and mysticism), not insisting they must always be kept separate, but allowing open, respectful dialogue on the implications for each field of study—one that can respect both a materialistic and theistic perspective without each mocking the other. One that refuses to become a fundamentalist on either the religious or materialistic side.

Lights in the Darkness

To be sure, there is a vibrant, open-minded spiritual movement in America. From progressives represented by authors such as Diana Butler Bass, Brian McLaren, Phyllis Tickle, Rob Bell, Anne LaMott, Rachel Held Evans, Brad Jersak, Doug Pagitt, and Frank Schaeffer to movements like the Wild Goose Festival, Darkwood Brew (a "convergence" of mainline Christians and post-evangelicals), and other "Emergent" streams, to nontraditional Jesus scholars, such as the late Marcus Borg and John Dominic Crossan. In addition, there are many more progressive evangelicals (envelope pushers) than most people realize that are comfortable rubbing elbows with these folks. People like N. T. Wright, Philip Yancey, and Greg Boyd. In fact, I have found myself at home within this progressive movement and find it exhilarating and refreshing in contrast to my legalistic, largely closed-minded, conservative evangelical past (yes, there were exceptions).

What's more, there appears to be a healthy melding of faith and science today as evidenced by the types of books that have arisen in recent years. For example, Antony Flew, a renowned atheist committed to following where the evidence would lead, wrote about his personal evolution from materialist to theist (nowhere near the fundamentalist variety) in his book *There Is a God: How the World's Most Notorious Atheist Changed His Mind*. Apart from a minor section in the Appendix, the book is solely about reason, the laws of nature, cosmology, and the teleological organization of life. It is not a "biblical" argument. And it doesn't have to be. Contrary to what some fundamentalists might claim about all truth deriving from the Bible, God gave us reason, logic, science, and reflection through which we can encounter the Divine.

Likewise, renegade evangelical and theistic evolutionist Francis Collins argues persuasively for a faith-science bridge in *The Language of God: A Scientist Presents Evidence for Belief*. Moreover, in his books *Proof of Heaven: A Neurosurgeon's Journey into the Afterlife* and *Map of Heaven: How Science, Religion, and Ordinary People Are Proving the Afterlife*, Dr. Eben Alexander urges readers to embrace a new open-minded spirituality that recognizes both the scientific pointers to a spiritual realm and the firsthand testimony and statistics of near-death experiences.

Another example is Krista Tippett exploring "the nexus of science and spirituality" in *Einstein's God: Conversations about Science and the Human Spirit*. In ten illuminating interviews with scientists—from cosmologist and astrobiologist Paul Davies to physicist and theologian John Polkinghorne, she explores the roots for a rational faith based on scientific findings. As Davies states, "For me the crucial thing is that the universe is not only beautiful and harmonious and ingeniously put together, it is also fit for life. . . . The universe has not only given rise to life, it's not only given rise to mind, it's given rise to thinking beings who can comprehend the universe. Through science and mathematics, we can, so to speak, glimpse the mind of God." And on the remarkable nature of the science behind the universe's fitness for life: "You soon discover you need to fine-tune those settings to extraordinary precision in order for there to be life. And the question is, what are we to make of that?"[27]

Finally, open-minded atheist Bradley Monton, while maintaining his philosophical stance, examines theistic arguments based on the science of

27. Tippett, *Einstein's God*, 35–36.

intelligent design theory (yes, the *science*, as he argues) in his book *Seeking God in Science: An Atheist Defends Intelligent Design*.

Both Christian and secular fundamentalists reject the ideas in such books because the conclusions are not doctrinally pure—either religious purity that insists on traditional faith, biblical creationism, or "Christian" terminology; or scientific purity that insists on materialistic evolution or non-theistic explanations. But a new spirituality welcomes them because they are honest, reasoned, and evidence based.

Despite these lights, I worry about the progressive Christian and "spiritual-but-not-religious" movements in America represented by some of these examples. I'm concerned that they don't realize how important well-studied history is to a grounded faith, and because of that, they will abandon an approach to follow where the historical evidence leads, and accept any and every idea that comes along even if it has no sound, historical underpinning.

This brings us to where this story really begins. How my friends and I discovered how much history matters. And how we learned in-depth examples of how history can and should inform our faith or lack of faith. How it sheds light on a new spiritual paradigm that we desperately need. It started with a group of spiritual seekers enjoying good food, wine, and beer and wondering about the origins of their spiritual heritage. It included a lot about the history and importance of beer and brewing. This is your invitation. Grab your favorite brew, and join us on this path to find a "craft brewed Jesus," one rooted in history. Not the traditional history you may have heard. Not revisionist history. Not bad history. But good, solid, historical scholarship.

Chapter Two

Why History Matters

"THAT'S A LOT OF books!" I told Dan. "Did you read them all?"

"Pretty much," Dan said. "But I have the advantage of being semi-retired."

It was the night of our regular discussion group we attend and Dan had laid out all these books on his dining room table for all of us to see. It was an impressive array, maybe thirty or so. Dan was equally impressive. A dentist who served in the Navy and a fellow craft-brewed-Jesus seeker (also a major character in my first book), Dan had embarked on an enormous research project last year. He began studying Christian history and its foundations without a sectarian agenda. In the course of one year, he read a plethora of books by a variety of authors. These books on the table represented the majority of them.

I glanced them over and in my mind added a few more that I had read to round them out. There was conservative Lee Strobel to agnostic Bart Erhman and most everyone in between. Moreover, there was pretty much every major scholar representing a variety of persuasions.[1] We also had a nice collection of historical studies and teaching on DVDs or podcasts.[2] So with Dan's leadership, our discussion group started down this path to study Christian history, which we called *The Timeline*. For some of us, it was a unique opportunity to look at Christianity with a critical eye. During the

1. Karen Armstrong, Diane Butler-Bass, Marcus Borg, Greg Boyd, Walter Brueggemann, Harvey Cox, John Dominic Crossan, Jacques Ellul, Bart Ehrman, Brian McLaren, Robin Meyers, Mark Noll, Robin Parry, Lee Strobel, Thomas Talbott, Frank Viola, Garry Wills, N. T. Wright, and many more.

2. "Saving Jesus," "Living the Questions," "Unbelievable" (Premier Christian Radio UK podcasts), "Bill Moyers Faith and Reason," "Beyond Our Differences," "The Place," and many more.

weeks and months ahead, much of what we read or heard and discussed in Dan's and his wife Gina's cozy living room and in local brewpubs was not even on the radar of our former evangelical or Catholic churches. It was the stuff your church never taught you.

Over the weeks we became engrossed in a historical drama that traced the origins, culture, communities, personalities, ancient texts, institutions, doctrines, and practices within Christianity over the centuries. We found lost history, unknown culture, obscure sects, an underground church, lost sacred writings, untold stories, neglected facts, and new paradigms on Scripture, the kingdom of God, and what it means to follow Christ. We had been stuck in the dark shadows behind enormous religious edifices the church and society had built and we were finally given the means to dispel the darkness and reveal the untold. Slowly, a more accurate picture of Christ, those he impacted, and their history began to emerge—one that in some ways, we scarcely recognized. It wasn't that everything was new, but that what was new made an enormous difference. This new paradigm made more sense and had the ring of truth to it. *Craft Brewed Jesus* is the way we traveled this historical journey. It taught us why history matters.

One of the first things we learned was that we can't be certain about many things. Mystery still abounds. But there are such things as historical facts and evidence. It's not a precise science, but nonetheless, it is a study with a scientific method that works in the realm of probabilities. Historians cite evidence or "traceable factors" to establish a high probability that something happened. No one can prove or know for sure whether Jesus was born of a virgin woman, but we can know with a virtually certain degree of probability that Jesus lived as a Jewish wisdom teacher in the first century and spurred a counter-cultural movement opposed to both the Jewish temple religious system and Roman imperialism. We know he was crucified by the Romans circa 30 CE in collaboration with certain Jewish religious authorities. We know his life and teachings have been documented, albeit with some disputes over what was original and what wasn't, in first-century sacred texts (the New Testament, the Gospel of Thomas, the Gospel of Peter, etc.) as well as other historical writings, such as Josephus, Tacitus, and Pliny the Younger.

We can know with high probability what many of those teachings meant to the original audience when we study them in the original Greek and place them into the mindset of Jewish and first-century culture. We can know with good confidence that Jesus was not a violent zealot as author Reza Aslan claims in his book *Zealot: The Life and Times of Jesus of*

Nazareth, because there is strong historical evidence that blatantly contradicts that conclusion and there is no conclusive evidence for it. In short, it's a wild stretch. When I saw leading Jesus scholars Marcus Borg and John Dominic Crossan speak in Seattle in 2014, a questioner asked their opinion of Aslan's thesis. Trying to be kind in their assessments, Crossan called it "bad history" and Borg declared it was "cheap journalism." Similarly, we can know that the oft-claimed statement (that the New Atheists sometimes make) that "religion has been the cause of all major wars in history" is simply untrue, as religious historian Karen Armstrong attests in her book *Fields of Blood: Religion and the History of Violence*. History matters.

Why Study History

Another important point was how many of us have gotten away from learning in-depth history, thinking we already know it. We trust the traditions we have been taught—whether fundamentalism, evangelicalism, or liberalism—are faithful to the record. We are blind to the possibility that they may not be. Moreover, there is new information at our disposal. As Harvey Cox declares, our generation now "knows more about the actual origins of the Jesus movement than any generation since the first century itself."[3] Discoveries in archeology, biblical studies, early Christian writings, etc., give us a clearer picture. We need to revisit the history.

The result of our historical ignorance is we often misread and misrepresent the Bible, "church," and Christ. In turn, both believers and nonbelievers frequently base their opinion of Christianity, and how they live it out or respond to it, on false paradigms. Our study of *The Timeline* was our attempt to create a "historical fact checkers" version of contemporary Christian belief and practice. One that, as far as is humanly possible (in other words, our conclusions are not infallible and we don't pretend to have studied all pertinent sources), follows the Socratic principle: uncover the core narrative and go where the historical evidence leads. Moreover, allow that evidence to impact the way we view God and live in the world. In so doing, we felt we were able to strip away misconceptions and uncover a forgotten or lost Path of Christ.

As Harvey Cox also states, what we think we know as Christianity through the ages and today is often a faulty perspective that does not reflect its central core.

3. Cox, *Future of Faith*, 56.

> There can be little doubt that many people who today feel a strong attachment to the life and message of Jesus become disenchanted, and sometimes even disgusted, with much of what historic Christianity became. Despite many glowing moments, it is often not a pretty picture. But the picture can be clarified when we notice both how much of that historic Christianity is a caricature of its essential core and that some of the liveliest and most promising Christian movements today are casting off this distorting crust.[4]

The question arises, once we get a clearer picture, what do we do with it? Are we called to emulate some romantic model of first-century Christianity? Actually, one of the discoveries is that there is no one right model. As Cox says, "Knowing about the past is vital not to *return to* it, but to *learn from* it, from both its mistakes and successes."[5]

So, how do we get that clearer image? As we started to study *The Timeline*, we realized there had to be some specific goals in our pursuit. We needed to find answers to a variety of thought-provoking questions that would put things in focus. First, about the world of Jesus and what he taught. What was the sociocultural milieu in which Jesus arose in the first century? How does that impact the message of Jesus? What really is the "the good news of the kingdom," given the original audience who heard it? Did Jesus found a new religion? If not, how should society engage his teaching? Given a fresh look at the Greek language of the New Testament and certain historical developments, what did Jesus really teach about salvation, judgment, the "end times," and the afterlife? What, if anything, did he and the earliest church say about original sin, the atonement, reciting creeds, or confronting "heresy"?

Then there are questions about the Bible. How was the Bible complied, copied, and translated? Given that, does it follow that it is the inerrant Word of God supernaturally inspired down to every word? If not, how should we view it? How relevant is it for today? Is it reliable? Are there parts of it that are not authentic? What of the other sacred Christian texts that have been discovered? Are they worth reading and considering?

Then there is "church." Are modern churches with professional clergy the true expression of Christ's body on earth? If not, what is "church," how did the earliest followers gather together, and where did our modern

4. Ibid., 80.
5. Ibid., 57.

institutions come from? What is the Roman emperor Constantine's and that empire's influence on our modern churches?

Next are questions about the variety of Christian communities and social practices. What are some of the largely unknown other versions of Christianity in early church history and why have we rarely heard of them? For example, not just the gnostics (of whom a lot is written about in our day), but the Church of the East, the Jacobites, the Nestorians, and Monophysites. What made them controversial? Why is Eastern Orthodox theology so different from Western theology and why aren't we taught those differences?

What about social classes in Christianity? What was the attitude toward children, the impoverished, and the diseased in societies of antiquity and how did Jesus' teaching make a difference? What did the earliest Christ followers believe about women in ministry and leadership? What does the Bible really teach about homosexuality?

Finally, there's the future. What did the original authors of the Bible mean when they spoke of Christ coming again? Did they really predict the end of the world, possibly in a modern time frame? In light of the past, where are we headed?

Once we got a clearer image of the original Path of Christ in its historical and cultural context, we could compare it to our movements today. How have historical and modern Catholic, fundamentalist, evangelical, and liberal churches misrepresented the movement Jesus began? Why does it matter? How does a closer examination of history help modern believers pursue a more historical-critical and genuine faith? What can we—whether conservative, progressive, liberal, "none," or agnostic—learn from history? What are the half-truths that some Christian traditions have embraced? Regardless of our spiritual preference, does the original Path of Christ have something to teach us?

Part of our group's passion for historical underpinnings was born from my own personal journey and search that I chronicled in *Confessions of a Bible Thumper*. I discovered the benefits of good historical study and Dan picked up on that. Knowledge of good history opens eyes to new perspectives closer to the truth. The revelations we uncovered didn't lead us to atheism, but rather to a deeper appreciation for historic Christian origins. For me, it led me to a more vibrant, intellectually satisfying faith. When an average person of faith becomes a student of history, good things happen, like gaining confidence to question religious authority. Or, causing fundamentalist and black-and-white ways of thinking to fall by the wayside. This isn't a trail to absolute certainty but rather a way of open inquiry where the toughest questions are welcomed and encouraged but where no one insists we all come to the same conclusions and sign a definitive statement of faith.

Searching Outside Organized Religion

Dan, his wife, Gina, my wife, Lori, and I, two other couples, and other friends who joined us at local pubs from time to time learned an important lesson during our journeys. Authentic searches for the meaning of life and spiritual truth work best outside the confines of religious or secular institutions. Organized religion stifles free inquiry and honest questioning while dogmatic atheism uses false certainties to discredit any spiritual belief. When religious or secular belief is institutionalized, boundaries are drawn, over which followers cannot cross.

"Why do you think it's better to search for answers outside organized religion?" a visitor to our discussion group asked.

"Because most institutions don't allow free inquiry," Dan said.

"But I've been in churches that permit questioning," the visitor replied.

"I have, too," Dan said. "Of course, there are exceptions, but for most churches, it's not so much that they don't allow questions, but how much they only allow *safe* questions and how they try to control the conclusions you come to."

Dan began telling the story of the time he brought up a new book he had read called *The Inescapable Love of God*, by Thomas Talbott, at an evangelical Bible study he attended. "Because the book questioned traditional views of the afterlife, I got a very strong reaction. The leader warned me to not read such books, declaring them 'dangerous.' No matter how much I tried to explain to them how truly 'biblical' the book was, they balked."

"Oh, I see what you mean," our visitor said. "That would be a hot-potato topic. Now, I'm curious. What were the points you brought up?"

"That the author wasn't arguing to trash the New Testament, but that we need to rethink the concept of hell based on the original Greek and the teachings of many of the early church fathers. But even that was too radical for people reared in the organized church."

I explained to our visitors the definition of a craft-brewed approach to Jesus and spirituality and how it opens doors to honesty and more genuine spirituality. How a brew pub setting is far enough outside the strict bounds of traditional religion to set a spiritual wayfarer free—unbound by predetermined statements of faith and "biblical" codes of conduct. Drinking beer in a pub has a way of fostering friendships and honest dialogue. And as I am fond of saying, craft beer—microbrews made by one of 2,800 microbreweries in the United States—have a big edge on Bud Lite. My fellow pub theologian Bryan Berghoef says it well:

> It turns out a pub creates a perfect setting in which to encounter people who are interested in spiritual topics, philosophy, life, and—yes—theology, and they are open to being honest about it. For some, it even becomes a place to encounter God himself.[6]

"Honest" is the operative word. Finding God (or redefining God) in church works for some people, but it is too limiting. Genuine honesty—about faith and doubts—is often squelched in such institutions because of the phenomenon of group think—when pressure to conform overrides free thought. Frankly, it's not the location that is important, but one's attitude. It could just as well be a local espresso café. *Craft Brewed Jesus* represents an inclusive way that acknowledges and respects others' religious or nonreligious views and practices—even a fundamentalist view. Like most of us, fundamentalists are only expressing the worldview they have been taught. This inclusive way realizes people of any faith and no faith have something important to add to the conversation about the meaning of life. It embraces our pluralistic society and seeks to unite, not divide people.

In another angle, craft beer represents a grassroots approach to engaging theology. Microbrewers start out as amateurs who brew in their garage for the love of beer. When they go professional, it's a small-scale-production microbrewery serving a local community, brewing varieties that the owners want, not a large corporation with national distribution and set brew recipes. They are like local, amateur theologians who are not constrained by an organized institution but free to follow where the evidence leads them and where their tastes lie. The pursuit of theology in this way is egalitarian just as microbrewers are empowered to create whatever beer they want. It's not controlled in a hierarchical structure like a large corporation or church. For some, that is scary and doesn't feel secure. Without some structure, maybe one's theology will fall off the deep end. But there is a balance. As we learned, good history provides the safety net.

6. Berghoef, *Pub Theology*, xiv.

Moreover, as beer lovers all have personal tastes—some prefer bitter IPAs and others more Belgian styles or dark porters and stouts—personal theologies do as well. We all encounter God in our own way and shouldn't feel like our experience isn't genuine unless it matches another's. And just as a beer lover's taste will evolve—that bitter IPA is an acquired taste for some—our taste in God experiences change as well. As one of the discussion group members put it, "I couldn't stand IPAs when I first started drinking beer, but now I really prefer my beer more bitter than sweet. And so my theology and my experiences of God have also grown and changed over time. I now savor the bitter (doubts, questions) just as much as the sweet (promises, comfort) in my faith."

Such a path is inclusive. A Christian on this path welcomes the Jew, Muslim, Buddhist, Hindu, agnostic, atheist, and spiritual-but-not-religious to the table. The goal is not to replace traditional, dogmatic faith with a new postmodern version of dogmatic faith, but rather to allow respect and love to rule. Although changing one's beliefs may take place while one is on the "path," converting souls is not the goal. The goal is honest pursuit of answers to the mysteries of life—in an open, respectful environment. The result is experiencing God, honoring how he works in the world, encountering Jesus in a new light, or at least becoming awestruck with life's grandeur.

This is why there are only two cardinal rules of those following a *craft brewed Jesus*. One, to fearlessly pursue historical, scriptural, and intellectual honesty, and two, to follow the way of love—one objective that remains the foundation of Jesus' teaching and one that most major religions and philosophies affirm. Historical honesty and love are the only structure that is required to create a safe environment. Those on this path trust that the pursuit of love for our fellow humans is the most important endeavor. For the theist, in so doing, we demonstrate our love for God. These two rules, honesty and love, are the foundation. When you add an optional third rule—only pursue consumption of quality craft beer—a spirited, meaningful, and satisfying conversation that binds people together will ensue!

Dan had compiled a half-inch thick document that represented *The Timeline*. As he passed it out that night, he explained how we would go through it, choosing books and/or DVDs to read or watch before discussing each section. We tried to choose the most credentialed and reputable scholars and historians, realizing they didn't always agree with each other. But we were determined to approach the material with an open mind, and to the best of our ability, follow where the evidence led.

As for the discussions, in reality, sometimes these discussions occurred inside Dan and Gina's home and sometimes other friends joined us for discussions in pubs. So, our journey began in earnest. It started by traveling back in time to first-century Palestine under Roman occupation. We were about to learn the religious culture and political environment in which Jesus taught. We had no idea how much Jewish purity codes played a role and how they shed light on Jesus' teaching. We were about to find out.

Yet, there was another history lesson I had to explore first to set up our journey. It had to do with the history of beer. I encountered it on a trip to a Seattle microbrewery.

Chapter Three

The Good News: Redrawing the Purity Map

DEEP INSIDE THE PIKE Brewery & Restaurant in downtown Seattle is the microbrewery museum. One evening as I was enjoying a Scotch ale called the Kilt Lifter, I had the privilege of meeting The Pike's owners Rose Ann and Charles Finkle, who called the room to my attention. Pointing to the walls inside a room voted by *Seattle Magazine* as "Best place to learn about beer," Charles proudly showed me the framed commentary, drawings, and photos that told the fascinating story of ten thousand years of brewing from the ancient civilization of Sumer (in modern Iraq) to cosmopolitan Seattle.

Incredible, I told myself. *Not only is this one of the best places in Seattle to drink beer, it's like the school of beer!* It really was.

When I saw the words "Beer and the Church" and the sign that read "900–1500 AD—Beer is introduced to the Western world by the Catholic Church," I knew I had found what I sought: the origins of the beer industry in the West, and more specifically, the connection to the brewing monks of old.

During the Middle Ages, Christian monasteries became some of the first enterprises to brew beer for trade, I learned from the material in the room and other research I did. "While monks led a solitary life of work and prayer, they also believed in hospitality and charity. Monasteries were renowned as places of refuge for travelers seeking a safe, clean place with decent food and drink."[1] With few if any healthy sources of water available, brewing, which included a boiling process, was a way to sanitize the water

1. Barnes, "Brief History of the Trappist Order," 1.

and add nutrients. It thus became popular with the lower classes and an important part of people's daily diet.

In 820 CE, the Saint Gall monastery, located in modern-day Switzerland, built what became the prototype for the medieval monastic brewery. The monks constructed three breweries: one for sojourners and paying customers, one for the monks' own consumption, and one to brew "charity beer" for the poor.[2]

Another day in Poulsbo, Washington (my current hometown), inside another favorite watering hole, while gulping Sound Brewery's specialty Belgian ale named *Monk's Indiscretion*, I learned of an even older connection between beer and faith. A fellow beer enthusiast gave me an article, "Did the Ancient Israelites Drink Beer?"[3] It states, "Ancient Israelites, with the possible exception of a few teetotaling Nazirites . . . proudly drank beer—and lots of it." Author Michael Homan and five other biblical scholars he cites make the case, based on linguistic and archaeological sources, that the Hebrew word *shekhar*, usually translated "strong drink," should be translated "beer." Thus, although the Hebrew Scriptures surely warn against drunkenness (Isa 5:11; Prov 20:1), beer was included in the daily sacrifices to Yahweh (Num 28:7–10), God commanded the Israelites to purchase beer (along with food) using tithe money as part of a celebration (Deut 14:26), and people were advised to consume it to erase their troubles (Prov 31:6). Who knew?

I was reminded of Jesus' first miracle of turning water into wine at a wedding in Cana. It was good wine, not cheap stuff. About 150 gallons worth. That's almost eight hundred bottles, in case you are wondering.[4] Did all this mean responsible enjoyment of beer and wine is part of Christ's way? Undoubtedly, yes.

But more than that, just as these historical, cultural, and linguistic facts about beer, the Jewish Scriptures, and monastic history shed light on our attitude toward alcohol consumption, it was clear that learning first-century Jewish and Greco-Roman culture would undoubtedly help us rediscover Jesus' original Path. Just as the microbrewery museum had uncovered the faith-based background of beer brewing over the centuries,

2. Ibid.

3. Homan, "Did the Ancient Israelites Brew Beer?," 49.

4. Scholars agree that the six purification jars of water turned to wine were between 20 and 30 gallons each, or around 150 gallons total, which is about 567 liters, representing 756 bottles.

our group had to discover the origins of our own faith—not only to learn from them, but to *unlearn* any misconceptions that we had.

First-Century Palestine

In our experience, most churches had taught either implicitly or explicitly that Jesus was sent by God to found a new religion called Christianity that circumvented Judaism. What's more, he supposedly called people to give up their personal sins and accept a set of doctrines about God, himself, and his atoning sacrifice on the cross (at least a Western definition of it). Moreover, we were to conform to a particular behavior code, obey the authority of the Bible—the Word of God—and submit to some form of institutional organization called *church*; all in order to be saved from eternal punishment—a state that supposedly all of us were destined for because of our inheritance of something called *original sin*. For evangelical-style believers there was an added admonition: spread this message to unbelievers, here and around the world, and encourage them to "accept" this view of Christ. When our group began putting the teaching of Jesus in historical context this popular view began to change. It wasn't that there was nothing right in popular Christian teaching, but that it was missing key concepts, definitions, and historical grounding that were essential to putting the Path of Christ into focus. The first thing we examined was the Jewish ritual purity code. With the help of scholars and historians like Marcus Borg, N. T. Wright, and Harvey Cox, we quickly learned how Jesus' message is easily misunderstood without understanding the first-century, Second Temple era view of purity and other historical facts.

The Purity Map

First-century Jews in Palestine were obsessed with a ritual purity code; part of the Jewish sacrificial cult centered on the temple in Jerusalem. By 30 CE, the second temple was an enormous thirty-six-acre set of courtyards and gargantuan buildings renovated and enlarged by King Herod the Great—the size of twenty-seven football fields. The temple courts were always crowded with people and the sacrifices proscribed in the Torah happened every morning and evening. The concept of ritual purity was about who was "clean" enough in God's eyes through following a strict set of behavior and purity regulations. It was perpetrated by the temple leaders and most of Jewish society bought into it. People looked at their world as if it was a purity map.

Both people and places at the center of the map were pure. These would be the temple and then the priests, scribes, and Pharisees, because they kept the purity code to a tee. Those out a ways were less clean and increasingly unclean the farther out you went to the margins—women were more unclean, menstruating women were really unclean, those physically stricken, like the blind, lepers, the lame and maimed were even more so. Then there were public sinners, like tax collectors, because they got enriched through the Roman Gentiles, and prostitutes; both were the scum of the earth.

Moreover, the poor were considered unclean because conventional wisdom said they were poor because of their sin. Dead bodies before burial were the ultimate in uncleanness. Samaritans and Gentiles weren't even on the map. To make matters worse for the unclean folks, in order to stay clean and pure, the so-called righteous ones would shun them and refrain from touching them or else they would become infected, albeit temporarily. It was a domination system based on fear of becoming unclean that also included economic exploitation.

But what made people or places unclean and where did this crazy idea come from? It was a hyper-paranoid way of interpreting some of the commands in the Torah. For instance, the dietary laws—what was kosher and what wasn't—and rules about bodily emissions (with only healthy people being acceptable for temple service and healthy animals for sacrifices), keeping the Sabbath, and other laws like which places in the temple were more holy. We learned much of this from the historian and Jesus scholar Marcus Borg.[5] We found a chart he created that helps define the different categories of purity. On the left were the "clean" categories and on the right the "unclean." It looked something like this:

> Righteous—Sinners (sin was a matter of being unclean, not acting in an unloving way)
>
> Male—Female (males were generally pure, automatically; females were automatically less pure)
>
> Rich—Poor
>
> Jew—Gentile
>
> Healthy—Diseased (or damaged or maimed)

5. Borg, "Social/Cultural World of Jesus," 1.

Further down the chart it differentiated between agricultural produce on which a tithe to the temple was paid (clean) and produce on which it wasn't (unclean, and therefore boycotted by the "righteous"). There was also clean and unclean places: the inner courts of the temple were the most clean and the outer courts less clean. The land of Israel was clean and Gentile land or homes were totally unclean, not even on the map.

The Good News for the Impure

It was into this sociocultural milieu and purity system that Jesus arose. One of his first messages was an announcement to peasants in Galilean villages about "the good news of God."

> The time has come. The kingdom of God is at hand. Repent and believe the good news.[6]

With the historical context of these peasants in our minds, we soon realized the good news of the kingdom Jesus spoke of had little to do with salvation in the afterlife and nothing to do with the end of our space-time world. It was about the here and now. A new just kingdom (or "reign" is a better translation, we learned) was about to replace the existing unjust one. As scholars have been saying for years, and Harvey Cox reminds us, "The phrase 'kingdom of God' is one of the most misused and misunderstood in the entire Bible."[7] The book of Matthew further complicates things by translating it "kingdom of heaven." But in this case, "heaven" is just a Jewish substitute for "God." The kingdom or reign of God is not pie in the sky. It isn't "heaven." It is a very real part of our world. As Jesus taught people to pray, "Your kingdom come, your will be done, *on earth* as it is in heaven."

Too often, people have interpreted the "gospel," which when properly translated is "good news," as good news about salvation from hell through Jesus dying on the cross for our sins. N. T. Wright reminded us, "But the usual heaven-and-hell scheme, however popular, distorts the Bible's good news. Over many centuries, Western churches have got the story wrong. They have forgotten what the backstory is (the larger story that gives meaning and context to the good news)."[8] Part of that backstory was the purity system and how burdensome it was for most people.

6. Mark 1:14–15
7. Cox, *Future of Faith*, 43.
8. Wright, *Simply Good News*, 1–14.

Moreover, Wright confirmed our conclusion that modern perceptions of the "good news of Jesus" are warped. Most people interpret Jesus' announcement as if it was good advice, not good news. They put it in terms of establishing a personal relationship with God, maintaining it through living a moral life, and securing assurance of a place in heaven in the afterlife. As important as those things may or may not be, they are not the good news. "These are not the center of the good news. We have placed the stress at the wrong point, like people putting the emphasis on the wrong syllable. The words may be true, but the way we say them gets in the way of that truth coming out clearly. The good news is about the living God overcoming all the powers of the world [evil and violence] to establish his rule of justice and peace, *on earth as in heaven*. Not in heaven, later on. And that victory is won not by superior power of the same kind [military might and violence] but by a different sort of power altogether."[9] That different force is the power of love.

It became obvious to us that this "good news" of the reign of God that Jesus first announced was directed toward the masses of people considered unclean or impure. Jesus quoted the prophet Isaiah as his mission to bring good news to the poor and oppressed. He was known for hanging out with the poor, drunkards, public sinners, tax collectors, prostitutes, women, and children, all people who were either outside or on the fringes of the purity map. Most everyone he healed were considered unclean—the blind, lame, lepers, those demonized, and women with "impure" bleeding. He forgave unclean people (often declaring them "clean"—e.g., Matt 8:2–3) without insisting they go through the temple sacrificial system. In the act of healing, he would touch them, in itself an unclean act, condemned in the Torah. As Wright affirms, "Jesus was offering forgiveness to all and sundry, out there on the street, without requiring that they go through the normal channels. That was his real offense."[10] He was breeching the purity code and naming the impure as members of the reign of God. "Repent and believe the good news" was not a call to personal piety ("repent" is a call to "turn" or "change" one's mind), but an admonition for the unclean to trust that God was on their side—that God loves *them* and does not favor the clean. He encouraged people to trust the reign of a loving God with no strings attached. He offered forgiveness with no conditions to follow purity codes, believe doctrines, or accept some future atonement on the cross.

9. Ibid., 35–56.

10. Borg and Wright, *Meaning of Jesus*, 39.

Moreover, Jesus' continual call announcing the reign of God was not what the Jewish people of the day expected. Whereas most people expected a messiah to come who would liberate the Jews from the oppression of the Romans and King Herod, Jesus had no such agenda. His was a message to embrace a whole new way of looking at the world, where freedom and deliverance comes, not by following a religious code of behavior or by defeating one's enemies in an uprising, but through love and compassion toward both the weak and the powerful. Marcus Borg sums it up:

> Whereas purity divides and excludes, compassion unites and includes. For Jesus, compassion had a radical sociopolitical meaning. In his teaching and table fellowship, and in the shape of his movement, the purity system was subverted and an alternative social vision affirmed. The politics of purity was replaced by the politics of compassion.[11]

Jesus' Call for True Purity

Jesus' taught purity of the heart and critiqued outward purity. He circumvented the law of Moses when he declared all foods clean (Mark 7:19) and insisted true purity was not found in following the temple code but simply having a loving heart. He challenged the conventional wisdom of holiness. Holiness wasn't simply following the purity code or even obeying the letter of the law. "You have heard it said, do not murder." But rather it was living with interior righteousness. "But I say unto you, anyone who is angry with his brother without cause is subject to judgment" (Matt 5:21–22). Jesus always zeroed in at the heart of sin. Likewise, refraining from stealing your neighbor's wife (the Jewish definition of *adultery* when applied to men) wasn't enough. Rather, one had to refrain from even desiring to steal a man's wife. His Sermon on the Mount was a correction for the conventional view of righteousness. It wasn't outward obedience to the letter of the law that is important. But rather, the heart of the law—love for one's neighbor beginning with an inward attitude.

So, whom did he say were blessed? The ones who obeyed the purity code to a tee? The ones who were the most religious, who believed the right doctrines? No! They were the worst in Jesus' moral system. The true righteous were the ones who had a pure heart—the merciful, mourning, meek,

11. Borg, *Meeting Jesus Again*, 58.

and those who hunger and thirst for justice (Matt 5:3–10). These weren't behaviors or doctrinal beliefs but attitudes of the heart. To Jesus, the heart of sin was acting in an unloving way, which begins with having unloving intentions. It wasn't violating purity and behavior codes or doubting statements of faith or creeds. This attitude drove the temple elites crazy because it could take away their power over the people.

It also drove them crazy because Jesus redrew the purity map and put them on the outer regions by his condemnation of religious leaders. He called the Pharisees and teachers of the law "blind guides." He accused them of performing religious deeds and prayers in the synagogues and on street corners for show. For Jesus, their public religious display was the height of hypocrisy; being religious on the outside while violating the more important inner purity code. Jesus also called them out for their two-faced practice of tithing, where they gave tithes for a minutiae of items, but "neglected the more important matters of the law—justice, mercy, and faithfulness." He exposed their uncleanness: "You are like whitewashed tombs, which look beautiful on the outside, but inside are full of dead men's bones and everything unclean. In the same way, on the outside you appear to people as righteous but on the inside, you are full of hypocrisy and wickedness" (see Matt 23).

For the temple elites of first-century Judaism, this was the ultimate insult. There was nothing more unclean than the dead in a tomb. They were the unclean ones because they had no purity of heart, while the "sinners" were actually clean. He once told the chief priests and elders that "tax collectors and prostitutes are entering the kingdom of God ahead of you" (Matt 21:31), not because they became religious, but because they began to do what God desires—treat others rightly.[12] In Jesus' new world, in the reign of God, inner purity or love was the measuring rod. He turned purity

12. Jesus' precursor, John the Baptist, also stressed repentance that translated into treating people rightly rather than performing religious acts or believing correct doctrines. When asked by devotees what should they do to change, he told them, "Anyone who has two shirts should share with the one who has none, and anyone who has food should do the same" (Luke 3:11). To tax collectors, he said, "Don't collect any more than you are required to" (Luke 3:13). To Roman soldiers, he said, "Do violence to no one, nor accuse falsely, and be content with your wages" (Luke 3:14 Young's Literal Translation; *note*: since soldiers routinely extorted money from Jews in Palestine, contentment with wages would end extortion). John's call wasn't a religious call to read the Torah, perform sacrifices at the temple, attend a Bible-believing synagogue, or organize prayer meetings. The call was to produce the fruit of loving your neighbor.

upside down. In the reign of God, the first become last and the last become first (Matt 20:16). Priests are sinners and prostitutes are saints.

With Jesus, the way of inner purity was open to everyone to follow, not just the Jews. The writer of Matthew had said Jesus had "come for the lost sheep of Israel" but that didn't mean he cast aspersion on the Gentiles. He came to remind Israel of their goal to be the light of the world (a theme of the prophet Isaiah). To the contrary, Jesus shocked his hearers in Nazareth, his hometown, by citing God's mercy to Gentiles recorded in the Torah when Elijah overlooked the widows in Israel and helped a Gentile and when Elisha ignored the lepers of Israel and cleansed a Syrian of leprosy (Luke 4:24–27). Jesus healed a Syrophoenician woman (a Greek living in Syria), came to the aid of a Roman army officer who he declared had greater faith than many in Israel, intentionally traveled through "unclean" Gentile territories, e.g., the Decapolis[13] (and welcomed crowds from there), and called his followers to make other followers of the Way among the "nations," meaning Gentiles. Finally, his call to "love your enemies," even those who forced you to walk a mile, a reference to being compelled to carry things for Roman soldiers, was one of the most radical things he taught. (He taught people to walk two miles when commanded to walk one). He taught acceptance and love for all outsiders without insisting they convert to Judaism.

Inner purity, to Jesus, included exceptions to the law of God. This is because Jesus' "law of love" demands it. There was no place for niggling legalism in Jesus' world. The Pharisees asked, "Why do you eat and drink with tax collectors and sinners?" They considered this an unclean act. To Jesus, it was the loving thing to do to ignore religious protocol, after all it wasn't the healthy ("righteous") who needed a doctor, but the sick ("sinners"). "Why are you doing what is unlawful on the Sabbath?" they asked. Jesus gives an example of King David making an exception to the Sabbath for the sake of feeding the hungry (Luke 6:1–5). Jesus healed on the Sabbath, considered unlawful, because it is always lawful to do good on the Sabbath. Whereas the keepers of the law of Israel were always looking at whether one kept the letter of the law, Jesus always made human need the priority. "Sabbath was made for man, not man for the Sabbath," he said.

We took note of how this could apply to today. Modern conservative Christians always insist on "submitting to Scripture." They can never allow

13. A region in Palestine that had ten Greek cities where the majority of the population were not Jews. Seven out of the ten cities were in what is now modern-day Jordan and Syria.

exceptions and rarely allow a nuanced interpretation. So, Jesus' teaching on divorce is taken as if it applies to all circumstances and legitimate grounds for divorce can only come from what Jesus taught. So, because Jesus never mentions physical or sexual abuse as grounds for divorce, it can't be lawful grounds, according to literalists. But this misses the whole point of Jesus' teachings—to make human need the priority with a view to purity of the heart. Today, some evangelicals are waking up to this fact in the case of divorce[14] when they allow women to divorce their unrepentant, abusive husbands. Yet, some still won't permit it. Neither will they consider other legitimate reasons for divorce; no matter how painful a marriage is, unless they see it spelled out in Jesus' teachings. But Jesus didn't lay down a new law to cover every conceivable scenario of marital strife. He showed how to interpret what God desires and how it applied to circumstances of his day. We have to interpret it for the circumstances of our day.

Finally, Jesus took on the spirit of the prophet Isaiah, who had called Israel to be the light of the world to the Gentiles and ultimately see the spread of salvation to the whole world (Isa 52:7–10). The short summary of Jesus' message, "Change your mind and believe the good news; the reign of God is at hand" was an echo of Isaiah's words. "How beautiful on the mountains are the feet of those who bring good news, who proclaim peace, who bring good tidings, who proclaim salvation, who say to Zion, 'Your God reigns!'" (52:7). Early on in his ministry, the Gospel of Luke records him quoting Isaiah in the Capernaum synagogue.

> The Spirit of the Lord is on me, because he has anointed me to preach good news to the poor. He has sent me to proclaim freedom for the prisoners and recovery of the sight for the blind, to release the oppressed, to proclaim the year of the Lord's favor. (Luke 4:18–19)

Jesus taught good news to the poor, the unclean, and the oppressed in Israel. Although he had much to say about "sin," this announcement of good news was not about rescuing people from immorality or "original sin" or saving people from hell, but rather encouraging the peasants they were not unclean in God's eyes. They were not poor *because* of their sin. The good news was mostly about rescuing people from the oppression of the purity code, the corruption of the temple system, the bondage of hatred for all things foreign, and the strict, legalistic adherence to the law. It was that the loving

14. See Instone-Brewer, *Divorce and Remarriage*; Callison, *Divorce*.

reign of God is in the here and now—a reign that sets people free from the worries of life because God is present to forgive, heal, encourage, and offer future hope—all outside the burdensome temple religion, and any religion. As we learned more about this cultural context of first-century Judaism, this became all the more clear. To the religious leaders, the source of Israel's oppression was the Roman military occupation. To Jesus, it was a national corruption of the heart trapped in organized religion. With that perspective, when Matthew (1:21) says his parents gave him the name Jesus (Yeshua in Hebrew, which is the name "Joshua" in English, and means "God saves" or more accurately, "God rescues") because "he will save his people from their sins," it was talking about this national corruption, not the stain of *original sin*, a phrase which is never mentioned in Jesus' teachings or in the Bible.

Today's Path to Purity

One evening, in Dan and Gina's living room with a fire blazing in the fire place, our group began a discussion on the historical background of Jewish purity, about which we had recently read.

"How can we apply all this about the purity code to today?" Dan asked. Fueled by *hors d'oeuvres* and glasses of wine or beer, we all took turns sharing our thoughts.

"I was thinking about many of the religious leaders of today," Gina said. "How they cite the source of oppression in America as the secular occupation of society and a loss of our 'Christian' values. In light of what we learned, I don't think Jesus would call that out."

"Why do you say that?" another member piped in. "Wouldn't it be good to recover Jesus' teachings in our society?"

"Absolutely, but how do we interpret which teachings to apply and how?" Gina said. "Like, with what we learned about purity, perhaps Jesus would call out the church for rejecting outsiders. You know, how the church tends to block membership, not on a basis of discerning people's actions that hurt others, but for merely believing things considered false doctrine."

"Yeah, we just learned how he spent all his time reaching out to outsiders, those marginalized from the religious system," Dan said. "He didn't address what they believed, like have them sign a 'statement of faith,' but how the religious purity system hurt them. So, to ask it another way, what is today's purity code in America, or in the church, and is it like ancient Israel's?"

"Oh, you mean, who in our society or in churches are considered unclean?" a third person asked. "And whom would Jesus declare clean and call to believe the good news that God is on their side?"

We continued to draw these types of questions out. Who among us practices inner purity but are condemned by religious leaders as impure? How do we confront religion and oppose it as Jesus did? How do we replace religion with inner purity?

As we continued, slowly, something became obvious. The impure today are those who offend without harming anyone.

The "sinners" in first-century Israel were the social outcasts: the poor, lame, bleeding, non-tithers, tax collectors, prostitutes, revelers, and Gentiles. They were deemed impure by who they were, not by what they did to harm others. Some of them had a reputation for doing harm, e.g., the tax collectors and Romans, but whether they treated people fairly or not, they were still considered unclean.

Who is like that today? It sank in. In an earlier century in the American South and among racists today, the unclean are African Americans and people of color. In Nazi Germany, the unclean were Jews, Gypsies, and homosexuals. Among non-Christian fundamentalist religions like conservative Islam, the unclean are non-Muslims or errant Muslims. For extreme atheists or materialists, any person of faith is unclean. For conservative Christianity today, the unclean are unbelievers—atheists, agnostics, Jews, Muslims, Hindus, Buddhists, Animists, and neo-Paganists. But also, in the evangelical/fundamentalist worldview, lesbians, gays, bisexuals, and transgender people (LGBT) are unclean, whether they are believers or not. To certain believers, even fellow Christians are considered unclean if they don't behave the right way, e.g., if they practice their homosexuality, don't remain virgins until marriage, decide to have an abortion, get divorced, or drink, smoke, or have children who do any of the above. Or, they are unclean if they don't believe the right doctrines, such as the infallibility of the Bible, or don't attend church or don't attend regularly enough. To the religious, harming other people isn't what makes you unclean. It's who you are and how well you follow religious codes of conduct.

Among the Religious Right, all unbelievers, the LGBT community, and Christians who don't believe the right things are not judged by the content of their character (purity of the heart) or on how they treat their neighbors, but by their place in religious society. They are unclean, not because they hurt their fellow human beings, but by virtue of who they are.

Fundamentalists, evangelicals, and conservative Catholics consider unbelievers or the "unchurched" as lost. It doesn't matter if they are upstanding people, they are "unsaved" and destined to face God's judgment unless they repent and convert. Likewise with the LGBT community, they are considered impure by their status, not because they practice behaviors that harm others. It doesn't matter if they call themselves Christian or are married to their gay partner. They too are "unsaved" at worst or "fallen away" at best, unless they repent and disavow their homosexuality and either remain celibate or pursue "reparative therapy" to become heterosexual.

Religious people today base this condemnation of homosexuals on the law of the Torah, which was written as a covenant to ancient Israel, not to our modern society. They also base it on later first-century commentary on the Torah and the life of Jesus, written by Paul of Tarsus, i.e., parts of the New Testament. Later, as we delved into historical events in Dan's *Timeline* that shed light on how to approach the Bible, we would learn the faulty underpinnings of such a basis.

"How would Jesus treat the modern 'unclean' and what would he say to them?" a member of the group asked.

"Which, by extension, would reveal how followers of his Way should treat them," another added.

How would Jesus treat unbelievers, the LGBT community, and those who have differing Christian doctrines? He would welcome them, accept them, heal them, forgive them, and love them, we concluded. To the most marginalized, he would say, "Change your mind. God is not against you. Believe the good news. In the loving reign of God, you are no longer last, but first." To those who feel like outsiders to the religious community, as Jesus never called an "unbeliever" or Jew to convert to a new religion, he would not tell them they must become a Christian or "accept him as Lord and Savior." This is a phrase that is absent from the New Testament and was never recorded as something he said or did.

He would call people to practice inner purity and not get hung up on legalities of religion, we concluded. He would tell them human need is always the priority, not following religious rules. He would challenge them, yes, to follow him, to repent of lack of love for others, but not to convert to a new religion and believe a set of doctrines, but to pursue a Way of Love—love for their local and global neighbors the same way they love themselves, and love for their enemies. He would tell them love is the fulfillment of what God desires.

To those who already followed a love ethic toward others, regardless of their faith or lack of faith, he would encourage them that their compassionate deeds, even those done "for the least," are "done for him" (Matt 25:40). We knew we were called to do and say the same. We felt like we had found one of the lost trails of Christ: a call to true purity, not to a religion.

We wondered, as we progressed through *The Timeline*, where else it would take us? One place, we realized, was Jesus' teaching on wealth and class. It was time to learn what the culture of wealth and class in first-century Palestine was like and how Jesus challenged it. His message was not just "good news" for the marginalized, but a condemnation of the systemic evils of the day. We needed to understand what those were, how Jesus confronted them, and what it meant to us today.

Chapter Four

Reforming Wealth, Class, and Power

Too often, people look at an ancient movement like Christianity through the lens of our modern culture. When we read that Jesus spoke on behalf of the poor, for example, we might think of the homeless, those below the federal poverty level, or the impoverished in Africa. When we consider things like children's rights and public education, we may take it for granted that people of antiquity had the same values. We are generally more attuned to the recent advances made with civil and women's rights, but still may be ignorant of what it was like to be of lower class or a woman where and when Jesus lived. We are also largely ignorant, despite whatever Sunday School teachings we might remember, of the different sects within Israel at the time of Christ, particularly the middle-class and wealthy religious elites. Our group's investigation into the historical context of Jesus' message helped open our eyes.

Through a number of weeks, we read books, watched DVDs, and discussed our findings at the group-discussion meeting or at one of the "pub theology" gatherings some of us attended in a local bar every two weeks. This is what we learned.

The 90 Percent and the Plight of the Poor

First, we discovered an alarming economic disparity in first-century Palestine. Being an agrarian society, 90 percent of people were poor peasants—notably farmers, shepherds, and fishermen—who were dependent on the rich. They either paid rent for land or sharecropped. Peasant fishermen, for example, could not afford to purchase exorbitant fishing rights from King Herod. So fishermen, like Jesus' disciples, worked for wealthy holders, who took a hefty cut for themselves. It was far from a free enterprise system. "Even fishers who may have owned their own boats were part of a state regulated, elite-profiting enterprise, and a complex web of economic relationships."[1]

The whole structure was regulated by a corrupt state and only the elites profited. Jewish peasants had to tithe their produce to the temple. Whatever they sold at the market that was not properly tithed was boycotted by those who wanted to remain pure. Then there was the temple tax. Every year, every Jew had to pay for temple "maintenance." There were also the several prescribed animal sacrifices Jews had to make in the temple—cattle, sheep, doves, or pigeons depending on their standing—at various times during the year in order to become "clean." Since most people lived far away from the temple, they would have to travel to Jerusalem and purchase the animals at the temple marketplace.

Purchasing animals for sacrifice had to be done at the temple market because all sacrifices had to be inspected for wholeness (again, this is about purity) by temple priests. And everything had to be bought with temple currency. This is why they needed money changers to convert local coins. Temple merchants sold sacrificial animals at excessive cost to the pilgrims. And money changers charged exorbitant fees for converting currency, whether to pay for animals or the temple tax. As a result, it was very costly for the 90 percent to remain "clean," that is, in right standing with God.

Those in charge of the temple had strict control over the populace. Ten percent of society was made up of the temple elites (particularly the Sadducees and chief priests, who oversaw the temple, but also the scribes and Pharisees), the rich landowners, who generally had something to do with the temple, and the governing Romans and Herod, who had their own oppressive taxes to extort. This 10 percent profited heavily from the system. They extracted around 66 percent of the value of all rural production from peasants through land rent, sharecropping, taxes, tithes, and temple currency exchanges.[2] Moreover, because of their obsession over purity, affluent Jews—a good chunk of the 10 percent—considered themselves "clean" and looked down on the usually "unclean" 90 percent.

1. Hanson, "Galilean Fishing Economy."

2. Borg, "Context."

The Elite and Judaism's Major Sects

Besides the 90 percent poor, who were the main actors in the Judaic system? What were the major sects within Judaism? We needed a refresher on all the major players.

The *Pharisees*, we learned, were a lay movement, one of the major sects of first-century Judaism. They emphasized the Torah and the importance of following the purity code to maintain everyday holiness. They also used an accepted oral tradition—longstanding explanations of the law—as a supplement to the Torah. These filled in details that the law of Moses left out. According to them, holiness was not merely for the priests, but for all the people, so the nation of Israel would display the holiness (purity) of God. This is why they taught the purity code with such zeal. On the other hand, there were varieties of Pharisees, including moderates, such as Rabbi Hillel (the grandfather of Gamaliel, another moderate who is mentioned in the book of Acts) whose recorded sayings were sometimes similar to what Jesus taught. Many Pharisees were part of the priesthood. A few, probably the more moderate variety, became followers of the Way of Jesus.

The *teachers of the law* are often cited in the New Testament along with the Pharisees. As the Pharisees were a type of revival movement, attempting to create a more "pure" Israel in accordance with the Torah and the oral tradition, the teachers of the law were professional, authoritative interpreters of the Torah. Both the Pharisees and teachers of the law therefore had a lot of power in their hands. They dictated to a largely illiterate majority the very laws of God.

Scribes traditionally were copyists, interpreters, and teachers of the sacred texts or Jewish Scriptures. At the time of Christ, they were the experts in judicial procedure, enforcement of Jewish law, and preservation of the Judaic system. They would be our modern equivalent of lawyers. Many apparently were priests. They were often associated with the chief priests and Pharisees.

The *Sadducees* were part of the Jewish upper class, the second of the major Jewish sects, whose role included maintaining the temple. As such, they were guardians of the sacrificial cult. Their number included many among the priesthood. They supported stable conditions in society, tried to get along with the Romans, and had a "reasonable" religion that rejected belief in the spirit world, the resurrection of the dead, and the afterlife, as well as the oral law promoted by the Pharisees. They saw the Torah as the only source of spiritual authority. The Sadducees and Pharisees apparently had many disputes around how to interpret issues of purity and details of the law, with the Pharisees coming to more strict and extra-biblical conclusions, partly because of their use of "oral law," which is "not written in the law of Moses." The Sadducees, too, had enormous power over the populace, as they, like the Pharisees, would use their perceptions of purity and the sacrificial requirements to enforce control over people. The high priest Caiaphas who presided over Jesus' trial before the *Sanhedrin*, as well as his father-in-law and former high priest, Annas, were apparently Sadducees.

The *priests* were responsible for performing and presiding over sacrifices in the temple, the major activity of worship of God for ancient Israel. In addition to the daily sacrifices, they oversaw the sacrifices of the three festivals of pilgrimage to Jerusalem—the Feast of Passover, the Feast of Weeks, and the Feast of Tabernacles. They were selected only from the tribe of Levi. There were various levels of priests. There was the captain of the temple, who would preside over the temple police, those in charge of the temple treasury, and various other overseers. Some historians say these would have been what the New Testament calls *chief priests* while others say the chief priests would have been relatives of the high priest, perhaps including former high priests. Regardless, historians conclude that in the days of Jesus, there was a wealthy priestly aristocracy that had a dramatically higher standard of living than common priests, and, of course, enormously higher than the majority of the people—the 90 percent.[3] Priests would have been made up of both Pharisees and Sadducees.

The *high priest*, traditionally a hereditary office, was the only one allowed into the holiest and most pure place on earth—the inner sanctuary of the temple called the holy of holies. He entered once a year on Yom Kippur, the Day of Atonement, to perform a sacrifice to atone for the sins of the whole nation. At the period during the life of Jesus, the hereditary appointment custom had died out. High priests began being appointed by King Herod the Great (a Roman client king of Judea) and then his Roman successors, and thus the office came under political control. The Romans could depose and appoint high priests at will. Although they were chosen from a small number of priestly families, to avoid losing power, the high priest would inevitably cooperate with Roman rule.[4] This infuriated purists and resulted in the people being unable to trust the highest Jewish authority to represent their best interests.

3. Allen, "Priests."

4. "High Priest," http://www.historicjesus.com/glossary/highpriest.html.

The *Sanhedrin* was the Supreme Court or council over ancient Israel. It was made up of seventy judges and the high priest. The members came from the chief priests, scribes, and elders (presumably older influential men and former high priests and chief priests), and would have included both Pharisees and Sadducees. At the time of Jesus, it only had jurisdiction over the province of Judea, the southern region of Israel. They had their own police force and heard both civil and criminal cases among the people. Although they could impose the death penalty, which according to Mosaic law would be stoning, during Roman occupation, it was against Roman law for Jews to carry it out.

The *Essenes* were an apocalyptic sect within Judaism. They lived in various cities throughout Judea and practiced a communal life, asceticism, and voluntary poverty. Some are said to have practiced celibacy. Some historians believe a community of Essenes inhabited the settlement at Qumran, the location where the Dead Sea Scrolls were discovered, and were the ones who wrote and hid the scrolls. The Essenes were separatists who believed they were the elect. They were against the worldliness of Jerusalem and the temple, most likely the way the temple authorities collaborated with the Romans and the Romans controlled the appointment of the high priest. They believed Israel was on the cusp of a coming new age and kingdom. Some of the writings of the Dead Sea Scrolls hint that the Essenes possibly believed in two messianic figures that would lead the coming new kingdom. One figure is like King David and would lead the coming war. The other is a priestly figure who would come to restore the temple to purity.[5] At times, the Essenes were also Zealots (see below). John the Essene was one of the Jewish generals in the Great Revolt (66–73 CE).

Samaritans were the people that lived in the region between Galilee in the north and Judea in the south. They claimed they were Israelite descendants of the northern Israelite tribes of Ephraim and Manasseh. The Samaritans claimed their descendants survived the destruction of the northern kingdom of Israel by the Assyrians in 722 BC. They also claimed Mount Gerizim, not Jerusalem, was the original Holy Place of the Israelites from the time that Joshua conquered Canaan and the tribes of Israel settled the land. They worshiped at their own temple at Mount Gerizim, hence the dispute with Jews whether the temple of Jerusalem was the true temple. Jews rejected these claims and treated Samaritans like pagan Gentiles, the

5. White, "Essenes and the Dead Sea Scrolls."

ultimate in uncleanness. Marriage between Samaritans and Jews was forbidden and social relations were greatly restricted.

Finally there were the *Zealots*, a revolutionary party opposed to Roman rule. Zealots were theocratic nationalists who preached only God was the ruler of Israel and urged no taxes be paid to Rome. They staged intermitted uprisings against Roman rule. In 6 BCE, a Jewish Zealot named Judas the Galilean protested Roman taxes and led a violent resistance. The rebellion was brutally crushed. The Jewish historian Josephus mentions a dozen minor rebel-bandit Zealots who arose from time to time. Josephus names *Zealots* as the fourth major sect of Second Temple Judaism. It's important to remember that these uprisings came in cycles and slowly grew larger over time. Josephus reports that at the time of Jesus, the Zealots were not a violent movement, but certainly the hatred for Roman rule they represented was prevalent. Over time, they grew to become a violent faction that influenced all of Israel. They eventually spearheaded the First or Great Revolt from 66–73 CE,[6] to which Jesus referred, when he prophesied that the temple would be destroyed and Jerusalem trampled on by Roman armies (Luke 21:5–24).

Roman Rule

In 63 BCE, Roman military commander Pompey the Great conquered Jerusalem, killing around twelve thousand Jews, an intervention precipitated by a civil war between rival Jewish sects. The conquest resulted in the land of Israel becoming a "protectorate" of Rome and thus subject to oppressive Roman occupation. Around the beginning of the Common Era, the land was ruled by Roman procurators whose responsibility was to maintain order and collect an annual tax for the empire. Whatever they raised beyond the quota, they could keep, hence they often enforced arbitrary taxation for their own benefit. There was no higher authority to appeal to for such a practice since it was allowed by Roman law.

In addition, King Herod the Great (an Idumaean—or Edomite; Edom was a country south of Judea populated by descendants of Esau—who converted to Judaism and rebuilt and enlarged the temple in 19 BCE) and his successors (three sons who ruled different territories), were Roman client kings or tetrarchs of Judea and Galilee. They had relative freedom of reign

6. The Great Revolt was the first and largest of three major Jewish rebellions against the Romans. See White, "Jews and the Roman Empire."

over their subjects, but still were servants of the Roman Empire. Herod the Great, who wasn't considered Jewish by most observant Jews, had a reputation for being a paranoid, brutal ruler. According to Matthew, in a passage that some historians dispute, he ordered the "slaughter of the innocents" in Bethlehem when he heard a new "King of the Jews" was prophesied to appear during his reign.

Rome's financial exploitation, which impacted the poor the most, its contempt for Judaism, and the way the Romans favored Gentiles living in the land, caused much discontent among the masses. It also influenced the emergence of the Zealots, who eventually evolved into a strong military force in the 60s CE.

The Plight of Women and Children

The poor had a rough life in Roman-occupied Israel. Human rights values irrespective of religion or class, that we take for granted today, were not instilled in Jewish or Roman society. This was especially true for women and children.

We have already learned that Jewish conventional "wisdom" placed women as automatically less pure than men. In general, this was true for all societies of antiquity, not just the Jews. Women were second-class citizens. That's probably why in the Gospel of John, it says the disciples were surprised that Jesus was even talking to a woman one on one. Women were like property. Although Jews didn't follow this practice, Roman families often rejected girl babies and even committed infanticide. In fact, there was a shortage of women in the Greco-Roman world as a result. This quote from a first-century letter from a husband to his pregnant wife was probably not uncommon: "I ask and beg of you to take good care of our baby son. . . . If you are delivered of a child [before I come home], if it is a boy, keep it; if a girl, discard it."[7]

The women shortage was actually an enormous gap. One hundred forty men to every hundred women. In the Law of Romulus in Rome, fathers were only required to raise healthy male children and the firstborn female. All others were disposable. So the bias was against both women and the diseased.

Although Jews didn't abandon girl babies, they had their own sexist ways. Women were only allowed as far as the court of women in the temple,

7. Bunge et al., *Child in the Bible*, 203.

for instance; they couldn't own property, and were considered the possession of their father and then later their husband. That's why older widows and divorcees were so vulnerable. If the father had passed away and they were left with no husband, there was no place to go. Younger women, when abandoned by their husbands—an illegal, quick divorce with no legal certificate—and had no family to which to return, often resorted to prostitution. There were no socially acceptable professions for unmarried women.

Jesus' treatment of women, to the point of elevating and extending forgiveness to prostitutes, compared to this, was scandalous.

Then there was the discrimination against children in the Greco-Roman world. Children, especially baby girls, were left to die. Both boys and girls were sold into slavery to earn money. In the modern world, most of us are shocked by reports of child slavery and sex trafficking that has come to light in both developing and developed countries today. But in the ancient world, forms of child abuse were rampant and the outrage against it was extremely rare. Norwegian scholar O. M. Bakke documents this in his book *When Children Became People*. It's eye opening. The ancients tolerated violence against children. Enslaved children were often sexually abused. Their owners would hire them out to brothels. Greco-Romans also had a common practice called pederasty, in which prepubescent boys were sold to or assigned to adult men, who used them sexually. It was considered a rite of passage for young males. Evidence suggests this was one of the practices the Apostle Paul referred to when speaking of homosexuality in the epistles.[8]

This attitude was probably why the New Testament records Jesus' disciples trying to shoo children away. The overriding culture had a negative assessment of children. There was no such thing as elementary education or orphanages. Unless a child was lucky enough to be born into affluence or "cleanness," he or she was destined to a life of poverty, slavery, or abuse. It was not unlike a caste system where one's lot in life was set in stone. The concept of equality for all human beings, including women and children, was absent from both Jewish and Roman society.

Lack of Social Justice and Compassion

There were other surprising characteristics of first-century Jewish and Roman culture. For example, social justice was not engrained in societal

8. Camp, *Confessions of a Bible Thumper*, 249.

structure. The ancient world honored characteristics like courage and wisdom but not humility or compassion. There were no such things as hospitals or places to care for the sick. There was no notion of emergency care. There was no public ambulance system. In medical emergencies, if family or friends didn't respond, people were literally left to die.

The concept of forgiveness toward one's adversaries was rare. Conventional wisdom told people to reward friends and punish enemies. Restoring relationships with enemies wasn't on people's radar, unless there was an ulterior motive. Justice and peace were primarily won by overpowering your enemy and subjecting them. This was the way of the Romans and the vision of the revolutionary Jewish Zealots. This was the method people expected a Jewish Messiah to follow—that he would release the Jews from the grip of Rome, most probably through armed conflict.

If armed conflict didn't work, justice was won by collaborating with your enemy so you could get a piece of their pie, as done by the Jewish tax collectors and the chief priests. Finally, another option for achieving social justice was to tune out and create your own parallel universe. This was the way of the Essenes, the religious separatists of their day, who rejected both society and corrupt mainstream religion to create their own communal system of justice.

Jesus and Conventional Wisdom

Marcus Borg calls Jesus a sage, a teacher of wisdom. His was an alternative wisdom that flied in the face of the taken-for-granted understandings of the day. Whenever he taught, he had to confront society's prevailing conventional wisdom and introduce a new paradigm. The paradigm of the reign of God.[9]

When Jesus proclaimed "Blessed are the poor" in the Sermon on the Mount (Luke 6:20), he wasn't talking about the inner-city homeless or the impoverished living in a distant continent. The poor were literally around 90 percent of the crowd sitting in front of him. This was truly good news for them. None of the religious leaders had ever told them they were blessed, only cursed. When Jesus condemned the temple elites in his famous "Woe to you" warnings to the Pharisees and teachers of the law, everyone knew who they were—the professional religious leaders in the temple. It was scandalous to critique the religious gatekeepers. When Jesus challenged the

9. Borg, *Meeting Jesus Again*, 75.

rich and called them to repent of indulgence (Luke 6:24–25), it was a shock to everyone. The rich were wealthy because God blessed them, went the conventional wisdom. Jesus turned this upside down.

When he taught that the reign of God is like children, it was unheard of. Children were not highly esteemed. Equating the emerging reign of God with them was elevating the least in society. When Jesus taught nonviolence in response to physical force, it was revolutionary, going against every conceivable philosophy. His call to love one's enemies restored a lost command in the law that had been all but forgotten (Exod 23:4). When he welcomed women into his entourage of followers to the point of making them emissaries, he destroyed society's conventional wisdom on class and power. Jesus was the ultimate feminist of his day. In teaching all these things, Jesus was introducing the way of a radical social justice.

Confronting Wealth, Class, and Power

We already saw how Jesus elevated the poor (90 percent of society) as fit for the reign of God because the heart of God has a special place for them—those impoverished, the sick, unclean, and marginalized. Now, we considered how he engaged the wealthy 10 percent, including the upper classes, and those in power.

Several of us in our group, along with other friends who liked to have "pub theology" discussions, were sitting at Hare & Hounds Brewpub in Poulsbo, outside of Seattle, each with a pint of beer in front of us. There was a wide array of colors of brews, from light hefeweizen to some ambers to black porters. "So, let's address this," Dan said, after sipping his glass of *Mocha Death*, a dark seasonal ale and a local favorite out of Bremerton, Washington. "How did Jesus confront the rich?"

"To Jesus, it was harder for a rich man to enter the kingdom of God than for a camel to go through an eye of a needle," someone said.

"True," I said. "But remember, he wasn't talking about the rich entering heaven, per se. The reign or 'kingdom of God' isn't about the afterlife primarily, but the influence of God in the here and now."

"Garry Wills has good stuff to say about this," Dan reminded everyone (Wills was one of the authors we had read a lot). Dan paraphrased Wills's summary of Jesus' scorn for the wealthy elite. The original quote read like this: "Over and over again, the gospels tell us that the forces arrayed against Jesus are conditioned by the ownership of property. 'When the Pharisees heard what he was saying, they belittled him, attached as they were to riches' (Luke 16:14). Jesus explains why wealth is at odds with the life he brings the world. 'No servant can obey two lords. Either he will hate the one or love the other, or pamper the one and scant the other. You cannot serve both God and Greed' (Luke 16:13)."[10]

"So, it's not just possessing wealth that he condemned," another said, "but greediness."

"Did Jesus ever acknowledge that the rich have a place in the kingdom?" someone else asked.

"The only wealthy person Jesus commends is one who gave away half his possessions to the poor and made restitution to those he cheated," Gina remembered (Luke 19:8). "He called the wealthy class to serve the needy, rather than the needy to serve the wealthy. He was rejecting the conventional wisdom about the rich and the poor."

As our discussion continued, we delved into how Jesus compared children to the powerful, what he taught about the use of force and violence, and how he elevated women as equals with men. There was a theme of humility, service, and leveling the playing field for all.

"Let the children come to me. Don't chase them away. For the reign of God belongs to them,"[11] Jesus declares according to Matthew (19:14). "Unless you change and become like little children, you will never enter the reign of God" (Matt 18:2). Jesus wasn't advocating for more Sunday School instruction for kids or adults, he was saying children are people, and by their nature (their humility and innocence) they are more pure than adults, and a great example to emulate in the loving reign of God. This was an affront to the powerful. The conventional wisdom on power was a sham. To Jesus, the most humble and weak among them were superior to religious, political, or economic elites. We also speculated on how this flies in the face of the evangelical teaching on *original sin*. If children are born with *original sin*, then why would Jesus call us to change and become like them? Rather than reinforce an innate *sinful nature*, this teaching seems to reinforce that we are made in the image of God and children are closer, by nature, to that image. Later, more of *The Timeline* material would cast light on this topic.

We then addressed violence. Ultimately, it is the greatest tool of wealth and power. Just as Jesus opposed self-righteous affluence and force, he stood against their major instrument: violence. The reign of God operates on a

10. Wills, *What Jesus Meant*, 41.

11. My paraphrase.

whole new level than this present order, Jesus said. If it wasn't, his followers would have fought to prevent his capture.[12] He ordered Peter not to use his sword and rebuked the disciples when they asked if they should call fire down from heaven to destroy a village that rejected him . He consistently taught nonviolence and defended it with an uncanny rationale:

> I say to all you who hear me: Love your foes, help those who hate you, praise those who curse you, pray for those who abuse you. To one who punches your cheek, offer the other cheek. To one seizing your cloak, do not refuse the tunic under it. Whoever asks, give to him. Whoever seizes, do not resist. Exactly how you wish to be treated, in that way treat others. For if you love only those who love back, what mark of virtue have you? Sinners themselves love those who love back. If you treat well those treating you well, what mark of virtue have you? That is how sinners act. If you lend only where you calculate a return, what mark of virtue have you? Sinners, too, lend to sinners, calculating an exact return. No, rather love your foes, and treat them well, and lend without any calculation of return. Your great reward will be that you are children of the Highest One, who also favors ingrates and scoundrels. Be just as lenient as that lenient Father. Be not a judge, then, and you will not be judged. (John 18:36)

Then there was his unconventional ways on women. An interesting fact we learned was that women traveling openly with a rabbi was unheard of in first-century Judaism. Yet, "many" women followed Jesus in this way. Garry Wills explains how the story of Martha and Mary (Luke 10:38–42), wherein Mary is praised for listening to Jesus teach rather than helping Martha in the kitchen, is often misinterpreted. In Jesus' day, this wouldn't have been construed as showing women it is better to live a religious life over a secular one, perhaps by joining a convent, but rather supporting the education of women. "Jerome Nerey, after a close study of social conditions in Jesus' time, shows that Jesus was defending the woman who would be criticized in his era for acting outside her condoned space, entering the world of the learned (signified by sitting at the feet of the teacher). So, far from closing women into a safe retreat from the world, he was beckoning them out into it, to join men in knowledge and action."[13]

Promoting the equality of women and men in this day was revolutionary. This was why Jesus' disciples were shocked that he would speak

12. John 18:36

13. Wills, *What Jesus Meant*, 53.

to women in public, even more so, if they were Samaritan women as was recorded once: "At this point his followers arrived and were thunderstruck [*ethaumazon*] that he was speaking to a woman."[14] Later, Paul latched onto Jesus' radical egalitarianism by boldly announcing, "There is no male or female in Christ" (Gal 3:27).

Confronting the Religious Elites

Later in that discussion at Hare & Hounds Pub, we drew on our group's research and talked about how Jesus confronted the upper-class religious leaders, who by their position were superior to everyone else. Jesus, like all good Jewish prophets, laid into these religious elites, the "clean" 10 percent. We marveled how Jesus spoke the most serious words of rebuke to these religious leaders. It wasn't sexual immorality or homosexuality (which he never addressed at all), or prostitution, or alcohol abuse or irresponsible reveling that he was concerned about. With the exception of adultery, which he specifically addressed in the context of men practicing casual divorce and "putting away" or abandoning women,[15] most of what we moderns consider as run-of-the-mill immorality, he never mentioned in his teachings. His most stern words were for religionists. He accused them of being two-faced hypocrites.

> Above all, Jesus attacks the arrogance of the spiritual leaders of his time. There is no reason to think this was a special attack on the Jewish religion. He would apply the same standards to every religion, including the ones later invoking his name. All three ranks of spiritual leadership of his time were arraigned by Jesus—the noble and priestly Sadducees, the zealous Pharisees, the learned Scribes. He scorches them. He flays them.[16]

Listen to his words to the teachers of the law, scribes, and Pharisees:[17]

> Woe to you . . . you hypocrites! You shut the reign of God in men's faces. You yourselves do not enter.
>
> You devour widows' houses and for a show make lengthy prayers. Therefore you will be punished most severely.

14. Ibid., 48.
15. See Francisco, "Does God Really Hate Divorce?"; Callison, *Divorce*.
16. Wills, *What Jesus Meant*, 49.
17. Matt 23:13–39.

> You . . . win a single convert . . . and . . . make him twice as much a son of gehenna as you are.
>
> Woe to you, blind guides! . . . You have neglected the more important matters of the law—justice, mercy, and faithfulness.
>
> You clean the outside . . . but inside [you] are full of greed and self-indulgence. Blind Pharisee!
>
> You are like white washed tombs, which look beautiful on the outside but on the inside are full of dead men's bones and everything unclean.
>
> You appear . . . righteous, but on the inside . . . full of hypocrisy and wickedness.
>
> You snakes! You brood of vipers! How will you escape being condemned to gehenna?
>
> Upon you will come all the righteous blood that has been shed on the earth.
>
> I tell you the truth, all this will come upon this generation.

As scholar N. T. Wright says, "Woe is called on the heads of the Pharisees, because they are so concerned with ritual purity that they cannot see the huge disease that is growing within Israel."[18] The disease of Israel was corruption of the true faith that abandoned love for fellow man—both the "impure" poor and sick and the "impure" foreigners (aliens) in their land—and focused on a legalism that failed to care for the oppressed in the name of obeying God's law. As Jesus said, they "strain out a gnat" (obey some menial command in the law) and "swallow a camel" (ignore what really counts—justice, mercy, and faithfulness). This is why parables like the Good Samaritan had such a sting to them. Samaritans were "unclean" but Jesus made one the hero of a story because unlike the "clean" priests and Levites, the Samaritan was the only one who had mercy on the victim of a mugging. In Jesus' world, the "unclean" was the clean one and the "clean" was the unclean.

The thing that infuriated the religious elites was that Jesus had the unmitigated gall to declare the "unclean" were purer than they were! Prostitutes and tax collectors were entering the loving reign of God ahead of the religionists. In as much as anyone embraces the love and mercy ethic of the

18. Wright, *Jesus and the Victory of God*, 331.

Way—that love for God and fellow man are more important than sacrifices, purity, and the law—they are the true "clean" ones, Jesus declared. Outsiders and the "unclean" who feed the hungry, give water to the thirsty, clothe the naked, and visit the prisoners are welcomed in the reign of God, and those who don't, no matter what religious heritage they claim, are cast out! Outsiders become insiders in Jesus' kingdom. The last become first, and the first become last.

Wealth, Class, and Power Today

Finally, our pub discussion took a turn to answer the question of how we should handle wealth, class, and power today. We speculated on how we could apply Jesus' radical call for social justice to our society. What historical movements have there been that emulate Jesus' teaching on this topic? In light of Jesus condemning the religionists of his day, what should our response be to institutional religion?

"First of all," one of the participants said, "It seems obvious that in the reign of God that Jesus announced, there is no class, caste, or social status based on being rich and poor." She went on to explain how there is only equality for all. The poor have a special place in God's heart as they are often oppressed at the expense of the rich. Jesus calls everyone to have that same heart. Jesus empowered the poor by elevating them socially and defending them economically. We should do the same, she said.

"Absolutely," another declared. "Jesus calls the wealthy to use their wealth to serve others, especially the poor. It seems to me that the Path of Christ calls us to expose the corruption of the rich and powerful wherever we find it—whether inside systems that favor the rich based on corporate greed or individual selfishness."

"Yeah, when you look at Jesus' teaching on wealth on the whole," the first person added, "it's the opposite of the Prosperity Doctrine that some churches push. God doesn't promise to enrich everyone but calls the rich to sacrifice on behalf of the poor."

"I struggle with how to handle and confront evil," a third person said. "Our world is still caught in an 'overcome-your-enemy' paradigm. Most Christians today understand forgiveness and love toward enemies only on an individual level. Society as a whole has not learned this lesson. Militarism still reigns supreme in our world. But, according to Jesus' love ethic, the solution to evil is not to squash it with military might but overcome it with good. I'm curious what others think about this."

"I agree," Gina said. "I think the evidence is plain that Jesus didn't merely teach nonviolence at an individual level but on a societal level. Like, how he actually predicted and condemned the Jewish Revolt [64–73 CE] and the devastation and destruction that would transpire if his Way of peace was ignored."

"Not to mention his clear teaching on how to respond to enemies," someone interjected.

"I think what really proves that, Gina," I said, "is the historical record of the early church. They were pacifists." I explained what I learned from Robin Meyers when he wrote, "Scholars are now united in this important finding: for at least two centuries, once a Christian was baptized, he could no longer consider military service."[19]

Dan piped in: "Yes, I think Meyers has uncovered another dirty little secret of Western Christianity. That the just war theory is false at worst or abused at best. Nonviolence was a hallmark of the early church.[20] Why isn't it today? The early church would probably be appalled at the way most of modern Christianity, except for maybe the Quakers and Mennonites, support the military and its solutions at the drop of a hat."

Someone asked about the record of the early church. Dan explained that we had found many quotes from early church fathers, including Justin Martyr, Clement of Alexandria, Tertullian, Origen, Hippolytus, and many others, from the second and third centuries. He paraphrased Justyn Martyr, when he said, "All of us [believers] throughout the whole wide earth have traded in our weapons of war." And Origen, when he wrote, "For we no longer take 'sword against a nation,' nor do we learn 'any more to make war,' having become sons of peace for the sake of Jesus." The record showed this was the dominant, if not universal, practice among the early Jesus Movement. It wasn't until the Emperor Constantine that the attitude toward serving as a soldier changed. Up until then, the attitude in this quote from Mercellus the Centurion, spoken as he left the army of Emperor Diocletian in 298 CE, was typical: "I serve Jesus Christ the eternal King. I will no longer serve your emperors. It is not right for a Christian to serve the armies of this world."[21]

19. Meyer, *Underground Church*, ch. 4.

20. Sprinkle, *Fight*.

21. Porterfield, "40 Early Church Quotes on Violence," quote 21.

I recalled another conclusion Meyers came to that we all agreed we should seriously consider and that would inform us how to rethink the traditional view. "Nonviolence is not optional for Christians. It is essential. There will be no recovery for Christianity as a vital and transformative force in the West without a return to our pacifist roots."[22]

I brought up our justice system. "Another good example is our mentality of retributive justice rather than personal restoration. You know, the focus on punishment for its own sake, rather than to restore someone to society. It's pervasive in our criminal justice system, with thirty-two US states still having the death penalty and our prisons busting at the seams with nonviolent criminals. I think our society has much to learn from the Way of nonviolence and forgiveness that Jesus taught."

We also touched on social justice. It occurred to us that when Jesus worked to level society's playing field, it was the foundation for human justice. Jesus was fighting for basic human rights of the poor, children, women, the sick, and the oppressed and followers of his Path should do the same.

"It seems to me that all movements that defend human rights are part of the Path of Christ," someone concluded, "whether they are Christian or not."

We were reminded of some of our own experiences carefully examining history. We were pleasantly surprised that society had made some great advances in social justice. And although the church was sometimes involved in such movements, it wasn't always or necessarily. It appeared that Jesus' teaching had influenced society's attitude toward children, women, and the sick, for example. Whereas it's been a long road, more advances are needed, and there are still pockets of oppression in the world, society has come a long way from the days of antiquity when it comes to the proliferation of hospitals, emergency healthcare, ambulatory services, children's rights, abolishing slavery, public education, worker's rights, women's rights, civil rights, human rights, racial equality, and international relief and development. Could it be that all these are examples of Jesus' loving reign of God coming into the world? That the "good news" includes the emergence of a radical social justice in society worldwide?

Between us, we thought of four examples of recent historical movements that in a large measure emulated Jesus' social justice teaching of love, forgiveness, and nonviolence. The abolitionist movement of the nineteenth century led by people like William Wilberforce in England and

22. Meyer, *Underground Church*, 88–114.

the Quakers, Mennonites, and Amish in the United States, the Mahatma Gandhi-led independence movement in India, the American civil rights movement led by Martin Luther King Jr., and the anti-apartheid movement in South Africa led by Nelson Mandela. Although only two of those movements were obviously Christian (the abolitionists and Martin Luther King Jr., as a Baptist clergyman), the other two were influenced mightily by what Jesus taught. Gandhi, as a progressive Hindu, took his nonviolent philosophy from Jesus and the gospels. Mandela, when he left prison after twenty-seven years found himself at a crossroads as to how to fight apartheid going forward. Should he foreswear some of his violent roots in the fight? He chose the way of forgiveness and racial reconciliation. "As I walked out the door toward the gate that would lead to my freedom, I knew if I didn't leave my bitterness and hatred behind, I would still be in prison," he said.[23] It wasn't a far stretch to surmise, this attitude would have been exceedingly rare in antiquity. The reign of God that Jesus announced, in the form of love and forgiveness, was having its way as history progressed. Should believers in his love ethic make things like prison reform and a return to pacifism next on a social justice agenda?

Finally, there was the question of religion. What should be the response of those on the Path of Christ to the religionists of our day? Undoubtedly, we agreed, we are to stand against the corrupting power of religion that divides people into "us versus them," those who believe the right thing pitted against those who don't, the pure versus the impure, as well as the power of faith-based institutions to control and spiritually (and sexually) abuse its members. But this was a much larger question that needed more examination. We would address it in detail when we looked at the portion of *The Timeline* that recorded the history of the "church" and how it had morphed from the original intention of Christ and his earliest followers.

Yet, there was one area that we were missing at this juncture. Jesus confronted the corrupt purity system and the powers of wealth and class in Jewish society, but the question is, what do we make of his calls for judgment on such systems and for individuals guilty of their perpetuation? We had examined the good news for the marginalized—the poor, sick, unclean, women, children, Samaritans, Gentiles, etc.—but what of the bad news he announced to those he considered corrupt and evil—the Pharisees, Sadducees, the teachers of the law, the priests, scribes, or some of the

23. "Nelson Mandela > Quotes > Quotable Quote," https://www.goodreads.com/quotes/278812-as-i-walked-out-the-door-toward-the-gate-that.

villages that rejected his message? What did Jesus mean when he spoke of judgment, woes, and future punishment? The answer, we discovered, wasn't completely in line with the traditional view we had largely been taught.

Chapter Five

The Bad News: What Jesus' Call for Judgment Meant

We had learned how Jesus brought good news to the masses. But we also became aware how he brought bad news for the elites and the religious system they had built. In truth, he challenged anyone who was oppressing the weak or hindering the "unclean" from enjoying the benefits of God's favor. Many times, he gave warnings and pronounced judgment on various people, most notably the religious leaders, but also on the wealthy and even on three villages; ones who opposed his message of the arrival of the loving reign of God. His warnings were for the whole nation of Israel. This included the Jewish Zealots whose answer to Roman occupation was hatred and eventually, revolt and violence.[1] It was these judgments that got him in trouble.

In general, Jesus' judgment was against the religion of the day. Historian Garry Wills reminds us.

> The most striking, resented, and dangerous of Jesus' activities was his opposition to religion as that was understood in his time. This is what led to his death. Religion killed him. He opposed all formalisms in worship—ritual purifications, sacrifice, external prayer and fasting norms, the Sabbath [codes] and eating codes, priesthoods, the Temple, and the rules of the Sadducees, Pharisees, and Scribes.[2]

1. The Zealots of Jesus' generation didn't develop into a violent movement until the 60s CE.

2. Wills, *What Jesus Meant*, 59.

These were some of the reasons for his calls for judgment. The religious leaders had turned the house of God into a "den of robbers," grew wealthy from the sacrificial system that was stacked against the unclean, and put religious burdens on people without lifting a finger to help them. The wealthy did not care for the needy. The populace, and especially the Zealots, had no interest in loving their enemies as a witness to a compassionate God "for all nations," which was the way of peace for Jesus. The legalistic purity system had circumvented the simple call to love one's neighbor.

To be sure, many people listened to his and John the Baptist's calls for change. Jesus may have confronted the conventional wisdom of the elites and seats of power and corruption, but he didn't condemn individual people that these sectors represented. One of his disciples, Matthew, was one of the despised tax collectors, who were actually wealthy tax profiteers.[3] He loved a rich young ruler according to Mark (10:21). Earlier, we saw how he commended a rich man who changed his indulgent ways. In Matthew and Luke, he healed a Roman centurion's servant. He honored a Samaritan in a parable and regularly traveled through Samaritan and Gentile territory, healing their sick and unclean. He told a Pharisee who had answered him with uncanny wisdom that he wasn't far from the reign of God. Jesus was open and inclusive to all. His call wasn't to drop out of society like the Essenes, nor drive off the pagans, nor completely write off the religious leaders, but rather, welcome all who were willing to change and enter into the community of the way of love.

But what should we make of his calls of judgment? As part of *The Timeline* study, we decided to investigate them from a historical perspective to shed light on their meaning for Jesus' audience and for us today. The following is an examination of the Old Testament historical record on the meaning of judgment.

What Judgment Meant in Jewish Tradition

Pronouncing judgment on the present regime was not unusual in Jewish prophetic literature, nor a sign of being anti-Jewish. Jesus was not unlike the Old Testament prophets who played the same role. Jeremiah warned Israel to turn back to God before the Babylonian destruction of Jerusalem. Isaiah likened Jerusalem to Sodom and Gomorrah, a symbol of judgment and destruction from the time of Abraham.

3. Nyland, *Source New Testament*, 25.

First, we noticed the reason for judgment. A typical reason was idolatry, serving other gods, and breaking covenant with God. But there was a root reason that had to do with social justice and the treatment of people. Ezekiel spelled out the reason for the judgment on Sodom: "Now this was the sin of your sister Sodom: She and her daughters were arrogant, overfed and unconcerned; they did not help the poor and needy" (16:49). Moreover, Isaiah proclaims "woes" on Israel for their neglecting the weak and poor.

> Woe to those who make unjust laws, to those who issue oppressive decrees, to deprive the poor of their rights and withhold justice from the oppressed of my people, making widows their prey and robbing the fatherless. What will you do on the day of reckoning, when disaster comes from afar? To whom will you run for help? Where will you leave your riches? Nothing will remain but to cringe among the captives or fall among the slain. (Isa 10:1–4)

These "woes" mirror the "woes" that Jesus delivered to the corrupt, temple elites. Next, we noticed how the prophets claimed that God used other peoples as a tool to punish Israel—the Babylonians or Assyrians, for example (Isa 10:5–6). But God's discipline of his people always ends and sometimes it is then directed toward the very ones God used to discipline them, as Isaiah states.

> Oh my people who live in Zion, do not be afraid of the Assyrians, who beat you with a rod and lift up a club against you, as Egypt did. Very soon my anger against you will end and my wrath will be directed in their direction. (Isa 10:24–25)

Finally, the usual cycle was this: God's blessings; then Israel breaking covenant and oppressing the weak; God's temporary punishment, which ends with God comforting Israel again.

> In that day, you will say: "I will praise you, O Lord. Although you were angry with me, your anger has turned away and you have comforted me. Surely God is my salvation; I will trust and not be afraid . . . with joy you will draw water from the wells of salvation." (Isa 12:1–3)

The key to gaining favor is humility and contrition. God's heart is to restore everyone. This theme came out over and over.

> I will not accuse them forever, nor will I always be angry, for then they would faint away because of me—the very people I have created. I was enraged by their sinful greed; I punished them, and hid

> my face in anger, yet they kept on in their willful ways. I have seen their ways, but I will heal them. (Isa 57:16–18)

As the psalmist says, "For his anger lasts only a moment, but his favor lasts a lifetime" (30:5), and, "The Lord is compassionate and gracious, slow to anger, abounding in love. He will not always accuse, nor will he harbor his anger forever" (103:8–9). In fact, the Apostle Paul, when writing about the fate of Israel in his day, boldly declared, "All Israel will be saved" (Rom 11:26).

Israel under Rome

Then we looked at the context of the Jews under Roman occupation in Palestine. Foreigners and soldiers had occupied their land. Rome was one of the most brutal regimes in all of human history. We had already learned how the Romans killed twelve thousand Jews when they first took Jerusalem in 63 BCE and how the revolt in 6 CE was crushed (chapter 4). In an earlier revolt in 4 BCE, Athronges the Shepherd was easily defeated.[4] In Jesus' day, the memories of these and other minor Zealot skirmishes remained strong in the mindset of the populace. Especially when you consider how the Romans routinely used crucifixion as a powerful deterrent to punish criminals and squash uprisings.

Jesus' Warnings of Judgment

We then placed Jesus' message in the context of the tradition of the prophets and Rome's occupation. N. T. Wright, the renowned New Testament scholar, who Marcus Borg called "the leading British Jesus scholar of his generation," helped us put things in focus. The big questions were: What was Jesus referring to when he talked of judgment or hell or eternal punishment? Could it be that he was only talking about a local, first-century judgment on those who rejected his Way? Like the destruction of Jerusalem and the temple that would occur thirty-three to thirty-seven years from when he spoke? Or, as we had learned in our church traditions, was he also, more importantly, referring to the final judgment at the end of our space-time world? N. T. Wright taught us that most liberal scholars like Albert Schweitzer (early 20th c.) think that he was speaking of the latter and that he was proved

4. *Wikipedia*, s.v. "Jewish Messiah Claimants," sect. 1.1, Before the Common Era.

wrong. Conservatives also think he was speaking of the latter and believe the final judgment is yet to come (they believe there is a double meaning to such judgment passages, one referring to the destruction of Jerusalem in 70 CE and one referring to the final judgment at the end of history). But, we discovered, there was another, more historically-grounded way of looking at it.

When we scoured the four gospels for Jesus' statements about any form of judgment or punishment, we found a sampling of statements like these in a typical English translation of the New Testament. Often they were announcements of punishment that was to come in the form or a prophecy. First, was Jesus' precursor, John the Baptist, who also told people to repent, for the reign of God is near.

> **To the religious elites:** You brood of vipers! Who warned you to flee from the coming wrath? Produce fruit in keeping with repentance. (Matt 3:7–8)

Then Jesus' many warnings of a time of judgment and impending destruction:

> **To the religious elites after exposing their hypocrisy:** Woe to you . . . You brood of vipers! How will you escape being condemned to *gehenna*? [Greek: *gehenna* is a metaphor for judgment, not eternal damnation, as we will learn]. (Matt 23:33)
>
> And so upon you will come all the righteous blood that has been shed on earth. (Matt 23:35)
>
> Your house [temple] is left to you desolate. (Matt 23:38)
>
> **Regarding the temple at the time of the end of the age:** Not one stone here will be left upon the other, every one will be thrown down. (Matt 24:2 and Luke)
>
> Your house [temple] is left to you desolate. (Matt 23:38)
>
> Jesus said, "I will destroy this house [temple] and no one will be able to rebuild it." (Gospel of Thomas, saying 71)
>
> **To Jerusalem at time of the end of the age:** The days will come upon you when your enemies will build an embankment against you and encircle you and hem you in on every side. They will dash you to the ground, you and the children within your walls. They

will not leave one stone on another, because you did not recognize the time of God's coming to you. (Luke 19:41–44)

When you see Jerusalem surrounded by armies, you will know that its desolation is near. (Luke 21:20)

This is the time of punishment . . . there will be great distress in the land and wrath against this people. They will fall by the sword . . . Jerusalem will be trampled on by the Gentiles. (Luke 21: 22–24)

To villages that did not turn and believe the good news: Woe to you . . . it will be more bearable for Tyre and Sidon [and Sodom] on the day of judgment than for you. (Matt 11:20–24)

To the crowds: Enter through the narrow gate. For wide is the gate and broad is the road that leads to destruction, and many will enter through it. (Matt 7:13)

To anonymous listeners: Do you think that these Galileans were worse sinners than all the other Galileans because they suffered this way? [referring to some who the Roman governor, Pilate, had executed]. I tell you, no! But unless you repent, you too will all perish.

At the time of the end of the age and the coming of the Son of Man: It will be like the time of Noah and the flood; many people will be taken away and perish. (Matt 24:37–41)

For then there will be great distress [tribulation], unequaled from the beginning of the world until now. (Matt 24:21)

To those who ignore the needs of the poor, sick, and those in prison, when all the nations are gathered when the Son of Man comes at the end of the age: They will go away to eternal punishment [Greek: *aionos kolasis*—the rehabilitation or chastisement of the age to come;[5] not hell, as we will discuss below].

To the wicked servant at the time of the end of the age when the Son of Man comes: Throw that worthless servant outside, into the darkness, where there will be weeping and gnashing of teeth. (parable of the Talents, Matt 25:30)

5. We had learned how this phrase, "eternal punishment," has been mistranslated over the years. See below and Nyland, *The Source New Testament*, 63.

> **To his followers at time of the end and tribulation:** When these things begin to take place, stand up and lift up your heads, because your redemption is drawing near (Luke 21:28) *and* Be always on the watch, and pray that you may be able to escape all that is about to happen. (Luke 21:36)

Then we noticed something. There was overwhelming textual evidence that Jesus was referring to events that would occur during the current generation in judgment of them, not to a generation in the distant future. He was referring to judgment that was "about to happen." These were very important time indicators and also point to why that generation was being judged; and why Jesus was not addressing generations in the future or people other than the Jews who rejected his way of peace.

"A wicked and adulterous generation demands a sign! But none will be given it, except the sign of the prophet Jonah," he told the Pharisees and teachers of the law (Matt 12:39). "I tell you the truth, all this will come upon this generation," he told the religious elites, after describing their seven "woes" (Matt 23:36). "Yes, I tell you, this generation will be responsible for it all," he told them again, referring to the blood of the innocent Jewish prophets who were persecuted (Luke 11:51). "I tell you the truth, this generation will certainly not pass away until all these things will happen," he told his disciples, referring to the time of the end of the age, the tribulation period, the coming of the Son of Man, and the destruction of Jerusalem (See Matthew and Luke 21:32). "I tell you the truth, some who are standing here will not taste death before they see the Son of Man coming in his kingdom," he told his disciples (Matt 16:28). "I tell you the truth, you will not finish going through the cities of Israel before the Son of Man comes," he told his disciples, who he sent into towns to spread the good news of the kingdom and to heal the sick (Matt 10:23).

All these passages that refer to the present generation or the very people Jesus was addressing (e.g., "*you* will not finish going through the cities of Israel"), when carefully examined, were in the context of the "coming of the Son of Man" or a coming day of judgment. They were not described as events in the distant future but rather as events in the very-near present day, within one generation.

And finally, we noticed, in our research on the afterlife, that many of the terms Jesus used for a coming judgment, had very sloppy translations. The word "hell" is actually the Greek term *gehenna*, the smoldering garbage dump outside Jerusalem. *Gehenna* was used by Jesus as a metaphor for judgment. Evidence is overwhelming he was not referring to the modern concept of everlasting damnation.[6]

Also, the phrase "eternal punishment" (in Matthew and Luke), is mistranslated. Many translators denote *aionios kolasis* as "punishment of the age" or "age-enduring punishment," for the Greek word *aionios* literally means, "pertaining to an age."[7] In the Greek version of the Old Testament (the Septuagint), its root is even used for very short periods of time, as in Jonah being in the belly of the whale for *aion*, which in this case was three days.[8] Greek lexicographer, Ann Nyland, translates *aionios kolasis* as a "rehabilitation for a set period of time." Moreover, the term for "punishment," *kolasis*, is a corrective, restorative term. "The Greek writers used *kolasis* to refer to rehabilitation, to the correction of wrongdoers so that they would not do wrong again. Generally, *timoria*, refers to retributive punishment and *kolasis* to remedial discipline."[9] *Timoria* is not used by Jesus in this passage. The New Testament authors record him using the term for remedial discipline (or the Aramaic equivalent, as that is the language Jesus spoke). There are many English New Testament translations that have these correct renderings of which most modern Christians are unaware.[10] So, the calls for the "time of punishment" and "day of judgment" were remedial, not retributive and everlasting.

As we took all these things into account, N. T. Wright helped us put things in perspective. He explained how these were warnings of an "impending national disaster: a coming, political, military, and social nightmare, as a result of which Jerusalem will be destroyed."[11]

> Jesus' warnings fit also quite naturally into the wider context of the first century, where Rome, provoked before, remained a threatening, brooding presence . . . Jesus' warnings carried a constant reference to the present generation . . . the story he was telling was not about some general or abstract truth . . . his message was specifically directed to that moment in Israel's history.[12]

6. Stetson, *Christian Universalism*, 32–35.

7. McDonald, *Evangelical Universalist*, 147.

8. Stetson, *Christian Universalism*, 41.

9. Nyland, *The Source New Testament*, 63.

10. Amirault, "Bible Translations That Don't Teach Eternal Torment," http://www.tentmaker.org/books/GatesOfHell.html.

11. Wright, *Jesus and Victory of God*, 320.

12. Ibid., 324–25.

Referring to judgment passages that don't specifically target the destruction of Jerusalem and the temple:

> The "normal" way of reading these passages within the Christian tradition has been to see them as references to a general *post mortem* judgment in hell; but this betrays fairly thorough lack of historical understanding.[13]

> [These passages] have been read as general warnings of hellfire in an afterlife, rather than the literal and physical-divine-judgment-through-Roman judgment that we have seen to be characteristic of Jesus' story.[14]

Referring to apocalyptic language Jesus used (e.g., the time of the end of the age, the coming of the Son of Man, heaven and earth passing away, the sun and stars and moon blocked of light): "The warnings that utilize such language are not to be siphoned off as dealing with only some far-off future final judgment, in the sense of the end of the space-time universe. Warnings of this sort, are on the contrary, exactly what we might expect on the lips of a [Jewish] prophet."[15] In other words, they are all familiar Jewish metaphors, taken from the prophets and referring to cataclysmic events that would occur in the near future.

> They do not speak of the collapse or end of the space-time universe. They are, as we have seen from passages in Isaiah and Jeremiah . . . , typical Jewish imagery for events within the present order that are felt and perceived as "cosmic" or, as we should say, "earth-shattering."[16]

Referring to the villages that Jesus warned would face judgment:

> Once again, this is not a prediction of a non-spatio-temporal "last judgment." It was a straightforward warning of what would happen if this or that Galilean village had refused the way of peace which Jesus had come to bring.[17]

13. Ibid., 323.
14. Ibid., 344.
15. Ibid., 325.
16. Ibid., 362.
17. Ibid., 329.

> The event that was coming swiftly upon Jerusalem would be the divine judgment of [God's] rebellious people, exercised through Rome's judgment on her rebellious subject.[18]

> This judgment was not a "last judgment" for the peoples of the earth, but a great national disaster looming on the horizon.[19]

Here are examples of how many seemingly general statements of Jesus were actually talking about this "looming national disaster":

> The way that Jesus was beckoning would pass through a narrow gate, and many who thought they were inalienably within the people of God would be proved wrong."[20]

> Here, as in the book of Daniel . . . , the coming of the Son of Man on the clouds of heaven was never conceived as a primitive form of space travel, but as a symbol for a mighty reversal of fortunes within history and at the national level.[21]

Clarifying the metaphoric meaning of the "second coming of Jesus" or "coming of the Son of Man," Wright states:

> The word "coming," so easily misread in English, is in Greek *erchomenon*, and so could mean either "coming" or "going" . . . The son of man figure "comes" . . . [or goes] from earth to heaven, vindicated after suffering.[22]

Wright shows how the "son of man" term is from the prophet Daniel, who sets the scene from the perspective of heaven not earth. The son of man or Jesus "coming in the clouds" is Jesus going to heaven entering the presence of God as a vindicated king, not coming to earth.

> The great city that had rejected Jesus' message, his way of peace, would be destroyed. He would thereby be vindicated as a prophet; yes, and more than a prophet.[23]

Reading N. T. Wright is quite a chore. It's not without its difficulties tracking such a brilliant scholar, especially his more scholarly works from

18. Ibid., 342.
19. Ibid.
20. Ibid., 327.
21. Ibid., 341.
22. Ibid., 361.
23. Ibid., 360.

which the quotes above came, which, by the way, were only the tip of the iceberg. Yet, it's a rich and rewarding experience. Personally, I needed a couple of beers after reading this most comprehensive and exhaustive examination that left no historical rock unturned. It just goes to show how important a historical-critical approach to reading the Bible is, and how much danger one can get into, when the Bible is only digested devotionally, with little historical context.

Three controversial conclusions (for some) were plain enough: One, historically, the "second coming of Jesus" was not seen as a literal event in the distant future, but a figurative coming into God's presence at the time the judgment of Jerusalem occurred, a vindication that Jesus was a true prophet and "anointed one." Something that happened in the first century. Two, Jesus never referred to the end of the world as we know it, but merely the end of the Jewish age of temple worship (Old Covenant) and the beginning of the new reign of God that is based on love not religion. And three, Jesus never spoke of a literal eternal conscious torment in hell. He only spoke of restorative punishment, which seemed to match what the prophets taught about God's heart to eventually heal evildoers and not harbor anger forever. These were evocative claims, yes, but ones that fit the facts we had discovered.

First-Century and Early Christian History

So, the question arose, does first-century history confirm this historical way at looking a Jesus' pronouncements of judgment? The answer is found in the Jewish historian Josephus, who wrote extensively about the Jewish Revolt from 66 to 73 CE and the destruction of Jerusalem and the temple in 70 CE in his volume called *The Jewish War*.

"So, you're saying that all the judgment statements by Jesus were about events that would occur within the time of his contemporaries?" a visitor asked me at our discussion group in Dan and Gina's living room.

"Yes, and even all the statements about his return," I said. "They were all about things that would happen within the present lifetime of most people alive in that day. His return was a figurative one, not a literal one. All that stuff about 'coming in the clouds' and 'when the son of man comes' were typical Jewish apocalyptic imagery that the Old Testament prophets used and were never taken literally, at least until centuries later when people started reading them with no Jewish historical or literary understanding."

"And all those statements about hell or eternal punishment or a day of judgment, too," Dan added. "They were about the coming judgment that happened when the Romans crushed the Jewish rebellion thirty-plus years later."

Our regular group was discussing some of N. T. Wright's material as well as the role of Josephus, who wrote about the Jewish revolt and the destruction of Jerusalem. His history was published in 75 CE, so it was only a few years after the events occurred. Since Josephus was an active participant in most of the events, it is amazingly detailed. Beginning as a Jewish rebel himself, he became a Roman negotiator when captured; hence, he has a broad perspective on the Jewish rebellion, the siege of Jerusalem, the destruction of the temple and the city, and the final resistance at Masada.

"What kinds of things are in Josephus' record?" Gina asked.

"Basically things that match Jesus' statements about 'tribulation' and the destruction of Jerusalem and other things," I said. "The lead up to the Jewish revolt. The existence of false prophets. Smaller conflicts and wars. Also, how Rome crushed the rebellion first through a long siege and then an attack of the city. Also, how the temple was destroyed and that part about it being 'desecrated' by both Jews and Romans. Even signs in the heavens. I think he recorded a comet in the shape of a sword in the sky over Jerusalem for a whole year.[24] Things like that. He called it the most horrendous experience any nation, before or since, had gone through."

"So, are you saying Jesus has nothing to say to us today about judgment of evil?" someone asked. "That there's no final judgment at the end or when people die?"

"No, I don't think that he has nothing to say about judgment to future generations," Dan said. "I think it tells us there's no Armageddon-type future end of the world. But, God still judges evil and when people harm others. It's just a different judgment than what we've been taught, though. It's a judgment, or correction, in this life or the next, which ultimately restores and rehabilitates evil or harmful people. It's not an everlasting damnation."

"A purifying, corrective punishment, you mean," another said.

"Yes, that's it. It doesn't mean it's easy, but it has hope for restoration. It also fits the theme of Jesus teaching on forgiveness; always reaching out to restore the lost sheep, never giving up on the prodigal son, saying there is never a time to close the door on forgiving your brother or sister. And Paul's statements that God gives all humanity over to disobedience so he

24. Hadas-Lebel, *Flavious Josephus*, 64.

can have mercy on them all. Or, as in Adam, all fall short, but in Christ, all will be justified."

"So, where did this concept of eternal damnation come from?" someone asked.

"It probably started when the Greek Scriptures were translated into Latin that the notion of everlasting punishment arose," Dan said. "It was then that the Greek word *aion* was mistranslated into a Latin word that meant *eternal*. Then the first person to write about hell was the Latin church father, Tertullian. But the main source of the doctrine came from Augustine, the fourth-century theologian.[25] He wrote about it extensively and was the first to condemn not only the wicked to eternal hell, but all non-Christians. He was also the first one that advocated using the fear of hell and physical coercion to try to turn heretics. He justified terror and persecution against apostates to save them.[26] The fear of damnation has been used ever since in varying degrees to try to convert people."

"That's sick," the questioner said. "A God of love draws people through loving kindness and hope. If he uses or allows suffering, like life's painful consequences for hurting others, it's to open our eyes, not scare us into heaven."

"I agree," I responded. "Also, another point on hell, almost all of the earliest church fathers had no such concept. They believed in what is called universal reconciliation—that ultimately, all people, both good and evil, would eventually be reconciled to God through Christ's Way of Love, in this life or the next.[27] When you examine early Christian history, you see this clearly in the record."[28]

"Okay, I have a few questions," the visitor said. "How do you really know that these terms were metaphors and shouldn't be taken literally as the return of Christ and the end of the world?"

There was a few seconds of silence. "Okay, I'll take a crack at that one," I said. "Well, first, is because the evidence for Jewish metaphors for such things is so strong. They are all over the Old Testament, including the terms Jesus used—the 'son of man coming on the clouds' is in Daniel, for example. Or, as it says in Isaiah that 'the Lord rides on a cloud and comes

25. Vincent, "Salvation Conspiracy."

26. Talbott, "Theological Justification for Terror."

27. "History of Universalism," http://www.christianuniversalist.org/resources/articles/history-of-universalism.

28. Hanson, *Universalism*.

to Egypt' [19:1]. These were never taken literally in Jewish history. And, as Wright says, there is no evidence historically that the Jews were expecting the end of the space-time universe.[29] They thought in terms of different ages, but with everything being in the present order. They spoke of the 'end of the age' and never used words that would mean 'end of the world as we know it.'"

"Alright, but there's also the question of real history," he continued. "How do we know that the gospels record in the New Testament about all this was genuine and not something the early church made up after 70 CE?"

"That is an excellent question," I said, "and one even good historians will disagree on. The answer is we have to treat the New Testament record like we do any other ancient document that claims to be historic. Approach it with an open mind and test it with historical tools."

"But there's the Jesus Seminar," the visitor continued. "That group of historians that graded whether Jesus' sayings were historical or not. They concluded only a small portion of the sayings of Jesus in the gospels were authentic."

"That's true," I said. "But they have been challenged by others, and not just conservative Christians. N. T. Wright and Garry Wills critique their methods, for example, because they start with premises that are suspect—like they already assume only a small portion of Jesus' sayings are truly his before they start investigating them. Garry Wills calls them 'the new fundamentalists' because they don't start with open minds.[30] Nevertheless, I find some of them reasonable in their conclusions, like Marcus Borg. The Jesus Seminar was not a monolithic block. There was disagreement among them. This is where you get into the hard work of following where the evidence leads, as best you can."

"An interesting point to add to that," Dan said, "is that the many Gospels sayings of Jesus that point to universalism received the most endorsement by the Jesus Seminar." Dan was probably thinking of the same thing I had read that said, "Virtually all Jesus' classic parables that have been interpreted as universalist since the beginning of Christian theology were judged by the Jesus Seminar to be genuine to him."[31]

"It may be," someone added, "that the Jesus 'zingers' [hard sayings] that many of them rejected were actually some of the verses that have

29. Wright, *New Testament and the People of God*, 333.

30. Wills, *What Jesus Meant*, xxv.

31. Vincent, *Salvation Conspiracy*.

been mistranslated, which would make sense why they thought them inauthentic."

The discussion continued. We could never solve this question or topic 100 percent conclusively. That is the way history works. But we had learned to think for ourselves and not blindly accept what others conclude without doing our homework. The way of looking at Jesus' judgments as outlined above seemed a reasonable course and much more probable than the way we were taught in our conservative theological backgrounds. It fit the record of good history.

Summarizing Jesus and Judgment

Regarding Jesus' calls for kingdom ethics and judgment, what did we discover? After announcing and physically demonstrating the good news to the masses and teaching them inner purity, Jesus, like a good Jewish prophet, laid into the supposedly "clean" religious elites. He announced they were unclean because they had no purity of heart. He purposely circumvented their strict laws. He healed on the Sabbath; he allowed the hungry to pick grain on the Sabbath; he ignored ceremonial washings, touched unclean people, and declared all foods clean. He condemned their extortion. He went into the temple and disrupted their corrupt market practices (taxes, money exchanges, and a sacrificial system that is stacked against the poor).

After revealing a heart of compassion for the inhabitants of Jerusalem (in Luke 19:4–5, he weeps over the city, lamenting it hasn't recognized his way of peace), he announced that their whole religious system is about to come crashing down, in the form of the destruction of the temple and the city of Jerusalem by their enemies, the Romans. A new socio-political era is about to begin. The end of the temple age and the beginning of the age to come—the loving reign of God was at hand; one that turns the world upside down. Anyone, who didn't change and enter into that new reign, that new way of defining Israel, was headed for destruction. He instructed his disciples to not support violence against Roman rule and to abandon the city at the sign of war. And, it happened very close to how he said it would. The current system came crashing down when Roman armies crushed the first-century Jewish Revolt (that also included Jewish factions who fought each other), razed the temple, destroyed Jerusalem, and killed at least one million Jews.[32] Those who followed Jesus' way of peace, who did not partake

32. "Great Revolt," https://www.jewishvirtuallibrary.org/jsource/Judaism/revolt.html.

in the Jewish Revolt, and fled the rebellion, were most likely spared.[33] As for the concept of eternal hell, it is erroneous and, as a doctrine, had no support among the earliest Jesus followers, let alone widespread acceptance, until Augustine and beyond. Notwithstanding some minor uncertainties, all of this is what history teaches us.

Our examination of Jesus teachings in historical context had ended. It was time to learn how to approach the Bible and a more responsible way of reading and using it. Is it altogether reliable down to every detail? What is authoritative for us today and what is not? It was time to rethink our sacred texts.

33. According to the 4th-c. church historian Eusebius, followers of Jesus fled Jerusalem to a city called Pella.

Chapter Six

The Bible: Rethinking Sacred Texts

YEARS AGO BEFORE DAN developed *The Timeline* and when we were still attending an evangelical Bible study, we both had trouble expressing some of our newfound discoveries to our evangelical friends. One meeting, after a particular New Testament passage was read, I brought up an argument from a book I had read that had convinced me that a phrase in that passage was mistranslated in most English Bibles. Because the mistranslation would have changed the meaning of the passage significantly, attendees thought I was crazy. They had never heard of such a claim. The thought that a familiar verse in the Bible was mistranslated was extremely disconcerting to them. Another time, I pointed out a minor but glaring inconsistency between the Gospel of John and Matthew and suggested an explanation (based on a historian's research) that Matthew had gotten a small, factual detail wrong, while the book of John had it right. Again, by people's reaction, you would have thought I had committed an unpardonable sin. There could be no mistakes in the Bible.

No telling what their reaction would be if I had told them what I later learned, that the evidence is strong that a small portion of the book of 1 Corinthians was not written by Paul but added by a copyist with a theological bias.[1] Earlier, we learned how Dan had similar reactions when he brought up an alternate interpretation of the afterlife to a group of evangelicals based on a well-researched book that examined early church history and meanings in the original Greek manuscripts of the New Testament. It became obvious to us we needed to get out of this closed-minded environment and into the freedom of a "craft-brewed path" to pursue the historical background about the Bible.

1. Fee, *First Epistle to the Corinthians*.

Based on our group's study of original biblical language and history in *The Timeline*, these examples pinpoint the need to rethink the Bible; to adjust from being a "literalist" with the Bible, to being a pragmatist.[2] This is based on six important conclusions about the Bible: one, English mistranslations of key words and phrases, although not widespread, are not uncommon. Over time, we discovered many examples of this based on historical scholars' study of first-century Greek, the language in which the New Testament was written, or ancient Hebrew. Two, popular misinterpretations abound due to ignorance of historical and cultural background. For too long, modern Christians, we learned, were looking at biblical passages with twenty-first-century eyes and missing what authors meant. Three, there are myriad minor and a few not-so-minor errors throughout the Bible, and no historical reason to believe the original manuscripts (which we don't have) are inerrant.[3] A careful, more objective study of the narratives and the history of the doctrine of inerrancy made this obvious. Four, throughout the centuries copyists have inserted or changed short passages due to bias or a compulsion to clarify. Studying and comparing the oldest manuscripts available brought this to light.[4] Five, the final "canon" of Scripture, although based on some solid, historically-critical rationale, was never as definitive as we were led to believe. This is based on historical evidence of how our New Testament emerged. And six, with the exception of the Torah and holiness code written for ancient Israel, the Bible was never meant to be used as a heavenly Rulebook or Blueprint. It never claims to be a collection of self-evident, unified, universally-applicable rules or dictates from above, but merely a human, historical record of how God engaged humankind.

As disconcerting as this is to fundamentalists and evangelicals, the irony is that our discoveries actually strengthened our faith. For when one takes what Bart Ehrman calls a "historical-critical" approach to the Bible, the result is a more thoughtful and intellectual faith that is based on sound evidence, not illogical traditional doctrines or wishful thinking. We learned

2. I define a "literalist," not as someone who never recognizes metaphor, hyperbole, or symbolism in the Bible, but someone who believes the Bible is always—that is, every passage equally—the literal, Word of God for us today and is therefore infallible. A "pragmatist" is someone who recognizes Divine elements in the Bible but uses reason, logic, and historical context to apply it to specific situations, and is not bound to "submit" to a particular passage if there are good reasons not to, based on internal and historical evidence.

3. Inerrancy is the belief that the Bible is free from error in its original form.

4. See Ehrman, *Misquoting Jesus*.

that the majority of biblical scholars, even ones who are strong believers, view the Bible with a critical, historical eye. They treat it like they would any historical document, and, even though they might come to different conclusions from each other regarding faith in Jesus, they have no problem viewing the Bible that way. They view the Bible as worthy of serious historical analysis with most of them having the intellectual honesty not to engage in idle speculation. Despite these facts, and in some cases because of them, we discovered for us the Bible is still an inspired collection of sacred texts with Divine fingerprints on it bringing a revolutionary message to the world. In our historical research of *The Timeline*, we found a middle way, between worshiping the Bible as an infallible instruction manual, and trashing it as an irrelevant collection of myths. Who knew?

The Bible Made Impossible

Christian Smith, author of *The Bible Made Impossible* notes a fascinating phenomenon. Despite the fact that conservative Christians believe the Bible is the infallible "Word of God" and the "only authority for faith and practice," countless Christian sects and denominations can't agree on what the Bible actually teaches! The history of Christian denominationalism is the history of Christians having variant interpretations of theological concepts in the Bible and splintering from another group to form a new one that they claim "rightly divides the Word of truth." These church movements have different views on charismatic gifts, prophecy, communion, worship, baptism, church polity, church discipline, morality, divorce, remarriage, evangelism, missions, social justice, the role of women, the "end times," the second coming of Christ, the millennium, homosexuality, and more.

Yet, literalists have a kind of internal logic. If it's true the Bible is the literal Word of God for us today and all of it has equal authority, then it stands to reason that it will make sense to the common person. God wouldn't make it confusing and contradictory. People can trust the "plain sense" of Scripture. Even though this makes sense, it hinges on whether the Bible is literally and equally God's Word for today. If it's not, and you rely on the "plain sense" of Scripture, you get yourself into trouble. You make the Bible impossible. James Bernstein, an Eastern Orthodox believer coming out of evangelicalism, describes his epiphany when he discovered this problem in his experience.

> To my surprise, this "common sense" approach led not to increased Christian clarity and unity, but rather to a spiritual free-for-all! Those who most strongly adhered to believing "only the Bible" tended to become the most factious, divisive, and combative of Christians—perhaps unintentionally. In fact, it seemed to me that the more one held the Bible as the only source of spiritual authority, the more factious and sectarian one became. We would even argue heatedly over verses on love![5]

The History of the Bible

One evening, Dan introduced us to a book called *Who Wrote the Bible?* by Richard Elliot Friedman. It made a strong historical case that the Torah—the first five books of our Old Testament, i.e., Genesis, Exodus, Leviticus, Numbers, and Deuteronomy—was a compilation of four separate narratives each written by a separate individual. Even though this contradicted the tradition we had been taught—that Moses wrote the whole Torah—it made sense. There was textual evidence that each narrative was written in a different style. The most glaring was the two creation stories within Genesis. In the first one, plants are created first, then animals, and finally Adam and Eve. In the second one, Adam was created, then plants, then animals, and finally Eve.

The most obvious inconsistency in the traditional view is how could Moses have written about things that occurred after he died? There are narratives that include just that. It became clear it is more probable that ancient Jewish authors—scribes or priests—wrote down their views of human and Jewish history based on their own oral traditions and later an editor or editors compiled those narratives into what became the Torah.

Other than the fact that Moses almost assuredly didn't write all these narratives, this wasn't particularly earth shattering to us. We found grounds that, rather than diminishing our view of the Old Testament, this study actually increased respect for it. Here was a historian using good scholarship and an analytical eye to objectively explain reasons for biblical contradictions with real evidence, rather than giving pat answers about simply trusting the "Word of God." It made us see the human element of compiling the Bible while still seeing various historical perspectives of ancient Jewish scribes.

5. Bernstein, *Which Came First*, 3.

Then we turned to the New Testament. That's where things got very interesting.

Forming the New Testament Canon

The night Dan outlined his findings on how the New Testament was formed was eye-opening to say the least. Most of us had been taught in such a way that made it seem like the New Testament miraculously fell from the sky in its current form and declared to be the Word of God. But careful examination uncovered a very different picture.

First we learned the Bible of the earliest church was very different than the one we have today. It contained no New Testament. What we call today the New Testament was not finalized in its present form until the third Council of Carthage in 397 CE (attended by Augustine).[6] That's over 360 years after Christ!

To be sure, the books of the New Testament developed slowly beginning in the 40s and 50s CE with some of Paul's letters. But it's not clear when his epistles came to be known as Holy Scripture. They were merely letters to specific gatherings of followers, not written to a general audience as "Scripture." Most scholars say the four gospels were written between thirty and sixty years after Jesus, with only Mark written before the destruction of Jerusalem in 70 CE.[7] Others say all of the gospels were written in the 60s CE—for example, secular scholar Dr. Ann Nyland comes to this conclusion.[8] Regardless, that means for at least three decades the earliest churches had no gospels and few New Testament documents, at least none that were universally accepted as Scripture. They relied on oral tradition for the story of Jesus' good news and didn't see the need to write down accounts until the original apostles started to die out. Even when they began to write down the accounts, most local gatherings of followers only had parts of what would become the New Testament. They only read accounts they could get their hands on in their area. Moreover, many early orthodox Christians (not just those later considered heretics) possessed other "books" or "letters" that never made it into the New Testament. So, at some point after all these decades, some Christians began putting the narratives

6. The Council of Laodicea met in 363 CE in Asia Minor and listed all the New Testament books we have today as "canonical" with the exception of the book of Revelation.

7. See Wills, *What the Gospels Meant*.

8. Nyland, *The Source New Testament*, 11, 163.

about Jesus and the writings of the apostles and Paul on the same level as Jewish Scripture. This eventually led to what some call, *local canonicity*, where a collection of Christian books considered authoritative were used in a particular region[9] but not in others.

What's more, before Christian writings arose, the earliest church's Bible was what scholars call the Septuagint, a Greek translation of the Old Testament written in the third century BCE that included the Apocrypha, a collection of expanded writings that are not included in any Protestant Bible today (written after the prophets and before the time of Christ). The Apocrypha books were accepted initially by the Jews at the time of Christ and by followers of Jesus in the early years of Christianity. Eventually, in reaction to the spread of Christianity, they were excluded from the Jewish canon because the Christians accepted them![10] Even more interesting, the modern Jewish canon of the Old Testament was not rigidly fixed until the third century CE.[11] So, even among Jews at the time of Christ, the concept of a rigid set of Scriptures was unknown! This is why the apocryphal books were easily accepted. No one had announced the Jewish Scriptures were closed. Finally, because the Apocrypha was accepted by the early church as Scripture, several Christian traditions accept it to this day, including Catholics, the Eastern Orthodox, and the Ethiopian Coptic Church.

Given these facts we came to a conclusion: The concept of Scripture among the earliest Christians was not well defined. They did not view the Bible the same way that our modern tradition does.

Next, we learned the compilation of the New Testament was not as straightforward as we were led to believe. For example, there was substantial disagreement on which gospels and letters should be included in the New Testament. Besides the four gospels we are familiar with, there were many gospel accounts of Jesus' teachings in the first and second centuries, in fact, up to forty of them![12] The Gospel of Luke attests to this when it says, "Many have undertaken to draw up an account of the things that have been fulfilled among us" (Luke1:1). These others included the gospels according to the Hebrews, the Egyptians, Peter, Matthias, and Thomas. In addition, there were many other letters and "apocalypses" that some considered Scripture. Those included, 1 Clement, 2 Clement, Barnabas, the Didache,

9. Lieuwen, "Emergence of the New Testament Canon."

10. Bernstein, *Which Came First*, 4–5.

11. Ibid., 5.

12. Ehrman, *Did Jesus Exist?*

the Acts of John, the Acts of Paul, the Preaching of Peter, the Protevangelium of James, the Shepherd of Hermas, and the Revelation of Peter. Clement of Alexandria, universally recognized as a church father, put together a New Testament canon in the second century for the church of Egypt that included all of these books just listed with the exception of the gospels of Peter and Thomas and the epistle of 2 Clement.[13] That's twelve books that we don't have in our New Testament today! His approach to Scripture was that it was an open canon. He seemed practically unconcerned about canonicity.[14] The Codex Sinaiticus from the fourth century adds the epistle of Barnabas and The Shepherd of Hermas to the traditional New Testament list. The Codex Alexandrinus of the fifth century adds 1 and 2 Clement.[15]

Moreover, even among the four gospels we have today, there was controversy over which to include. Western Christians resisted the Gospel of John and favored Matthew, Mark, and Luke. Eastern Christians resisted Matthew, Mark, and Luke, and favored the Gospel of John.[16] Jewish believers tended to use Matthew only. A gnostic group called Valentinans only used John. Marcion, who was considered a heretic, only used parts of Luke. The church father Irenaeus argued there should be four gospels to counterbalance the others.[17] Yet still, there was a debate over whether to use a composite gospel rather than separate ones. In the second century, Justin Martyr's student named Tatian published a single harmonized gospel called the Diatessaron, which many churches used. Even up to the fourth century, the Syrian church considered this Scripture. They didn't accept the four separate gospels until the fifth century.

Furthermore, from the second to the fourth century, Western churches excluded the epistle to the Hebrews from their New Testament listings. The controversial book of Revelation, known as the Apocalypse, wasn't accepted by the Eastern Orthodox Church for centuries, and then only partially. Many respected church fathers of the East, including Dionysius, Eusebius, Cyril, John Chrysostom, Theodore of Mopsuestia, and Theodoret, as well as the Council of Laodicea in 363 CE, all rejected the book of Revelation! It was omitted from the Syriac and Armenian New Testament. Many Greek manuscripts of the New Testament written before the ninth century do

13. Bernstein, *Which Came First*, 8.

14. Lieuwen, "Emergence of the New Testament Canon."

15. Bernstein, *Which Came First*, 6.

16. Ibid., 7.

17. Ehrman, *Misquoting Jesus*, 35.

not contain it. Evidence suggests the Western and Eastern Church made a compromise on Revelation and Hebrews. Each church finally decided they would accept the other's disputed book. It was a "we'll accept yours if you accept ours" agreement. On the other hand, to this day, the Eastern Orthodox Church doesn't treat Revelation equally with other Scripture. It is not used in their liturgy.[18]

Interestingly, there were several other books in today's New Testament that were disputed by early church leaders. In the second century, the Muratorian Canon did not include Hebrews, James, and 1 and 2 Peter. On the other hand, it did include the Apocalypse of Peter and the Wisdom of Solomon, a book that is considered part of the intertestamental Apocrypha. The church father Origen (often considered to be the first systematic theologian) questioned the authenticity of 2 Peter and 2 John in the third century. Some churches rejected 2 Timothy and Jude. Eusebius, considered the "Father of Church History," in the fourth century, lists James, Jude, 2 Peter, 2 John, and 3 John as disputed books and totally rejects Revelation.[19] For centuries, 2 Peter was rejected by many more and the Nestorians reject it even today.[20]

Even more fascinating, several church fathers, including Origen (185–254 CE) and Eusebius (260–340 CE) divided the available historical writings into three categories: (1) recognized, (2) disputed (in other words rejected by some churches and accepted by others), and (3) spurious (or forgeries). Although eventually there were a chunk of books that many did generally agree on as "recognized," e.g., the four gospels, Acts, the epistles of Paul, 1 Peter, and 1 John, there was still disagreement over what other books should be recognized. Origen would cite Barnabas, Didache, and the Shepherd of Hermas as "Scripture" and initially accepted Revelation, but later in life became more cautious regarding Revelation and Shepherd. Disputed books were James, Jude, 2 Peter, 2 John, and 3 John. Eusebius said this about them: "Those that are disputed, yet familiar to most, include the epistles known as James, Jude, and 2 Peter, and those called 2 John and 3 John, the work of the evangelist or of someone else with the same name."[21] Eusebius placed Barnabas and Shepherd as spurious books while Origen didn't. Moreover, in the end, even outside the "disputed books," there were

18. Bernstein, *Which Came First*, 9.

19. Ibid., 9–10.

20. Lieuwen, "Emergence of the New Testament Canon."

21. Ibid.

many books that were not accepted into the canon of Scripture but were still considered worthy of reading. Finally, there were a set of books that were considered by many to be forgeries written by heretics under the name of the apostles.

Some of the gnostic writings fall into this last category. Out of this spurious group, some of the teachings are just strange or obviously contradictory to the generally accepted teachings of Jesus or Paul. Others are just confusing and border on nonsensical. As Bart Ehrman says, "There is scarcely any religious literature written in any language at any time that can be more perplexing and deliberately obscure than some of the Gnostic writings of Christian antiquity."[22]

Gaining Perspective in the Pub

One night, a week or so after we had finished reading some of the material on the formation of the New Testament, we had a chance to gather our thoughts about it all. A group of us—some from our discussion group and some of our other pub theology friends—were sitting at a table inside Sound Brewery's tasting room in Poulsbo, munching peanuts and drinking beer.

"When you actually study in detail how the New Testament was formed, it kind of makes your head spin," Dan began, after explaining to some of the others what our study entailed, including Eusebius' three categories of sacred texts. "Even when trying to make sense of it all with the classification of these categories, people still couldn't agree 100 percent which sacred text should be in each category!"

"What blows me away," someone said, "was the number of books that were disputed through the first three centuries of Christianity. I mean, there was a core of books, like the four gospels and some of Paul's letters that most everyone seemed to agree on, albeit with some variation on how to put them together, but there were so many others that people had trouble with." We remembered that half the church favored the Gospel of John and the other half Matthew, Mark, and Luke. And, part of the church used a combination of all four called the Diatessaron. Moreover, our research had revealed the disputed or spurious books to be several of those that are in the New Testament today and several that are not.

22. Ehrman, *Lost Christianities*, 113–34.

"Weren't there a lot books that were obvious forgeries or had really crazy theologies?" someone asked.

"Yes," Dan replied. "There were streams of thought and writings that people had good reason to censure, I think. Like the Ebionites who insisted converts to Christ must become Jews and follow the whole Torah.[23] Or the gnostic writings that said that creation is not good and it's futile to improve it or society. They believed we have to escape our evil world through finding some secret knowledge. Even to the point of saying all sex, even married sex, is evil.[24] That stuff is bizarre and contradicts the core teachings and themes of Jesus and Paul."

We briefly mentioned a few other examples of this. The Gospel of Peter has a lot of "orthodox" teaching in it but the resurrection account has a giant Jesus with a head that reaches above the sky and a walking, talking cross.[25] The controversial Gospel of Thomas has many sayings of Jesus that match the synoptic gospels, but includes a saying that claims women must become men to be saved.[26] We concluded there is a basis for rejecting certain teachings in certain early Christian writings. But then again, we observed that there were some books that made it into the New Testament that many "orthodox" leaders disputed or rejected, like Revelation, James, Jude, 2 Peter, 2 John, and 3 John, and sometimes 2 Timothy.

"Even after the New Testament canon was finalized," I added, "those disputes did not entirely end." I explained how the date usually attributed to the finalization of the NT canon was 397 CE, when all the books in our modern NT were "approved." An earlier council at Laodicea in 363 CE had accepted all our current NT books except the book of Revelation. "But after these councils," I added, "other traditions still listed books outside the Western canon, for example the Codex Alexandrinus and Codex Sinaiticus.[27] Like a letter of Barnabas, the Shepherd of Hermas, and the Clement letters were included in some of these. And, there were still doubts about certain books like Revelation, 2 Peter, and others."

"Then there's Martin Luther's concerns," someone said. "I think it was fascinating what we learned about his take on the New Testament. That he thought they should be graded, that is, some should be accepted as more

23. Ehrman, *Jesus Interrupted*, 190.

24. Ehrman, *Lost Christianities*, 113–34.

25. Ehrman, *Jesus Interrupted*, 209.

26. Pagels, "Gospel of Thomas," saying 114.

27. Ehrman, *Jesus Interrupted*, 211.

inspired than others." We had learned that in the sixteenth century, Martin Luther argued for this and held that Hebrews, James, Jude, and Revelation should be secondary to the others.[28] And also, even today, there are church traditions that have different lists of books in the Bible. The Eastern Orthodox and Catholic Bibles include the Apocrypha, for instance.

"So, what do you guys do with this information?" another asked. "I mean, you don't toss the Bible out, do you? I've never heard any church I've attended question the New Testament this way. Most churches universally accept it."

"I always say that perhaps we should stop gripping the Bible so tightly," Dan said. "You know, maybe this tells us there's a better more responsible way of reading it. After all, the earliest Christians didn't view it the same way modern believers do. While they accepted a particular core of the writings [eventually the four gospels, Acts, and most of Paul's letters were generally accepted], they disputed or ignored much of it, while reading other texts not part of it. Why can't we do the same?"

Gina piped up. "Yeah, like recognizing that, although there's a lot that is inspirational and historically reliable, it's not all a cohesive whole . . . not an infallible communication from God. We need to wrestle with it more and not be so cock-sure everything we read is straight from the mouth of God to be obeyed today. I mean it seems like half the early church didn't pay attention to half of what we call the New Testament."

"So, how do you tell difference?" someone said. "Between what's authentic and what's doubtful."

"To me," Gina continued, "many inspirational parts are obvious. Where the teachings of Jesus or Paul ring true, touch our heart, bring comfort, or make sense. Where major themes or conclusions that are consistent in other places jump out at you; we can put those themes ahead of isolated verses. But it also takes understanding the historical context."

"It just seems so subjective," someone objected. "Like anyone can pick and choose what they like and disregard the rest."

"Yeah, I know what you mean," I said. "But you have to remember a couple things. First, that people in the first through fourth centuries got to pick and choose what sacred Christian texts rang true to them, so why can't we? Why are we obligated to accept a fourth-century council if many of the earlier church fathers didn't agree with their conclusion? Moreover, even people who believe the Bible is all 100 percent infallible have to pick

28. Bernstein, *Which Came First*, 9.

and choose how to interpret it. That's why there are thousands of Protestant denominations. Believing the Bible is all true doesn't solve the problem with subjectivity."

I gulped my ale and then went on. "Second, there has to be a good historical reason for discounting something. So it's not just one's personal feelings. Like, if there's minor contradictions that can be shown to be historical errors, that's a good reason. Or, when we have evidence that many church fathers didn't accept as genuine some books, like Revelation or 2 and 3 John or Jude. Or when most modern scholars today argue that only seven of Paul's thirteen letters in the New Testament were definitely written by him while three are most probably not written by him, and three others are disputable.[29] So, you don't throw everything out, but are free to put more stock in those deemed more universally accepted or authentic."

I'm not sure everyone that night could agree with these sentiments—that there is a core of material in the New Testament that seems obviously inspirational and most probably historical, but that it's okay to question parts of it, especially those parts that were historically disputed. But everyone seemed to agree that it would be worthwhile to go one step further in our research. We had looked at how the canon was formed and finalized more than three centuries after Christ. We also needed to look at how well the Bible was preserved down through the centuries until today.

How the New Testament Texts Were Compiled, Copied, and Translated

Bart Ehrman helped us understand how the New Testament was copied and retained through the years. Because of the way we were taught in evangelical circles, we had the impression that the New Testament was miraculously preserved starting from a set of original manuscripts down to our English translations today. Some of us were not aware that today we don't have the original Greek manuscripts of the New Testament, but copies that are a

29. Garry Wills, in *What Paul Meant*, 15–16, says modern scholars are in consensus that 1 Thessalonians, Galatians, Philippians, Philemon, 1 and 2 Corinthians, and Romans are genuinely written by Paul but that 1 and 2 Timothy and Titus were probably not and that there are disputes about Colossians, Ephesians, and 2 Thessalonians. Again, this doesn't mean we toss the inauthentic or disputed ones as having no value but rather recognize there are good reasons to focus on some letters over others to discover Paul's original meaning and intent.

few centuries at best removed from the originals. So, how were the original New Testament books copied, the ones finally agreed on as authoritative?

In antiquity, books were copied by hand through a painstakingly slow process. As strange as it seems to modern literates, with ancient Greek, copyists did not use punctuation or spaces between words, but a continuous writing style called *scriptuo continua.* Although there was such a thing as professional scribes who copied for a living, among Christians, scholars think the early Christian texts were copied by literate members of a congregation who volunteered to do the job for personal or communal purposes. It wasn't until the fourth century that professional scribes were used. These facts lead scholars to believe that mistakes in transmission were common. In fact, the church father Origen once complained about the quality of the gospel texts he had:

> The differences among the manuscripts have become great, either through the negligence of some copyists or through the perverse audacity of others; they either neglect to check over what they have transcribed, or, in the process of checking, they make additions or deletions as they please.[30]

These changes to the original texts took several forms. The majority of them were just common mistakes; misspellings, accidental omissions, or inadvertent additions. Copying was a grueling task and it was easy to slip up from time to time. Others were intentional changes a copyist made to correct something or bring clarity, perhaps a mistaken reference or confusing statement. Although intentional, their motives were pure.[31] Finally, there were the more serious types of changes. The ones done for theological or ideological reasons to reinforce a copyist's or editor's bias. Sometimes those considered heretics were accused of maliciously altering manuscripts to conform them to their own views. Marcion, who started a movement known as the Marcionites and who didn't believe the Old Testament God was the same as the God of Jesus, was charged with doing that to the book of Luke. But also, those considered orthodox, would sometimes change texts to try to prevent others from misusing them for "heretical" purposes. Or, they would just want to insert their perspective to control the message. Several of these have been identified by scholars, although some of them are still hotly debated.

30. Ehrman, *Misquoting Jesus*, 52.

31. Ibid., 55–56.

John 1:1–18 is written in a poetic style not found in the rest of the book. It refers to the Word becoming flesh in Jesus, even though the rest of the account never refers to Jesus being the Word. Could this have been added to reinforce a scribe's perspective? And if it was, does it minimize the validity of the message, or just show us the New Testament authors were human? In another example, some readers believe chapter 21 of John is an add-on. The narrative appears to come to an end at 20:30–31 and the next chapter is like an afterthought. Could a copyist have added this? In these cases, there is little concrete evidence to go on beyond what was just stated.

However, in other instances there is very strong evidence of copyist additions. Even conservative scholars agree that the story of the woman caught in adultery in John 7:53—8:12 was not in the original. Even the evangelical NIV translation, although it includes it, it sets it apart and notes that it "is not found in our oldest and best manuscripts." Its writing style is different from the rest of John and it contains many words alien to the rest of the story. The same can be said for the end of Mark's gospel. All scholars agree the last twelve verses of Mark were not part of the original but added by a scribe. The reasons are the same as for the passage in John. Again, even the NIV version has the passage set apart and explained in the footnotes as "absent from our oldest and best manuscripts, along with other important witnesses."

There are other examples. Earlier and in my first book, I explained the case that the passage in 1 Corinthians 14 that states women should remain silent and not speak in church was added by a copyist to limit the role of women in the church. Even conservative evangelical scholar Gordon Fee holds this theory.[32] Paul wasn't the misogynist, the scribe or editor was, according to this very possible theory of alteration.

Then there is the question of how accurate historical details are in the original compilation of the texts. Evidence shows there are minor errors and contradictions regarding factual details in many passages. These are found in our oldest and best manuscripts, not just newer copies. Mark attributed an Old Testament quote to Isaiah when it was really from Malachi. He states the last supper was the Passover meal while John says it occurred the night before the Passover. Luke says Joseph and Mary returned to Nazareth from Bethlehem after completing the ritual purifications for a newborn child. Matthew says they immediately went and settled in Egypt until King Herod died before returning to Nazareth. How can they both be right? Matthew

32. Fee, *First Epistle to the Corinthians.*

claims Jesus' disciples brought him two donkeys and he rode on *them*. Mark says there was only one. These are obvious discrepancies. Historically speaking, they don't discount the whole narrative, but merely show those who recorded the stories are human—they made mistakes or didn't confirm details or possibly added events that were not verifiable.

There are many other similar contradictions, most of them small, but some consequential. In addition, there are thousands of textual variants in the thousands of Greek manuscripts we have. Although most differences don't impact the meaning of the text, some of them do. Some affect the interpretations of entire passages. Biblical scholars have known these facts and wrote about them for years.[33] Biblical archeologists agree. As the *Biblical Archaeological Review* states, "The New Testament, like the Hebrew Bible, is not always literally accurate."[34] But again, this is not a revelation that should alarm us. It's how history works. Peter Enns calls this reading the bible as it is, rather than as we would like it to be.[35]

We almost had enough information to begin rethinking how we should change the way we use the Bible. But there was one more area we needed to address: how the New Testament has been translated.

Translating the Scriptures

One of the best kept secrets of Bible translation is that it is frequently not straightforward. Just like there are in modern languages, there are often words for which there is no direct translation into English. Moreover, in an ancient language such as Koine Greek (the language of the New Testament) there are often words for which translators don't know the exact meaning. In such cases, they take an educated guess (i.e., they form their own interpretation), and if a Bible reader is lucky enough to have a version with good footnotes and takes the time to read them, they are made aware of the problem. But more often than not, readers are clueless to such translation issues.

Another secret the general public is not aware of is that many of these translation problems are being solved by new historical discoveries. Unfortunately, many if not most of them are being ignored by Bible translators. Dr. Ann Nyland, a scholar of ancient Greek, has written extensively about this phenomenon. In the 1880s, she explains, volumes of Greek papyri from

33. Ehrman, *Misquoting Jesus*, 253.

34. Shanks, review of *Zealot*, 18.

35. Enns, *Bible Tells Me So*.

New Testament times were discovered. They include private letters, marriage and divorce contracts, tax and business documents, official decrees, and birth and death notices. The use of words with unknown meanings in context in these papyri revealed the precise meanings of numerous words in the New Testament that were unknown to translators. Over years, these papyri were studied and published but not in an exhaustive way, so the meanings of many words remained a mystery even as others came to light. As of 1929, there was still no documentary attestation for 800 Greek words found in the New Testament manuscripts. Over the years that changed. As Dr. Nyland describes it, "Scholars had thought the previous finds of papyri sensational and dramatic, yet the subsequent discovery and editing of papyrus fragments revolutionized our understanding of words that appear in the New Testament."[36] This happened to a large degree in 1976 when fifteen volumes of new papyri were published. Moreover, new findings were ongoing. In the last two decades over four thousand inscriptions have been discovered in Ephesus alone! Dr. Nyland makes the following conclusion:

> These discoveries have been largely overlooked by Bible translators, despite greatly exciting New Testament scholars and lexicographers. Laypersons and a significant number of Bible translators alike are unaware of the main body of scholarship, as it is tucked away in technical journals. Thus the dictionary work we see in today's Bible translations is based on a centuries-old view of word meaning.[37]

In my studies, I have found numerous terms that have been mistranslated from the Greek of the New Testament to modern English. Some of them are due to ignorance. Others due to resistance to some of the discoveries that Dr. Nyland has explained. Still some are due to some denominational or traditional bias. In other words, by mistranslating a word or phrase a translator or team supports a particular theological position. I will be citing some of these mistranslations in forthcoming chapters. Here are a few examples for now.

More and more people are learning that the word translated "church" is a poor translation from the Greek *ekklesia*, which simply denotes a gathering of people. The phrase "kingdom of God" is a poor translation and is better depicted as "reign" or "realm" of God. The word has no political connotation like "kingdom" does. Oftentimes, the Greek word *oikenosis*

36. Nyland, *The Source New Testament*, 7.

37. Ibid.

is mistranslated "world" (as in "this gospel must be preached in all the *world*"), even though it denotes a region or political sphere, not the entire earth. Matthew was saying the message of the good news would be spread throughout the known *Roman* world. One fascinating mistranslation is found in Romans 16 where Paul cites a woman named Junia as "foremost among the apostles." In the original Greek, Paul is consistent with other teachings in his letters and in the gospels that women are equal to men "in Christ" and can hold any role in the community gatherings. Yet it is easily demonstrated that later copyists or translators changed this feminine name to a male form, Junias,[38] to prevent readers from concluding the obvious leadership implications of women in the church. As we've also seen, our research discovered several other mistranslations for words or phrases denoted in English as *eternal punishment* and *hell.*

Can the Bible and New Testament be Trusted?

In light of these discoveries, we were forced to ask these questions. How could the New Testament be the authoritative Word of God when the earliest church didn't have it? Or, when it was disputed from its inception? How can Revelation be the Word of God when so many rejected it? Or the other disputed books like 2 Peter, Jude, James, and Hebrews? What is the nature of inspiration in light of textual errors, the impossibility of finding the original texts, copyists' mistakes, and variant texts that are well documented?

What about the books that never made it into the New Testament? Shouldn't we at least examine them since some of the earliest Christians considered them Scripture or at least worthy of study? Who's to say that some of these have portions that are inspired by God? Or, that some of what did make it into the New Testament is not inspired? Why shouldn't we take Martin Luther's approach and grade the books of the New Testament as primary and secondary? And the granddaddy of all questions about the New Testament, Why do Christians in the fourth century get to decide what is considered "Scripture" and we don't? Why are we obligated to accept their decision? (Which, by the way, wasn't unanimous.) Finally, once something is considered "Scripture," how does one discern whether it is the Word of God or contains a Divine message for us today?

Fundamentalists and conservative evangelicals claim the Bible is infallible and fully reliable in theology, history, and science. So, the answer

38. Ibid., 10.

to this question—can the New Testament be trusted?—for them is a simple yes. Any effort to scrutinize the historical accuracy of the Scriptures is sacrilegious. Any critique that uncovers errors or problems is immediately discounted or claimed to be capable of harmonization. More astute defenders will admit the doctrine of inerrancy only pertains to the original manuscripts but will rarely follow that to its logical conclusion: we don't have an infallible Bible because we don't have the originals, only copies of copies of copies, sometimes centuries removed from the originals.

As we are starting to see, there are many contradictions and errors in the Bible, and for our purposes here, the New Testament. So how can we trust the Bible and the New Testament at all?

To many secularists, agnostics, and atheists, the answer to that question is, "We can't." But this is the fundamentalist position on the other side. As Bart Ehrman says, "The (sometime) atheist opinion of the Bible as non-historical is no better than the (typical) fundamentalist opinion."[39] Both the secular or religious fundamentalist camps refuse to acknowledge this fact: The New Testament authors did not know or imagine their writings would one day become canonized as sacred Scripture and probably had no intention of doing so. They were writing their memories or accounts of others about Jesus. It was human literature, whether one believes it was inspired by God—either wholly or in part—or not. We need to treat them like any other piece of human literature. We should examine them, not relegate them beyond investigation because we think God inspired them or religionists consider them sacred. Just like any other piece of literature, it may or may not be historically accurate, and there will be some bias in it, but it still can be used for historical purposes. As Ehrman says, "We don't dismiss early American accounts of the Revolutionary War simply because they were written by Americans."[40] So, we shouldn't dismiss accounts of early Christianity merely because they were written by Christians.

So what is the consensus of biblical scholars on the New Testament? Well, that would probably take a few volumes to answer that question! There are disputes about all kinds of details. Nevertheless, there are some major agreements as well as solid historical and archeological evidence that much of the New Testament can be trusted, barring certain theologies that really can't be verified in a historical manner. In fact, you can say this about the whole Bible. Just as there are doubts about some of its historicity, there

39. Ehrman, *Did Jesus Exist*, 69–93.

40. Ibid., 74.

is historical confirmation about much of its claims. Archeologists have confirmed fifty individuals in the Hebrew Bible alone as real historical figures and the number keeps rising with new finds.[41]

As for the New Testament, nearly all critical scholars agree that Jesus was a Jew from a small village in northern Palestine called Nazareth. He was an adult in the decade of the 20s CE, was for a short time associated with John the Baptist, and became a moral teacher to rural Jewish communities in the region of Galilee and sometimes Jerusalem. He preached a message that the reign of God was close at hand, that it was good news for the poor and marginalized and often taught by telling parables. He gathered a small inner following and broader outside following, including women, and gained a reputation for healing the sick and casting out unclean spirits (whether one believes he literally healed people or not). At the end of his life, around 30 CE, he made a trip to Jerusalem during the feast of Passover, where the Jewish leaders of the temple instigated an opposition to him and convinced Pontius Pilate, a precept of Rome in Jerusalem, to put him on trial. Pilate, whether he thought him dangerous or not, had him crucified for his claim to be king of the Jews.[42]

This determination is based on both internal evidence inside the New Testament and external sources outside. Bart Ehrman cites seven independent witnesses that attest to core historical facts about Jesus. The first three are the books of Matthew, Mark, and Luke, all written between the late 60s CE (Mark) to early 80s CE (some scholars like Anne Nyland believe all these books and John were written in the 60s CE). Although similar, all have their own original material on the life of Jesus. Erhman's fourth witness, the Gospel of John, which most scholars believe was written much later, has the most original material not found in the other gospels. Independent accounts are very important for historians because they show more than one source. The fifth witness and another independent account is the Gospel of Thomas discovered in 1945, possibly dating to before the other gospels but no later than 120 CE. Historians have reason to believe Thomas got his material from other sources outside Matthew, Mark, and Luke. Ehrman adds to these, a sixth source, the Gospel of Peter not discovered until 1886, which is only a fragmentary account of Jesus' trial, death, and resurrection. The seventh and last account Ehrman cites is an obscure

41. Mykytiuk, "Archeology Confirms 50 Real People in the Bible."

42. Ehrman, *Did Jesus Exist?*, 269.

highly fragmentary manuscript called Papyrus Egerton 2, which contains four episodes of the life of Jesus, one of which is completely original.[43]

Add to this a number of non-Christian and secular sources and on the whole, the textual evidence for the life and influence of Jesus is indisputable in historical terms. Josephus, the late first-century Jewish historian refers to Jesus twice and briefly mentions John the Baptist in his *Antiquities of the Jews*. He cites James, "brother of Jesus who is called anointed one." In another longer, more controversial passage, a majority of scholars and experts on Josephus believe the original writing mentioned Jesus and later Christian copyists touched it up to reinforce their faith. But they agree that Josephus cited Jesus as a historical figure who was considered by some to be "the Messiah." Roman historians Tacitus, Pliny the Younger, and Suetonius cite Jesus and his earliest followers as a historical figure and movement.[44] As to the claim that none of the New Testament accounts are true eyewitnesses to Jesus' life and teachings, and therefore, that fact makes them unreliable, here's what Bart Ehrman says:

> The absence of eyewitness accounts would be relevant if, and only if, we had reason to suspect that we should have eyewitness reports if Jesus really lived. That, however, is far from the case. Think again of our earlier point of comparison, Pontius Pilate. Here is a figure who was immensely significant in every way to the life and history of Palestine during the adult life of Jesus . . . politically, economically, culturally, socially. As I have indicated, there was arguably no one more important. And how many eyewitness reports of Pilate do have today? None. Not a single one. The same is true of Josephus. And these are figures who were of the highest prominence in their own day.[45]

Historically speaking, the Bible and the New Testament has an amazing amount of historically reliable material, even though it's not an infallible document.

How to Discern the Logos of God

The word we translate "Word" in the phrase, "Word of God" in the original Greek is "logos," a word that is more accurately denoted as "the reason" or

43. Ibid., 74–77.
44. Mykytiuk, "Did Jesus Exist?"
45. Ehrman, *Did Jesus Exist?*, 49.

"rationality" of God.[46] It does not mean a set of sacred texts. Furthermore, when you get right down to it, the definition of the "Word of God" or the "Word" in the New Testament is Jesus himself, not a collection of writings. "The Word became flesh," John tells us. He didn't mean the Bible became flesh. So if the Word of God is Jesus, what is the Bible? We needed to find out.

"Why don't all these discoveries you made cast doubt on the reliability of the Bible altogether?" a person new to our pub theology meetings asked one evening.

"They cast doubt on how to discern the 'logos' of God—God's way of thinking and reaching us—but not on how to determine if the Bible is reliable," I answered. "We can determine the reliability of the New Testament the same way we evaluate any piece of historical literature. The discoveries show that the core of the New Testament is substantially reliable, although not error free. With a few exceptions, most of the errors are immaterial to the main story.[47] But the core story must be very close to the truth."

"Wait, so you believe the virgin birth, the miracles, and the resurrection are all historical facts?"

"That part of the story can't be verified historically," I answered. "They aren't things that have been scientifically substantiated as possible—but, logically, I believe, they can't be ruled out either. So, there's room for debate on those things. But, if believed, they are taken on faith. I actually still believe in the virgin birth, the miracles, and the resurrection, even as a progressive Christian. My belief in them is not based on hard historical evidence, but personal faith and some logical reasoning. On the other hand, I don't think it's right to insist everyone believe them, like evangelicals do, in order to be a genuine believer. It's not necessary to believe those things to be a modern follower of Jesus. The historical core of Jesus' life and teachings is very reliable. But the fringes? We can legitimately argue about those, e.g., the miracles and other details."

"How do we know what part of what Jesus or Paul taught is historically accurate?" another asked.

"We use our God-given minds to critically examine them," Dan said. "For the most part, Jesus' teachings show me he's a spiritual genius of the most loving character. Where I see contradictions to that, I dig deeper. Often, we discover there are mistranslations or misinterpretations of some

46. *Merriam-Webster*, s.v. "Logos."

47. Erhman, *Misquoting Jesus*, 259–61.

of his teachings. Or, sometimes, we discover the texts weren't accurately copied. After that, if something remains a mystery, we are under no obligation to accept everything we read as 100 percent true. The New Testament doesn't say, 'You must believe everything written in these twenty-seven books, or else.'"

Dan and I were trying to articulate how we had changed our view of Scripture. It's okay to doubt some of it or wrestle with it, we realized. It can be treated like any historical document of antiquity. It's a human book, yet to a believer, it contains Divine elements. I agree with Dan that Jesus is a spiritual genius. And so is Paul, as one of his first-century followers. The love ethics of Jesus are astounding and, I believe, the answer to all human social problems. They are Divine fingerprints.

Human books on history, when validated as substantially accurate using historical tools, are largely accepted as true. There may be doubts about certain details, but no one doubts the general historicity of the writings of Josephus, Tacitus, Pliny the Younger, and Suetonius, all historians of that era. No one doubts the existence and story of Julius Caesar. No one has serious doubts about Plato and Socrates. Can't we judge the Bible, particularly the New Testament, the same way we judge these? The answer is yes.

"Then how do we discern the Logos of God?" someone asked.

"I think it's found in the essence of a passage or book of the Bible, or the themes across books," Gina said. "These take precedent over each individual verse or passage."

"And the themes must be taken in their historical and cultural context with attention to the original intent of the author," I added. "A verse may be important, but only if it captures a conclusion or theme."

"That makes sense," another piped in. "Perhaps it's the prevailing themes in the Bible that point us to the 'Word of God,' not the Bible itself. That's a view not unlike what theologian Karl Barth had taught."

I was reminded of and shared what Robin Meyer says, that the macro message of the New Testament is more important than the micro message.[48] I also was aware of the explanation of Anabaptist Michael Hardin, who argues that the Bible should always be read through the lens of Jesus and his teachings. They take precedent over anything else in the Bible.

We kept discussing this. I brought up a specific example. I explained that it's really not the "plain sense" of Scripture you're after, but consistency, logic, and reason. For example, the "plain sense" of Scripture would say that

48. Meyer, *Underground Church*.

"women shouldn't speak or teach in church," according to 1 Corinthians 14:34. But logically, this doesn't make sense for several reasons. First, a few verses before this verse Paul says women pray and prophesy in church (the gathering). You have to speak to do either of those things. Second, Paul says "there is no male or female in Christ" in his letter to the Galatians. The equality of gender in the Jesus Movement demands that women be given the same rights as men when it comes to a voice in the church. Finally, our study showed us that that particular passage in 1 Corinthians 14 was almost assuredly either added to Pauls' original letter by a biased copyist or twisted by translators to fit the misogynist world view of the prevailing culture.

Both Jesus and Paul consistently taught several themes in their ministries. Love is more important than religious practices. Love for God and neighbor, including love for one's enemies, sums up or fulfills the law of God. Practically speaking, when we do to others what we would want them to do to us, we do what God desires. Love supersedes specific rules and dogma. Jesus circumvented the Torah at times to express love for people. He sometimes made exceptions to the law (defending David eating bread consecrated only for priests, his disciples eating on the Sabbath, and his own practice of healing on the Sabbath) and other times totally rewrote it, as when he declared all foods clean, said it is unnecessary to worship at the temple, and came out against the practice of temple sacrifices.

Another theme is that the Path of Christ takes us from being under the law to being under grace. We are released from the law, Paul says, and serve in the new way of the Spirit, not the written code. Christ is the end of the law. Jesus said he came to "complete" or "finish" the law.[49] Paul says that anyone seeking justification under the law is under a curse. In Acts 15, the apostles concluded that as a concession Gentiles should be encouraged, not commanded, to obey only four points of the Jewish law. When literalists ignore these overriding themes and try to make a law out of a particular verse or passage of Scripture, e.g., wives should always submit to their husbands (and try to shoehorn that into a situation with an abusive spouse), they are contradicting the Logos or rationality of God. One, they are making the New Testament into a new law to be obeyed to the letter and putting people back under a "curse," and two, they are ignoring Jesus' and Paul's love ethic, that we practice love and love does no harm to its neighbor. When we see admonitions in Scripture that appear unloving in modern circumstances,

49. See Matt 5:17; see also the meaning of the Greek "pleroo," in Bromily, *Theological Dictionary of the New Testament*, 867.

the principle of love over law must prevail. This is not ignoring the Bible, it is following the model of Jesus. It's using the Bible the way Jesus and Paul used it.[50]

What is the loving thing to do? is the question we can ask when met with a moral dilemma, rather than always looking for some rule in the Bible. This is one of the reasons that many Christians, including some evangelicals, are rethinking the debate over gays in the church and gay marriage. The traditional view—that the Bible says homosexuality is always a sin—has been found to be faulty. Studying historical context and original language reveals the biblical authors when discussing homosexuality were talking about things like the covenantal sins of Israel, same-sex shrine prostitution, idolatrous sexual relationships (women or men leaving natural relations to dedicate themselves as cultic prostitutes), the Greco-Roman practice of pederasty (men having sex with boys), sexual slavery, and sexual exploitation. The Bible doesn't condemn homosexuality across the board; only certain of its practices, the same way it condemns certain practices within heterosexuality.[51] When confronted with the questions of what to do with gays and lesbians in the church or gay marriage, the Bible's theme of love is our guide. What's the loving thing to do when addressing gays and lesbians who harm no one by their sexuality or their behavior who want to get married or join a Christian community? Keeping in mind that "ex-gay" techniques have been discredited and cause psychological harm? The loving thing to do is to welcome them and support them, not condemn them and deem them as immoral. Love demands we accept without judgment anyone considered "unclean" by religionists as long as they are committed to loving their neighbor. Jesus' and Paul's teaching calls for correction and rehabilitation for those who harm others. Not for those who merely live out their sexuality.

"So what if people still disagree on what the Logos of God is?" someone asked. We discussed this and came to a consensus. Love for people and respect for individual conclusions must rule. The only place for vehemently defending "the truth of the Bible," was when people abuse Scripture to justify harming others. Lack of love and hurting people is the real heresy, not "unorthodox" belief.

50. See Flood, *Disarming Scripture;* Shore, "Betraying the Spirit."

51. I give a lengthy argument on this issue in *Confessions of a Bible Thumper*, 237–59. Also see Gushee's "Tackling the Hard Questions" and "Disputable Matters."

We had learned much in our study on the Bible and its origins. We certainly weren't pretending that we had solved every issue but felt like we had come to a more intellectually honest, historically accurate, and spiritually consistent view of how to handle the Bible. Now, it was time to venture into one of the pillars of organized religion—the institution of church. Had Jesus founded a "church?" When he referred to "church," what did it look like? How did the earliest followers of his Path form communities? Have we deviated from that model, and, if so, are we called to return to it? It took an encounter in a Viking-themed brewpub to set up how to share the discoveries we made about "church."

Chapter Seven

The Earliest Church: Communities of "The Way"

I PULL ON THE heavy wood door, noticing its antique metal hinges and large handle. The centuries-old character of the small pub's entryway opens up to an equally impressive interior—a cozy decor with square beam posts and worn-wood tables and bar. One of my favorite watering holes, Valholl Brewing in Poulsbo, Washington, had just moved to new digs. I grab the one untaken stool at the bar and ordered a Valkyrie Red Ale from Katy the bartender. "Where's Jeff?" I ask, referring to her husband, one of the owners.

"He's here somewhere." Katy replies, as she places a glass of beer in front of me. "Probably in the back."

Right then Jeff emerges from the large backroom area with its rows of silver brew kettles. As I turned toward him, he notices me. "Hey Mike, good to see you."

I reach out to shake his hand. A large-framed man with buzz-cut hair and facial stubble, Jeff is always upbeat but often appears to be on a tight deadline. He liked my first book about my spiritual evolution. We had discussed it briefly several times over the months.

"I happen to be reading your book again," he says.

"Oh, so you're a glutton for punishment?"

He laughs. We get into another conversation. At one point, Jeff divulges more about his past. "Yeah, I went to Billy Graham's college in Minnesota for a while and eventually left because the professors didn't like all my questions."

"I can relate."

"That's what I like about your story. You confront much of the same doubts I had and uncover an unconventional point of view. I think it's a more credible way of looking at theology."

Later, after Jeff goes back to his brewing, I stare at the large graphic above the line of taps on the wall. It's the Valholl logo—a black-and-white image of a long-haired Viking with a beard so long it's braided. It was a typical microbrewery brand. Unconventional. Out-of-the-box. Far afield from the leading corporate brands of Budweiser, Coors, or Miller. Yes, just like the unconventional theology Jeff said he liked in my first book.

That unconventional spirit reminded me of one of the books in our group's collection of sources—a Garry Wills book entitled *What Jesus Meant*. The first time I read it I received a startling unconventional revelation. It was as if a phrase jumped off the page and clobbered me to the side of the head. "Christ was not a Christian," the author had penned the title of a chapter. *What sense does that make?* But as I continued reading and began to put that thought in perspective, along with other concepts and historical facts I had recently learned, that simple statement suddenly made perfect sense. Jesus does not fit our modern definition of Christian. He did not found a new religion. In fact, he was against all religion. He didn't begin "Christianity." He never founded an institutional church. He was a Jewish rabbi, a mystic of the Spirit, and teacher of alternative wisdom, not unlike Buddha and Socrates. He came in the spirit of the Jewish prophets to confront corruption in the religious establishment and announce and demonstrate good news for the poor and oppressed. He came with the authority of God. To his followers, he was the "Anointed One" cited by the Jewish prophets. In that sense, he was a divine mystery, whether one believes in his deity or not. In his day and under his authority, no churches were formed. No ecclesiastic organizations. No denominations. In fact, his followers were not called *Christians* until thirty years after he died. They called themselves and were referred to as "followers of the Way." Jesus began a counter-cultural movement within Judaism, not a new religion. It is critical we understand the difference.

Jesus Against the Temple and Religion

To understand why Jesus would have been against replacing Judaism's organized system of religion with a new Christian version, we had to rethink how he felt about the existing Jewish temple. Jesus was categorically set against it. He declared the temple and its worship and sacrificial system were destined to fall. This critique was by no means flowing from a kind of anti-Jewish prejudice, but was deeply rooted in the tradition of the Jewish prophets, who also called for an end to empty sacrifice and temple worship and declared a more acceptable way. In the gospels, we noted how much Jesus quoted the prophets' view of the sacrificial system.

When confronted by the Pharisees for eating with "sinners," Jesus quotes the prophet Hosea, telling them to "go and learn what this means: 'I desire mercy, not sacrifice'" (6:6).

In his most famous conflict inside the temple, he asserts his own authority to disrupt and put an end to the system. He turns over the tables of the moneychangers, drives out both the buyers and sellers of sacrificial animals, and prevents anyone from carrying merchandise in the temple. He then declares, "Is it not written: 'My house will be called a house of prayer for all nations'? But you have made it 'a den of robbers'" (Mark 11:17). The first quote is from Isaiah, who envisioned foreigners who love and serve God as welcome at the temple. The second is from Jeremiah, who warned the people to not trust in the temple but rather to act justly and refrain from oppressing foreigners and the weak.

> Do not trust in deceptive words and say, "This is the temple of the Lord, the temple of the Lord, the temple of the Lord!" If you really change your ways and your actions and deal with each other justly, if you do not oppress the foreigner, the fatherless or the widow and do not shed innocent blood in this place, and if you do not follow other gods to your own harm, then I will let you live in this place, in the land I gave your ancestors for ever and ever. But look, you are trusting in deceptive words that are worthless. . . . Has this house, which bears my Name, become a den of robbers to you? (Jer 7:4–8, 11)

Jesus could have quoted from a rich collection of prophetic utterances that call the sacrificial temple system into question. For example, the Psalmist declared, "Open my lips, Lord, and my mouth will declare your praise. You do not delight in sacrifice, or I would bring it; you do not take pleasure in burnt offerings. My sacrifice, O God, is a broken spirit; a broken and contrite heart you, God, will not despise" (51:15–17). Perhaps Isaiah, summarized the sentiment best when he declared the limits to the concept of a dwelling place or temple of God and that the heart of God's desire is not found in sacrifice but humility:

> This is what the Lord says: "Heaven is my throne, and the earth is my footstool. Where is the house you will build for me? Where will my resting place be? Has not my hand made all these things, and so they came into being?" declares the Lord. These are the ones I look on with favor: those who are humble and contrite in spirit, and who tremble at my word. But whoever sacrifices a bull is like one who kills a person, and whoever offers a lamb is like one who breaks a dog's neck; whoever makes a grain offering is like one who presents pig's blood, and whoever burns memorial incense is like one who worships an idol. They have chosen their own ways, and they delight in their abominations; so I also will choose harsh treatment for them and will bring on them what they dread. For when I called, no one answered, when I spoke, no one listened. They did evil in my sight and chose what displeases me. (Isa 66:1–4)

These passages echo Jesus' call for a "religion of the heart," not outward appearances and practices. A call to "deal with each other justly," to "not oppress the foreigner, the fatherless or the widow," and to exercise humility rather than to perform sacrifices. In fact, God "does not delight in sacrifice" or "take pleasure in burnt offerings" at all.

Once Jesus commended a teacher of the law, in an incredible declaration of religious sanity, who responds to Jesus' own radical statement that love for the one God and love for neighbor are the greatest commandments: "Well said, teacher," the man replied. "You are right in saying that God is one and there is no other but him. To love him with all your heart, with all your understanding and with all your strength, and to love your neighbor as yourself is more important than all burnt offerings and sacrifices" (Mark 12:32–33). Jesus told him he is not far from the reign of God.

Jesus loved to break the taboos of his day. On more than one occasion, he travels through unclean Samaritan territory, a scandal to any devout Jew. One day, having gone to the base of the Samaritan's alternate temple mount called Gerizim, he begins a conversation with a doubly-unclean Samaritan woman. Remember, his disciples are flabbergasted. At one point, she asks him where should be the proper place to worship God, intimating the conflict between the Samaritans and Jews about which of their holy houses of worship is authentic. Jesus tells her the time is coming, and has now come, when people will worship God in neither temple. True worship comes when one worships internally, "in Spirit and truth," not through performing external religious practices in "consecrated" man-made structures

(John 4:21–24). Most modern readers don't catch the significance of Jesus' statements, thinking that eventually true worshipers will meet in Christian churches not in a Jewish or Samaritan temple. Garry Wills drives home this point: "Jesus did not come to replace the temple with other buildings, whether huts or rich cathedrals, but to instill a religion of the heart."[1]

Another time, in confronting the Pharisees for their niggling legalism regarding the Sabbath, he told them, "I tell you that something greater than the temple is here" (Matt 12:6). If something greater was here (an anointed Messiah for all people), then there was no further use for the temple. And, in fact, Jesus predicted its demise several times, in apocalyptic, graphic detail. "Not one stone will remain upon another," he told his disciples after they marveled at its grandeur one day walking through its courts. When will this happen? his disciples asked, and he proceeded to describe the trials and tribulations that would arise in the coming years with its culmination in the destruction of both the temple and Jerusalem, and how "this generation will not pass until all these things take place" (Matt 24:1–44).

It was fascinating to learn how history confirmed the end of the temple era. Later, in the latter half of the first century, Johanan ben Zakai, who was a primary contributor to the development of rabbinical Judaism, independently came to the same conclusion as Jesus. The way of peace was superior to the conventional wisdom of political and military power struggles. He argued in favor of peace after seeing the anger of the populace during the Jewish Revolt and siege of Jerusalem. When the Jews had to face the reality of worship without the temple, he helped persuade a council to replace animal sacrifice with prayer, quoting the prophet Hosea, like Jesus, "For I desire mercy, not sacrifice, and acknowledgement of God rather than burnt offerings"[2] (6:6).

Jesus did not call for a reformed temple or a new "Christian" version of a temple absent the sacrifices. He consistently called for a purity of the heart—humility, mercy, interior love, just treatment of each other—as more important than religious practices and institutions and had no concern that the destruction of the Jewish temple he predicted would hinder true spirituality. Yet, there was the question about the Jewish synagogues and whether later Christian churches were meant to be patterned after them. To answer that, again, we turned to their history.

1. Wills, *What Jesus Meant*, 76.

2. JewishEncyclopedia.com, s.v. "Johanan B. Zakkai."

The Diaspora, Synagogues, Hellenized Jews, and "God-Fearers"

In order to understand how the earliest Jesus followers organized themselves in gatherings, we had to also know the landscape of Jewish communities throughout the Roman Empire. This was some of the background information we learned in *The Timeline.*

Because of what is known as the Jewish Diaspora (dispersion of Jews by the Assyrians and Babylonians), by the first century there were ethnic Jews living all over the empire and in the East beyond. Sometimes called *Hellenized Jews,* they acclimated within Greco-Roman culture and spoke the Greek language. Their "Scriptures" were a Greek translation of the Torah, Prophets, Psalms, and Apocrypha called the Septuagint, which ultimately became the Scriptures of the early Christian church.

It is assumed that *Hellenized Jews,* since they were a minority among Greeks and Romans, were less strict with Mosaic rules on mixing with Gentiles than their Judean counterparts. Because Jews followed their own historical religion (something Roman culture had respect for), Rome granted them exemptions to certain obligations that Romans had. For example, taking part in Roman civic religion and the emperor cult, as well as service in the army. Thus *Hellenized Jews* thrived in the Roman Empire at the time of Christ.

Hellenized Jews met in synagogues because they lived too far away from the temple in Jerusalem. The synagogue system was actually begun by the sect of the Pharisees. Pharisees, technically moderates on the theological Jewish landscape, argued that God could and should be worshiped outside the temple and Jerusalem (although, unfortunately, they didn't go so far as to promote meeting in taverns). They developed the idea that the synagogue is a legitimate institution of religious practice apart from the temple, a place of worship, school of Torah, and communal meeting place. So, everywhere Jews were dispersed throughout the Roman Empire a system of synagogues sprang up. This is why Paul was in the custom of first visiting the local synagogue when he arrived in a city. This is where he could readily share the message of Jesus with an already established community of Jews, who would have been mostly Hellenized Jews.

In addition to the *Hellenized Jews,* there was also a movement of Gentiles who converted to Judaism called *proselytes.* Historians believe that this occurred because of a trend in the Roman Empire toward monotheism and away from the non-scriptural traditions of the Greco-Roman gods. For example, classical philosophers increasingly leaned toward monotheism. Many sophisticated Romans were turned off by traditional polytheistic paganism with its reverence for animal-like gods or half-human beasts. Moreover, a movement began to identify a supreme God over the other gods in order to address the troubling confusion that developed with the expansion of the number of gods in paganism. For example, one innovation was to organize the gods into a hierarchy ruled by a supreme, all-powerful Creator. Rather than call him Zeus or a traditional name, one movement named him Serapis. Another example was one of the new oriental gods popular in the Roman Empire in the first century called Isis. She was known as the Goddess Supreme, "the savior goddess" or "savior of the human race" and her superiority was considered "almost monotheism."[3]

Another option was to embrace the ancient monotheistic religion of Judaism, the only faith that had a distinct set of Scriptures, which was another appealing draw for the educated in the empire. These developments undoubtedly influenced the Jewish proselyte movement. Moreover, it presumably moved other Gentiles to become what were known as "God-fearers." God-fearers were a class of non-Jews sympathetic to Judaism who followed the Jewish way of life, but did not fully convert and obey the 613 laws in the Torah. Many of these Jewish proselytes and God-fearers later became followers of the Way of Jesus. Especially for the "God-fearers," this new Way of worshiping the one, true Jewish God (through his Anointed One) was especially appealing because the early church decided that Gentiles did not have to obey the whole law of Moses in order to be fully accepted into the community (Acts 15). In other words, for males, that meant no circumcision!

The Emergence of Ekklesia

With that background information, we began a study on the roots of "church." We realized that most of us are preprogrammed to believe that Jesus began a new religion called Christianity and formed a new institution called "church." But from our study of first-century history, it became obvious that this is read into the New Testament not derived from it. Moreover, there is recent interdisciplinary biblical and historical scholarship that has revealed more facts about earliest Christianity than previously known.

3. Stark, *Cities of God*, 98–101.

Thanks to these remarkable findings, "like the walls of Jericho, our myths about the early church are tumbling down. . . . What's more, these new discoveries from what Cox calls 'the age of faith' confront both liberals and conservatives with real challenges."[4] Could the truth about our modern concepts of "church" and early Christianity be that far off wherever one falls on the theological spectrum? We would soon find out.

The Organization of *Ekklesia*

The word in the Greek that is translated "church" is *ekklesia*. It literally means "gathering." In Acts (19:32, 41), the same word is used to describe a mob of people who besiege Paul and his companions in Ephesus. Jesus used the word only twice, recorded in Matthew, where he describes his followers of the day and his followers of the future. This is the only time the word occurs in the gospels. Paul used it to describe the groups of people in each city he visited or to whom he wrote, who were "followers of the Way." Historically, the word was never used to describe a Christian meeting place until 190 CE.[5]

It's interesting to note that the other Greek word for "gathering" is *sunagoge*, from which the word synagogue is derived. Neither Jesus nor Paul used that term for gatherings of Christ followers, probably because its common understanding by the first century was that a *sunagoge* was a religious assembly of Jews. Using the word *ekklesia*, may have been strategic, as it was not distinctively Jewish like *sunagoge* had become, but was meaningful to both Jew and Gentile alike. Moreover, Jesus was not saying he was raising up a different type of synagogue, a Christian one, that would become the church.

Jesus was clear that those who followed his Path were not to organize themselves in a hierarchy as did the temple or synagogues of the day. For Jesus, equality of followers was paramount: "But you are not to be called 'Rabbi,' for you have one Teacher, and you are all brothers. And do not call anyone on earth 'father,' for you have one Father, and he is in heaven. Nor are you to be called instructors, for you have one Instructor, the Messiah. The greatest among you will be your servant. For those who exalt themselves will be humbled, and those who humble themselves will be exalted" (Matt 23:8–12). Paul, too, echoed this sentiment, when he boldly declared the

4. Meyers, *Underground Church*, 43.

5. Viola and Barna, *Pagan Christianity*, 11–12.

most radical claim of any movement known in his day that "there is neither Jew nor Gentile, neither slave nor free, nor is there male and female, for you are all one in [Messiah] Jesus" (Gal 3:28). Even women, thought to be among the most unclean and least qualified, were equal among Jesus followers. As were Gentiles (not even on the Jewish purity map), and slaves, who traditional wisdom would call some of the worst sinners. So, the first observation one makes about the gatherings of Jesus followers or *ekklesia* is that they are egalitarian with no one having a leadership title or office.

Close examination reveals that *ekklesia* is a nonhierarchical body of people with no priests or bishops. No disciples of Jesus were designated priests. Bishops, who became local administers of churches, do not appear until the second century. We know this from the letters of Ignatius of Antioch.[6] There were titles in the earliest gatherings named by Paul, in fact twenty in all, but these were all ministries that were functional in nature, from apostles (emissaries or "sent ones") to elders to teachers to pastors to stewards. They were not offices. They did not derive from some kind of bureaucratic organization nor form a hierarchy. They were not professional clergy presiding over a church. They were functional skills; natural gifts and motivational abilities that people already had or had developed. Nowhere does Jesus or Paul name one of these ministries as having authority over a gathering. Nor over consecrating the bread-and-wine in the traditional meal of Jesus followers. When the word priest is used in the New Testament (only three times), it refers to all believers being priests. The word pastor is only found once in the New Testament and it is plural, meaning it is one of the functions in the church—it means, *shepherd*. It is not a top officer with authority over others.[7]

Jesus gave a simple definition of these early gatherings (*ekklesia*) when he said, "Where two or three meet together in my name, there I am in their midst" (Matt 18:20). As Garry Wills asks, why would followers need a bishop or priest or pastor when Jesus' spirit is among them?

This didn't mean there were no leaders in the *ekklesia*. To be sure, there were. Elders were leaders. People who had the twenty innate gifts or ministries Paul mentioned were leaders. Yet, they were not bureaucratic overseers making decisions for the gatherings. They were servant leaders. Frank Viola makes the point that elders, or any other leaders in gatherings, were not *ordained* by a governing body, in the modern sense when we think

6. Wills, *What Jesus Meant*, 78–80.

7. Viola and Barna, *Pagan Christianity*, 106–7.

of clergy ordination. In Acts 14, Paul and Barnabas return to three gatherings they helped form in Lystra, Iconium, and Antioch. They appoint elders in each one. The Greek word used *to appoint* "carries the idea of endorsing, affirming, and showing forth what has already been happening. It . . . conveys the thought of blessing."[8] People were appointed elders or recognized as having one of the ministry gifts when others saw they had the appropriate skills. Elders and other leaders had no authority to control the church. All in the gatherings were equal. There was no clergy/laity or professional/non-professional distinction in the earliest churches.[9]

It's important to note that Paul called gatherings *ekklesia* even before he appointed elders. No formal eldership was necessary to have a "church." It appeared he appointed elders (or advised others to do so) either for practical reasons, when a church had grown enough that they needed organization, or after a period of time when people had time to recognize their gifts. But these were always a *plurality* of elders with no one being appointed a senior pastor or top elder. The early church was following the teachings of Jesus who turned the conventional wisdom of leadership and authority on its head.

Our research on the early "church" also uncovered the historical reality about women in the early Jesus Movement. We had seen that Jesus was a leading feminist in his teaching. So it would be no surprise that the earliest "church" included women as full participants and leaders, even apostles. Again, Dr. Ann Nyland, an expert in Greek lexicography, shed light on this. She reveals the many mistranslations modern English Bibles have on women. "The translations of most New Testament versions are based on a lack of understanding of Greek word meaning,"[10] she argues. Sometimes they are also based on theological bias.

Nyland cites nine popular Bible versions that deliberately changed the Greek female name for "Junia" to a masculine name.[11] In Romans 16:7, Paul names Junia among the Apostles. In the fourth century, the Eastern Orthodox Church father Chrysostom, said, "Indeed, how great the wisdom of this woman must have been that she was even deemed worthy of the title of apostle."[12] The King James, the New King James, and the Living Bible

8. Ibid., 124.
9. Viola, "Myth of Christian Leadership."
10. Nyland, *The Source New Testament*, 10.
11. Ibid.
12. Ibid., 305.

versions changed the female name "Nympha" to a masculine name (Nymphas, Col 4:14) and changed "the church that is in her house" to "the church that is in his house."[13] Nympha was obviously a leader in a house gathering, a "church." The King James and the New King James reversed the order of Priscilla and Aquila when Paul referred to them in a teaching context.[14] Nyland says, "The most senior person was always greeted first and this was a strict protocol of the times."[15] Priscilla, listed four times before her husband, was apparently a teacher in the "church."

Finally, the woman Phoebe, whom Paul cites in Romans 16:1–2, is referred to in Greek as *prostasis*. Nyland says the correct translation is "presiding officer" or "leader and protector" as it referred to someone who stands in front of people and protects them. Phoebe was obviously a leader in a local gathering, a "church." Paul even says she was "over me, also."[16] But how does this read in most versions? In all my years as an evangelical, I read those words in the New International Version as "she has been a great help to many people, including me," a phrase that doesn't even acknowledge the leadership qualities of the term, *prostasis*. These examples of deliberate mistranslations and unbeknownst misreadings on women in the early church are a grave injustice for women today.

What's more, on *ekklesia* organization, we learned how different the Eastern Orthodox tradition views leadership and decision-making in the church. Even though they have titles of leaders in their church, like bishops and pastors, follow clergy-laity structure, and recognize the importance of historic church "councils," they don't look at them the same way as Western churches. All Eastern Orthodox congregations are people centered. Clergy and laity are equal. Forming theology or making decisions are not matters reserved for the professionals, i.e., pastors, denominational leaders, or councils. Decisions must be confirmed by the whole congregation. It is not a top-down approach. Even a council of bishops in the Eastern Orthodox Church has no authority over local churches. Their decisions, much like a denomination's or a senior pastor's or a pastoral team's, are not binding unless confirmed by each local church, that is all the individual members together. Historically, pastors and teachers in Orthodox churches explained theological positions to the people, but "everyone in the church

13. Ibid., 10.

14. Ibid.

15. Ibid., 305.

16. Ibid., 304.

was involved. The whole body had not only the right, but the duty to certify the Faith. Besides, the bishops' individual opinions did not hold any special authority." And, as far as church councils, "No local church was forced to agree with the decrees of a Council."[17] Although not exactly the same, this fit the organizational style that we learned the earliest church had much more than the Western church traditions.

Finally, we learned how contemporary scholarship has debunked the idea of apostolic succession and the whole notion of an authoritative hierarchy in churches. Even Paul never claims apostleship as a lineage bestowed on him or others by previous apostles, but rather as simply a "gift of the Spirit" distributed as the Spirit desires and in subjection to the greatest spiritual gift of love. Apostolic authority was a convenient fiction created later in the history of the church as a way of justifying ambitions to control the congregations.[18]

The Early "Church" Did Not Go to Church

"Are you saying that the early church didn't go to church?" a man asked, one of the people who had gathered at Valholl Brewing for "pub theology" night after I had talked to Jeff.

"Well, yes!" Gina said. "That's a great way to put it. The earliest followers met in homes. There was no institutional church." Gina then summarized some of what we had learned. With the exception of the earliest gatherings in Jerusalem who sometimes met in the temple courtyard before it was destroyed, throughout the first three centuries of Christianity, followers of "The Way" met together in private residences. The earliest gatherings had no proscribed liturgy, worship practices, hierarchical system, or professional clergy. All members were equal, she explained.

"The concept of 'church' was different for these earliest followers," Dan added. "They didn't consider themselves creating a Christian version of the Jewish temple or synagogue with priests and synagogue rulers. To them, the new paradigm was that the people following Jesus' Way were the house of God, the new temple. Nowhere in the New Testament do we find terms referring to the people of God as a building or place. The house of God was wherever followers gathered, even as little as two or three, in a courtyard or

17. Bajis, *Common Ground*, 120–24.

18. Meyers, *Underground Church*, 52.

under a tree. It happens that the easiest place to gather was in homes, so it became an informal home-centered movement."[19]

I added a few points about how striking this was, considering the earliest Christians were surrounded by religious places of worship, i.e., synagogues and pagan temples. "The earliest followers never built a structure for their place of worship, nor did they establish a hierarchy of leaders."

"But Acts says it was the custom of Paul to go to the synagogue and preach Jesus as Messiah," the man said.

"True," I said. "But Paul and other apostles only used the synagogue as an easy meeting place from which to share their message with Jews. Eventually, Paul abandoned this strategy when some synagogues began rejecting him. There is no record of early Christians creating new synagogues or temples or church buildings for places of worship."

Gina paraphrased a passage from one of the books we read, *Pagan Christianity*, that she said had special meaning to her. The original quote was this: "When Christianity was born, it was the only religion on the planet that had no sacred objects, no sacred persons, and no sacred places . . . The Christian faith was born in homes, out in courtyards, and along roadsides."[20]

Dan then talked about how fascinating it was to learn that the earliest Jesus gatherings met on Sunday—to commemorate Jesus' resurrection day—before the day was a national holiday. That meant they met early in the morning before going to work. The Jewish Jesus followers, if they were still keeping the Sabbath, would have done that the day before they met, on Saturday. The point being the day the first followers typically met to honor Jesus was just an ordinary work day not a special "day of worship."

"This kind of blows my mind," that same man said. "So, what does it mean to 'go to church' today?"

"Things are warped today," Dan said. "We are still learning how that happened. I mean, how Catholics and Protestants developed religious institutions and denominations. I think we need to seriously rethink 'church,' in light of this. Like maybe, meeting at a pub like this is just as good as any Christian 'church' gathering.

"Or, maybe meet in homes or just meet to work together to make the world a better place, wherever or whatever organization that may be. It's not that organized 'church' should be abandoned—people should be

19. Viola and Barna, *Pagan Christianity*, 11.

20. Ibid., 14.

free to meet how they want and have a leadership structure that works for them—but that it should be put in perspective. It's not mandatory to go to an organized church to follow the Path of Christ."

"That attitude might put some churches out of business," someone else said.

"And, make it unnecessary to have professional pastors and priests," another added.

"That might be a good thing," Gina said.

"Or, perhaps, lead us to be creative about forming communities of followers," I added. I told people about a community I discovered called *The Refuge* in Denver, Colorado. "It's a community or 'church' for people who are burned out on organized church. They call it 'part-church-part-social-service-agency-part-family.' People aren't shoehorned into a set of beliefs but allowed to question and doubt and come to their own conclusions while rallying around the call to simply help hurting people."[21]

We had learned a lot about what the earliest gatherings of Jesus were like and some of the implications for today. Later, we would delve into how the earliest church changed into a mega-institution in the Catholic Church and how little things had really changed since the Reformation in Protestant churches. But first, there was more to learn about why the earliest Jesus gatherings attracted people and how followers of the Way grew to be a major movement in the Roman Empire.

What the *Ekklesia* Did

To learn the appeal of the earliest followers of Jesus' teaching, we needed to learn what the practices of these first followers were. Robin Meyers, in revealing some of that recent scholarship on the early church, reminded us there was never a pure original church that had a definitive theology, single form of governance, uniform liturgy, and universally accepted Scripture[22] (as we had also learned in our study of origins of the Bible). What's more, there had always been some level of theological and doctrinal disagreements between the earliest congregations. The move of some to try to rediscover the perfect model for church and replicate it today is futile. There was never a perfect model, and in fact, it would have been counter to Jesus' and Paul's teaching to claim there was one. The overriding principle of Jesus'

21. Escobar, *Faith Shift*, 227

22. Meyers, *Underground Church*, 42–50.

teaching and the New Testament—that love supersedes specific rules—is in direct contradiction to any legalistic model of how "church," or more accurately "gatherings" of Path followers should operate. The New Testament principles of love and freedom insist on it.

It appears the only real common denominator in the earliest Christian gatherings was that all focused on Jesus and his love ethic, for this was their major distinctive. They had one pledge of allegiance: "Jesus the Anointed One is Lord," which was not a doctrinal statement about his deity or a mandatory dogma, but a statement of who one serves. Lord is from "Kyrios," in the Greek, which means *master*. "Jesus is Lord" was a declaration of loyalty to Jesus and his Path of love, rather than to Caesar and his way of power and control. Kyrios was a title for Caesar, for the emperor, and part of the relatively new emperor cult that had developed. "Jesus is Kyrios" was a statement in contrast to the emperor cult, and also a statement in contrast to classical paganism, that worshiped Zeus, Apollo, Juno, or Dionysius and made them "Kyrios." It was also a declaration that Jesus' Path was superior to the Jewish temple cult. And Jesus' Path was twofold: one, the counter-cultural way of love, and two, an internal religion of the heart, not external rituals.

So what did the earliest gatherings do when they met? The only thing remotely approaching a ritual for the earliest church was what some called a "love feast," a festive, community meal that followers shared, in which they incorporated the taking of wine and bread in remembrance of the death of Jesus. Sharing food together is an act of hospitality and a symbol of love and fellowship. The Love Feast was just that. No clergy or spiritual leader was necessary to officiate.[23]

To be sure, at times they probably read or had someone read the Jewish Scriptures. But this was not necessarily a hallmark of their meetings. As we had learned earlier, their Scriptures were not the New Testament. Throughout the first century, there was no New Testament. In time, documents surfaced that eventually became the New Testament (or others that never made it in), but there was no official list of books that make up the New Testament Scriptures until the fourth century. For decades, local congregations would not have relied on a written record of Jesus' or the apostles' teachings. For hundreds of years, there was no universal set of Christian writings that every church recognized. History teaches us the earliest church used the Septuagint when they read the Bible, which was the Greek translation of the Old Testament that included the Apocrypha (which is rejected today by

23. Viola and Barna, *Pagan Christianity*, 192.

all Protestants). Any specific mention of Jesus' teachings would have been people recollecting the oral tradition, not quoting the gospels, which didn't appear until thirty to sixty years after Christ (historians can't all agree on the timing of their appearance) and to which not all congregations would have had access. Paul began writing letters to some congregations around twenty years after Christ, so some followers would have access to these, but not all. Moreover, it would be decades, even centuries before these writings would be considered definitive, sacred "Scripture."

At times, gatherings probably practiced prayer as well, but again, this was not necessarily a hallmark of their meetings. There was no set ritual, order of worship, Bible readings, sermon, music, or liturgy. Jesus' way was a religion of the heart, not outward piety. That would have been reflected at their meetings. In time, documents that spelled out set ways of doing things began to appear, as in the Didache, a type of Christian manual from the early second century, but these were not from the beginning.

What else did this earliest church do? Well, in short, things counter to the surrounding culture. Things Jesus would do. Harvey Cox calls this early period of the Jesus Movement the Age of Faith, where "'faith' meant hope and assurance in the dawning of a new era of freedom, healing, and compassion that Jesus had demonstrated. To be a Christian meant to live in the Spirit, embrace his hope, and to follow him in the work he had begun."[24] The early church did not go to church and perform religious duties. They followed *a way of life*[25] that looked at the world differently, broke down the barriers of class, and reached out to all, especially the marginalized and "unclean." This new way of life clashed with the conventional wisdom of both the Jewish and Greco-Roman philosophy. Harvey Cox summarizes what the earliest communities of *ekklesia* were like:

> During the first two and half centuries of its life, this nascent Christian movement ("the Way") flourished despite periodic persecutions and did so without relying on theological agreement. What we now call doctrines or dogmas, let alone creeds, were yet to appear. Historians of that period agree that what bound Christians together in their local congregations was their common participation in the life of the Spirit and a way of living that included the sharing of prayer, bread, and wine; a lively hope for the coming of God's *shalom* [peace] on earth; and putting the example of Jesus into concrete practice, especially his concern for outcasts. With

24. Cox, *Future of Faith*, 5.

25. Bass, *People's History of Christianity*, 27.

> regard to theological questions, opinions differed widely. In other words, in this most vibrant period in Christian history, it was *following* Jesus that counted; there were no dogmas to which one had to adhere, and rich variety of theological views thrived. It was the era of a thousand flowers blooming, and the idea of "heresy" had not yet stepped onstage.[26]

The Growth of the Jesus Movement

What made the earliest Jesus gatherings attractive to outsiders? To answer that, we had to understand what communities of antiquity in the Roman Empire were like. We already learned what first-century Palestine was like, with the 90 percent of the population being poor and a lack of public services. What about the rest of the Roman Empire?

Historian Rodney Stark describes Greco-Roman cities as "extremely crowded, filthy beyond imagining, disorderly, filled with strangers, and afflicted with frequent catastrophes—fires, plagues, conquests, and earthquakes . . . life in antiquity abounded in anxiety and misery." He goes on to reveal that cities like Antioch and Rome were more densely populated than modern Calcutta![27] Remember, there were no societal concepts of public service, healthcare, economic development, and opportunity for all. These are modern ideas. Nor is there any historical evidence that Christianity grew because miserable people were promised eternal bliss in heaven.[28] No, the evidence confirms that people became followers of Jesus' Path largely due to the practice of Christian benevolence and hope for a better life in the here and now. Followers of Jesus were known for nursing the sick (even during epidemics), supporting orphans, widows, and the elderly, helping the poor, honoring women, and showing concern for slaves. "In short, Christians created 'a miniature welfare state in an empire which for the most part lacked social services.'"[29]

When the earliest Jesus followers spoke of this new way of life, it was put in terms of loving others, not "accepting Jesus" and not in order to be right with God and saved from wrath and hell. The Didache, an early Christian document circa 120 CE, said there were two ways, one of life and

26. Cox, *Future of Faith*, 77–78.

27. Stark, *Cities of God*, 26.

28. Ibid., 30.

29. Ibid., 31.

one of death. The way of life was Jesus' major teaching, to "love God who made you; second, love your neighbor as yourself, and do not do to another what you would not want done to you."[30] The reputation of Christians putting this teaching into practice spread far and wide. By 362 CE, when the Roman emperor Julian sought to revive paganism, he said in a letter to a pagan priest, "I think that when the poor happened to be neglected and overlooked by the priests, the impious Galileans observed this and devoted themselves to benevolence . . . [They] support not only their poor, but ours as well; everyone can see that our people lack aid from us."[31]

The attraction wasn't that Christians were part of some newly organized religion with superior doctrines nor, was it because of some new formula for salvation that guaranteed a heavenly reward. No, what attracted the ordinary person wasn't religious in nature at all. It was a practical demonstration of love and hope for the future, a rare commodity in that culture. It was the practical application of Jesus' teachings and his announcement of good news, drawn from the Jewish prophets' call for social justice that got people's attention. Suddenly, the poor and disenfranchised, including unclean women, peasants, and slaves, were worthy of acceptance and promise. The playing field of class was leveled and all were equal. A unifying spirit prevailed. The desire for wealth or power over others as the solution to the problems of this world was replaced with radical generosity, common ownership, elevating the needy, and reaching out to enemies.

Initially the movement attracted the marginalized of Palestine and eventually the Hellenized Jews and Gentile "God fearers," who were drawn to monotheism and a more personal spirituality and community. It was that *new way of life* that attracted the first followers, not a religion. "It was an underground, populist movement so distinct from the joyless brutality of the age that it grew from twelve followers to six million in three centuries."[32]

In an age when courage and power were the values most aspired to, the earliest Jesus Movement advanced a most unlikely virtue: mercy. Seen by classical philosophers as a weakness since it extended assistance to those who had not earned it, it struck a chord with the masses of people. The practices of mercy, community, love for neighbor and enemy, and equality for class and women, drew many to join the movement.

30. Bass, *People's History of Christianity*, 28.

31. Stark, *Cities of God*, 31.

32. Meyers, *Underground Church*, 58.

History was teaching our group an important lesson. As best they could, the earliest followers of Jesus' Path emulated Jesus when he walked the earth. They did not build an institution nor create a hierarchal authority but rather promoted and practiced equality for all classes. As Jesus focused on inner purity that culminates in outward acts of love, so did they. As Jesus opposed religion, so did the they. Garry Wills reminded us what his opposition to religion looked like:

> What is the kind of religion Jesus opposed? Any religion that is proud of its virtue, like the boastful Pharisee. Any that is self-righteous, quick to judge and condemn, ready to impose burdens rather than share or lift them. Any that exalts its own officers, proud of its trappings, building expensive monuments to itself. Any that neglects the poor and cultivates the rich, any that scorns outcasts and flatters the rulers of this world. If that sounds like just about every form of religion we know, then we can see how far off from religion Jesus stood.[33]

As much as the early church drew followers attracted to their radical communities, it was this opposition to religion that paved the way to persecution, first by the Jewish population still loyal to the corrupt temple system, and later by Rome. We learned how the Way of Jesus was counter-cultural to Roman philosophy of loyalty, family, and religion—whether the traditional gods or the emperor cult. In Jesus, all were equal, not just Roman citizens. All were family, not merely blood relatives. With Christ, the traditional gods and their temples were irrelevant because true religion was one of the heart. And ultimately, Jesus and his superior Path of love was Lord, not Caesar, the power of Rome, or the pagan gods. Initially, because the Jesus Movement was first seen as a branch of Judaism, which Rome tolerated as a traditional religion, it was ignored by Rome. Later, as these differences became more apparent, the powers in Rome began to see it as a dangerous sect and persecution began.

But we weren't so much interested in persecution by Rome as we were with how this grass-roots egalitarian first-century movement of love morphed into one of the most powerful clerically dominated religious institutions on the planet—that is *Christianity*, as we know it today—on par with any multi-national corporation. To understand that, we had to learn what went wrong.

33. Wills, *What Jesus Meant*, 77.

Chapter Eight

Poisoning the Path

WHAT WE HAD LEARNED about the early Jesus Movement was refreshing. It trusted the spirit, not doctrines, to maintain unity, founded on Jesus' inclusive love ethic. There was an egalitarian leadership approach to community with a plurality of elders appointed only when necessary, not as a requirement. Women were included in leadership, even among the apostles. There was no line of authority with professional clergy, let alone senior pastors or priests. Gatherings of believers met in homes and courtyards. There were no religious buildings. Formal meetings were on a normal work day in society, not a special religious "holiday." Although we recognized that people should be free to organize and attend modern churches (as long as they don't impose that system on others as the only proper "church"), we yearned to see that same spirit of the early church flowing freely today.

What Went Wrong?

We wondered what transpired to create what we knew to be the dark ink blotches of Christianity—institutional control, the suppression of women, heresy hunting, a corrupt medieval church, the Crusades, and the inquisition, to name a few. Moreover, despite a bright light in the Reformation, there were the shadows of denominationalism, loss of vibrancy in many mainline churches, sexual abuse in the Catholic Church, and spiritually abusive and politically motivated nature of many fundamentalist and evangelical churches. There is the shadow of churches—Catholic or Protestant—that seems more interested in protecting its reputation, power, and expansion than dealing justly with people. What went wrong?

It was in the fourth century, we learned, with the conversion of the emperor Constantine, when a major shift began. But even before Constantine, the seeds of change were already being planted. In what Robin Meyers calls "The Great Reversal," the early Jesus Movement gradually turned from this non-hierarchal, non-creedal collection of followers meeting in homes sharing a way of life together, into a full-blown mega-religion. One of the most fascinating parts of our *Timeline* study was investigating the details of this phenomenon.

Roman Organization

Roman society had a profound impact on early Christianity, especially when it introduced the idea of hierarchal control. One such influence was the Roman Empire's political and military organization. In 96 CE, a church leader wrote a letter that eventually came to be known as 1 Clement (the one that some placed in early versions of the New Testament). In it, the writer, whose identification is not indicated in the letter, seeks to solve a leadership dispute in a congregation in Corinth. Apparently a youth rebellion had occurred in which younger members had replaced the older elders and taken the reigns of leadership. The letter argues that the older elders were the rightful leaders because they were the successors to the apostles and had a right to lead. Its rationale is not based on the cause of the conflict, whether there was a claim that either group were heretical, immoral, or corrupt, but on the example of the Roman army and its clear lines of authority. Later, a tradition developed that said the letter's author was a bishop in Rome named Clement, which added fuel to the emerging notion that churches should be organized in a hierarchical way, patterned after the Roman military.[1]

Some years later, four church fathers and another important document introduced ideas that furthered the move to a new hierarchal structure in congregations. Ignatius (ca. 110 CE) and Ireneaus (ca. 180 CE) were authoritarian-styled leaders who fought early Christian heresies through solidifying church hierarchy. Ignatius was the bishop of Antioch, one of the early bishops, a position and title that was just starting to appear in the second century. He had a strict autocratic view of governing churches. He argued for apostolic succession. He also elevated one church elder above the others in congregations, a position known as *bishop*, and the position

1. Cox, *Future of Faith*, 90–91.

he held over believers in Antioch. As we will soon learn, this position later became known as *priest* or *pastor* while the bishop position became one over many churches. He believed "we ought to regard the bishop as the Lord Himself."[2] Although, he introduced it, during his time, this autocratic church leadership wasn't widely practiced.

Irenaeus "was even less democratic" and exalted the apostolic line of authority even more. What's fascinating is what drove these men's concern was not heresy in the form of false doctrine, but rather the "charismatics" in local churches who claimed to have prophetic words from God and needed to be reined in. Another point is they were not looking to enforce a uniformity of belief nor to excommunicate members. Ignatius insisted that unity in love was more important than uniformity in belief. As for Irenaeus, he was strongly opposed to excluding anyone from the gatherings, even someone accused of being a "false prophet."[3] These more strict practices came later. It appeared Ignatius and Irenaeus were not only introducing authoritative structures to maintain order, but unbeknownst to them, they were laying a foundation for future, more controlling practices.

Then, sometime in the third century, a manuscript called *Didascalia Apostolorum* emerged in Syria. It was initially alleged to be written by Jesus' original disciples. Scholars today unanimously agree it was not. The document claims that those with the title *bishop* should have almost absolute power over members of churches. It elevates them to a status of representing God, as a priest, teacher, father, governor, mighty king, and mediator. "Let him who rules in God's place be given [honor] by you," it states. As organizational teaching, it flies in the face of Jesus' position on equality.[4]

Finally, there was Origen (ca. 230 CE) and Cyprian (ca. 258 CE). Origen still has much respect today as the first genuine Christian theologian. He held several views that later came to be thought as heretical. He didn't believe Jesus was equal to the Father in every way (a position easily arrived at when reading certain New Testament verses), had a spiritualized view of the resurrection, and was a universalist, believing Jesus and Paul taught that all souls would eventually be reconciled to God. Unfortunately, there was one position he held that never was questioned in later years. That was his view that common church members were required to obey bishops even if they were unjust. He respected the practice of ordaining clergy as leaders,

2. Viola and Barna, *Pagan Christianity*, 111.

3. Cox, *Future of Faith*, 93.

4. Ibid., 95.

whom he believed had a more sacred quality than the laity, although he did acknowledge they could abuse their power.

Cyprian, too, despite being a sacrificial leader who gave his wealth to the poor, pushed the bishop office, advocating that unity and love among bishops was more important than among the laity, implying common followers may not be capable of it.[5] It was during this period that the role of bishop caught on universally and eventually every church had its own bishop. This new clergy class of "bishops" became the only ones who could preside over the "Eucharist" or communion, which by then was evolving from being an informal "love feast" to a religious ceremony. Slowly, the view of human organization found in the earliest church eroded. It was supplanted by the view of the dominant people, for "Greco-Roman culture was hierarchical by nature."[6]

All these views, some of them not entirely out of touch with Christ's teachings, were the stepping stones to what came next. Harvey Cox concludes, "By the end of the third century, the earlier more egalitarian fellowships were fading into a dim memory, and the imperial version of Christianity—with its princes and monarchs above and its common folk below—had won the day."[7]

As another historian put it referring to the original Jesus Movement before more controlling practices gained a foothold: "The organizational structure, the great institution of the church—signified for Roman Catholics today by the Vatican and its complex hierarchy—simply wasn't there. There was an apostolic band of followers. There were missionary efforts in major centers, first in Jerusalem, then Antioch, then Rome, but certainly no sense of headquarters. Instead you had this tiny, vulnerable, poor, often persecuted group of people who were on fire with something."[8]

Enter Constantine

Apart from Jesus, no person has influenced Christian history more than Flavius Valerius Constantinus. Known as Constantine, he became the Western Roman emperor in 312 CE and emperor of the entire empire in 324 CE. According to Christian historian Eusebius, it was in 312 CE, on the

5. Ibid., 97.
6. Viola and Barna, *Pagan Christianity*, 117.
7. Cox, *Future of Faith*, 97.
8. Todhunter, "In the Footsteps of the Apostles."

night before Constantine's defeat of the current Western emperor in a battle called Milvian Bridge, that he claimed to have converted to Christ after seeing a vision of the cross in the heavens that revealed the words, "In this sign conquer." He reportedly ordered his army to display the sign of the cross on their weapons and they won the battle despite being outnumbered. The fact that this account did not surface until years later, makes it suspect to some.

Was Constantine a true believer whose vision was some sort of personal revelation? Or did he merely invoke one of the gods, this time the god of the Christians? During this period, the older Roman religions were declining and Christianity was growing. In an attempt to ensure victory, as was the practice of Roman generals in battle, did Constantine merely try out another god? Was his conversion genuine or was he only appeasing various deities, as many historians attest, such as Tyche, the god of chance, or Helios, the sun god?[9]

Later, he was most likely responsible for the death of both his son and mother. Given that, the case against his genuine dedication to the Prince of Peace is suspect. Although historians continue to argue over the legitimacy of his conversion, one thing seems certain. As Harvey Cox says, the Christian communities of the Roman Empire, with their emerging hierarchies patterned after Rome and its military were probably suffering from "empire envy" and were ripe for a Christian Emperor to use Christianity to hold the masses together. After all, religion was always the "social cement" for the Romans. Constantine, many historians argue, just used Christianity as a tool to unify the then fractured empire. Regardless, in time, to be Christian was no longer a handicap under Constantine. Apart from a few exceptions, he essentially ended Roman persecution against Christians (although, as we were to learn, he would ultimately begin official church persecution against heretics).

What caught our attention was how Constantine began to pattern the church after the Roman top-down political society, as well as the ecclesiastical structure of pagan religion. He built church buildings that mirrored pagan temples and spaces for Roman government. He was the one who organized churches into dioceses, which were Roman regional districts. He elevated church leaders and gave them special privileges on par with Roman officials. Historians believe all this was part of his unifying-empire strategy, patterned after his imperial predecessors, to form a single ideology, one

9. Cox, *Future of Faith*, 100.

that he could control.[10] And it worked. Now protected and promoted by the emperor, Christianity outgrew its minority status and drew more and more people into church membership. But now, the attraction was different. It didn't mean they were necessarily walking the egalitarian Path of Christ. A new national Roman religion was forming and, like all good Romans do, people got in step with it.

Sacred Places

Not until 190 CE was the term *ekklesia* used by Clement of Alexandria to refer to a meeting place. He was also the first person to use the phrase "go to church," referring to a private home not a religious building.[11] Yet, it wasn't until Constantine (ca. 340 CE) that a movement began to have distinct sacred places in which to gather and worship. Constantine ordered the construction of "Christian" church buildings and great basilicas, something that was never done before.

A collection of sacred buildings for Christians, as the pagans and Jews had, would help legitimize the faith in the eyes of the populace. Often built over the tombs of Christian martyrs and all named for saints, he built nine churches in Rome, including St. Peter's and St. Paul's, and several more in Jerusalem, Bethlehem, and Constantinople. Later, throughout the empire, other Christians converted pagan temples into churches or built church buildings on the sites of pagan temples.

Both the buildings and certain practices were patterned after pagan customs and temples as well as the Roman basilica, the common government buildings of the day. These included the altar, the "bishop's chair," candles and incense, special garments for clergy, and the requirement that worshipers do a purification ritual before entering a sacred space. In the earliest gatherings of Jesus followers, the community looked on the people corporately as the new temple or house of God. But in Constantine's era, the sacred place inside the hearts of followers was being supplanted by brick and mortar. "Fourth century Christianity was being profoundly shaped by Greek paganism and Roman imperialism."[12]

Today's church building structure still follows this pattern in many ways. Church sanctuaries, like the Roman basilica, serve the same function

10. Viola and Barna, *Pagan Christianity*, 119.

11. Ibid., 12.

12. Ibid., 21.

as school auditoriums or theaters—a place for passive crowds to watch a performance. There is an elevated platform or stage where clergy minister. Some still have an altar (or replaced by a communion table) like the original basilica, the holiest place of the building, where the Eucharist is served by Christian clergy. The original basilica had a larger judge's chair and other chairs for elders, facing the audience, which became the bishop's chair. Christian sanctuaries today often have similar chairs for the priest or pastor and the associate ministers. In original basilicas, the speaker spoke from the large judge's chair in front of the people. Eventually, the Christian practice introduced speaking from an elevated pulpit on the stage. Finally, the basilica design had some sort of separation between the elevated stage and the people below, a separation that was retained in Christian buildings.[13]

Although there were quite a few changes to church buildings over the years, from basilicas to Byzantine to Romanesque to Gothic cathedrals, particularly the elaborate art work, stained glass, and enlarged construction, the essential interior architectural style remained the same. This is also the case in today's Protestant church buildings and even the typical evangelical mega-church building.

One fascinating fact was that original basilicas and church buildings had no chairs or pews for the audience. People stood to hear the speaking or watch the worship service. Pews were not introduced until well over 1000 CE. To this day, all Eastern Orthodox Churches still follow this practice of standing rather than sitting during a service.

Sacred Time

In 321 CE, Constantine made Sunday a legal holiday. Some historians believe he did it in honor of Mithras, the sun god, a deity to which they believe he never stopped worshiping. So, even though Christians had already been meeting on "the first day of the week"—*Sunday* to Romans but the "first day" to Jews—in memory of the day Christ rose from the grave, Constantine legitimized it as a day of worship. Its origin, however, is a day named after the *sun* in honor of a pagan god. Before Constantine's edict, Christians presumably worked on Sundays after having gathered for fellowship in the early morning.

13. Viola and Barna, *Pagan Christianity*, 23.

Sacred People

After Constantine's conversion, the authority structure of bishops that Ignatius, Irenaeus, Origen, and Cyprian had supported ballooned into a full-blown hierarchy and control mechanism. Constantine took on the title of Pontifex Maximus, a title the pagans used for their "high priests," the bridge-builders between humans and the gods, and that Roman emperors used to signify their control over all state religions. Catholics will recognize it is even used today as one of the titles of the pope. As the title implied, Constantine appointed himself as the chief administrator of the new religion he was creating—the governor of the Christian church.

Under Constantine, clergyman (*bishops*, who presided over a church and *presbyters*, their deputies) were honored as the highest officials of the empire. He gave bishops of Rome more power than Roman governors. He ordered that clergy receive annual pay allowances, hence the beginning of a professional class. Clergy became exempt from paying taxes, being tried in secular courts, and serving in the army. Eventually bishops and presbyters shaved their heads and wore the same clothes as Roman officials.[14]

All this solidified the newly developed clergy-laity distinction and introduced the idea of sacred and secular roles and professions. With all religious power and societal privilege in the hands of the bishops and their deputies (and later priests and pastors, as we were soon to learn), lowly members of local congregations became second-class citizens. The irony of this didn't escape us. This class divide was completely absent from the original teachings of Jesus, who vehemently confronted and opposed it in its Jewish and Gentile form in first-century Palestine.

A further shift developed during the Middle Ages. It was then that the bishops began to take on political duties, overseeing groups of churches, and the presbyters (who had already years before begun to be called *priests*) took the role of the overall leader of a local church. We were surprised to discover, with the possible exception of Anabaptists, how little the Reformation changed this system. Having been taught in evangelicalism that the reformers had recovered the original, pure structure of the church, I was amazed how the hierarchy of senior pastor and associate pastor mirrored Constantine's church leadership and the Catholic priesthood. Senior pastors were Cyprian's and Constantine's bishops and associate pastors were presbyters. A clergy class lived on. Despite saying the right words about all

14. Ibid., 121.

church members being "a priesthood of believers," reformers kept hierarchal control in place. "Only in their rhetoric did they state that all believers were priests and ministers. In their practice they denied it."[15] The only real change the reformers made was to oppose the position of pope and give every believer access to God without the help of a priest. Yet they retained the ecclesiastical structure of the church. As Frank Viola aptly asserts, "So in Protestantism an old problem took a new form. The jargon changed, but the error remained."[16]

Sacred Practices

In the book *Pagan Christianity*, Frank Viola and George Barna have done a great service by painstakingly cataloguing the evolution of the "church," from the earliest gatherings to our contemporary churches, complete with how various movements within Catholicism and Protestantism influenced its development. Their conclusion is one of the best kept secrets in Christendom: the overwhelming majority of church meeting customs practiced today are rooted in pagan culture and rituals. They are not the original practices of the earliest followers of Jesus.

We have already seen how the church building was foreign to the early church and how it developed under Emperor Constantine's push for "Christian" uniformity in the empire. Beyond buildings, there were other practices that became sacred that were not part of the earliest church, or if they were, later generations poured new meanings into them until they were almost unrecognizable from their original form.

Viola and Barna list at least eight practices that were never part of the original gatherings of Jesus followers. First, there's the *order of worship*. Although there are variations, it is essentially the following: Greeting, prayer, music (or "worship"), announcements, offering, sermon, communion, prayer, and benediction. This order did not come from Jesus' teaching but from the original Catholic Mass developed after Constantine and solidified in the sixth century. Viola cites Will Durant: "The Catholic Mass was 'based partly on the Judaic Temple service, partly on Greek mystery rituals of purification, vicarious sacrifice, and participation.'"[17] The worship elements were centered on the Eucharist or communion. Later reformers like Luther

15. Ibid., 129.
16. Ibid.
17. Ibid., 51.

shifted the focus to the sermon and preaching and adjusted communion so every member could partake, not just the priests. Yet, the basic worship order was retained.

Second, was the *sermon*. We think of it as biblical because there seems to be sermonizing in the New Testament. But a careful examination shows the teaching of Jesus in the early church was not a weekly formal occurrence proclaimed by the same person nor a one-way discourse. Jesus' teaching in Matthew 5–7 was not called "The Sermon on the Mount" until the fifth century at the time of Augustine. Oral teaching among the Old Testament prophets, in the synagogues, and by Jesus and the early apostles and church leaders were sporadic, issue-driven, and included feedback and interruptions from the audience (e.g., Acts 2). They were not rhetorical in nature. The roots of our modern sermons are from Greek culture and the sophists, who invented rhetoric, persuasive speaking, and the fine points of debate around the fifth century BCE. Sophists used emotional appeals and clever language to make their case. Their delivery became more important than the accuracy of their logic or appeal to facts. Eventually, the church from Constantine through the Reformation and beyond used this style and made preaching and one-way communication paramount in services. It was not so in the beginning. There was no need for a "sermon" in an early church gathering.[18]

Third, is the practice of wearing *religious costumes* and garb. Tracing the origins of clergy clothing doesn't lead one to early church practices, but to various cultural preferences and prejudices,[19] such as the secular dress of the Greco-Roman world, Clement of Alexandria wearing white garments to set apart clergy from laity, Constantine's influence toward official Roman dress for clergy, elaborate vestments of the Middle Ages, and the replacement of priestly garments with the black gown (customary of scholars') during the Reformation.[20] Likewise was the custom of dressing up for church, which didn't become popular until the late eighteenth century during the advent of the Industrial Revolution when fine clothes became more affordable for the average family.[21] Today, a welcome trend in evangelicalism is the resistance to these practices. Many churches welcome

18. Ibid., 87–88.
19. Ibid., 159.
20. Ibid., 150–53.
21. Ibid., 146.

casual wear by both members and pastors. Nevertheless, both Catholic and Protestant traditions retain many of these practices.

I always wondered how biblical our *music-based worship* was in the various evangelical churches I attended over the years. I was encouraged that the church was using contemporary music, even soft rock, when writing and playing worship songs. Contemporary Christian musicians and/or worship teams on guitar, bass, drums, and piano drew many of us into the Jesus Movement in the 1970s and 80s, whereas traditional hymns never could. Yet, in time, I noticed something awry. "Worship" was almost entirely defined as the practice of listening to contemporary folk-style songs, singing their simple-minded lyrics, raising one's hands, and experiencing the emotions that good music elicits. What was missing were practices that tapped deeper, more spiritual and even intellectual devotion, such as the appreciation and study of nature and the cosmos, enjoying intimate relationships, performing meaningful work, and practicing reflective meditation—whether based on Scripture and other inspirational literature. So, to me, it was confirmation to discover that worship through music was never the primary focus of the early church.

Church choirs arose in the fourth century and have their roots in pagan temples and Greek dramas performed on a sacred stage. As in Greek religion and culture, trained singers slowly emerged in the church. By 367 CE, congregational singing was banned. Papal choirs, boys' choirs created from orphanages, and professional singers became commonplace. They derived from the audience-performer culture of the day. The Reformation brought back the practice of congregational singing to Protestant churches but the choirs and special worship players remained. The use of organs became popular at this time, although some denominations, such as the Calvinists, actually banned them. Today, many churches have replaced the choir with "the worship team" and the guitar has become the new musical organ. As I said earlier, I'm grateful for music in Christian gatherings. Yet, most Christians see it as mandatory, not as an optional avenue to worship the divine. Nor do they realize it was never the center of worship in Jesus' ministry or the earliest church.

The fifth practice cited by Viola and Barna is the *elevation of a pastor or priest* as the head of a Christian community or church. They observe that the entire New Testament only has one verse with the word *pastor*. It is in the plural, is a translation for a Greek term that means *shepherds*, and is a metaphor for a particular function, not an official title or office. It is talking about people in gatherings who care for others in need of guidance,[22] much like a mentor or advisor. Conversely, the word in the New Testament for *priest* is only used in reference to every person being a priest under Jesus' new covenant. It turns upside down the whole concept of the priesthood in pre-rabbinical Judaism.

First-century churches had organic, untitled leaders with no direct control over members. When elders were appointed or recognized they all had equal standing. There was never a senior pastor or priest over the gatherings. As we learned above, through the influence of church fathers in the second century on, Constantine, and later the Reformers, the practice of appointing bishops, priests, and pastors, i.e., professional clergy, gradually became formalized in a hierarchal church system.

Along with the formation of official professional clergy, came the sixth practice of *tithing and paying for clergy salaries*. But a careful study of the origins of tithing clearly shows the early church did not practice this. The original tithe in the old covenant law was the practice of giving a tenth of one's produce in an agricultural society. The tithe went to support the Levites (who had no inheritance and were part of the priesthood), religious festivals, and the poor—orphans, widows, and foreigners in the land.[23] It wasn't until the third century that the idea of using church member tithes to financially support clergy arose, not until the fourth century that it began to be defended seriously, and not until the eighth century before it became commonplace![24] As is argued from the historical evidence, the Old Testament practice of tithing was not carried over to the earliest church, let alone used to pay for professional leaders. Generous giving was encouraged, for sure, but not in a proscribed way, but as much as each individual decided and for the poor and needy.[25]

Next, was the practice of *baptism*. Granted, we did not do an exhaustive study on this subject, but there are several fascinating points we discovered. First, evidence shows the practice of baptism did not originate with John the Baptist or early Christians. Before the beginning of the Christian era, Jews adopted the practice of baptizing male Gentile converts seven days after their circumcision, which also was preceded by a type of interrogation to judge one's true intentions. "In the baptism, he was immersed naked

22. Ibid., 106–7.

23. Ibid., 173.

24. Ibid., 176.

25. 2 Cor 8:1–15.

in a pool of flowing water; when he rose from the pool, he was a true son of Israel."[26] John the Baptist apparently took this practice (and possibly the practice of symbolic cleansing in water for priests in Leviticus) and re-purposed them for a symbol for "true repentance and forgiveness of sins." He stressed the importance of "producing fruit in keeping with repentance" and rebuked the Pharisees and Sadducees for thinking their standing as "sons of Abraham" was enough to be right with God. He implied that true sons and daughters of Israel change their actions to share their excess clothing and food with the poor, that repentant tax collectors don't collect any more taxes than they have to, that soldiers (possibly temple guards or even Roman soldiers) should not extort money or accuse people falsely (Luke 3:1–4). All these things fall under the love ethic Jesus was about to bring to Israel. John focused on loving behaviors not religious practices as paramount.

Moreover, the word "baptizo" was a Greek word, common in that day, for immersion in water, but not necessarily for the whole body. Luke 11:38 uses baptizo for the washing of hands. The noncanonical sacred text, the Didache, records the practice of pouring water upon the head as a baptismal method in situations where little water is available. Finally, Paul was apparently baptized in a home (Acts 9). Homes in that culture did not have tubs nor pools, therefore, he probably had water poured on his head. It appeared the early church was very flexible with how baptism was practiced and there was no reason to believe that they taught baptism was necessary for salvation. This would have contradicted John the Baptist's teaching on outward change in treating others justly and Jesus' on inner purity as more important than religious practices.

Finally, was the practice of taking the *Lord's Supper* or communion. Historians agree that for the early church, the practice originated as a festive, community meal called a "love feast." A group of followers would gather over food to celebrate their way of life. They would start by breaking and passing around bread, eat a full meal together, and culminate by passing a cup of wine.[27] It was a celebration and remembrance of Jesus and the new life and hope and love he had brought. But with the influence of the new Roman official "Christian" religion, slowly the practice of the love feast ceased until the Council of Carthage in 397 CE when it was actually banned![28] Gradually, the love feast morphed into the "Eucharist,"

26. Barnes, "Baptism."

27. Viola and Barna, *Pagan Christianity*, 192.

28. Ibid., 193.

a sacred ritual administered by sacred priests—only containing the bread and wine—and representing a somber, religious act of sacrifice that only the clergy took part in. Members only observed. Later, Protestants restored the practice to include all members, but it still retained the serious mood not the original celebratory practice of sharing a meal together.

Sacred Objects

There is fascinating, historical evolution of the practice of collecting, idolizing, and marketing sacred Christian relics. It probably began with Constantine's mother, Helena, who Constantine appointed to locate relics in Judea and bring them back to Rome for inclusion in the imperial treasury. Tradition says she discovered the true cross of Christ and brought back parts of it to Rome along with other relics, including Jesus' tunic.[29] The practice of collecting relics was not part of early Christianity.

Moreover, in actuality, the ubiquitous cross symbol so common throughout church history was not a major symbol of the early church. For the first three centuries of Christianity, we learned, it was not widely used, as it represented "a purposely painful and gruesome method of public execution and Christians were reluctant to use it."[30] In fact, the fish symbol was considered the most important symbol used by early Christians.[31]

Learning from the Past

We had just begun another evening of discussion at another favorite watering hole, this time, a place called ChocMo's, known for an unorthodox menu, fine wines, and a variety of local microbrews. Before Dan asked his question, he referred to the path of modern Christendom we recently learned, initiated largely by Constantine that ended in what we have today—hierarchical organization, religious control, professional clergy, clergy salaries, a clergy-laity divide, Catholic or Protestant institutions, church buildings, cathedrals, tithing for "church" funding, sacred holidays, an order of worship, sermonizing, the loss of the love feast, a modern-style communion or Eucharist, and music-based worship. Not necessarily bad

29. *Wikipedia*, s.v. "Helena (empress)."
30. *Wikipedia*, s.v. "Christian Cross: Early Christian."
31. *Wikipedia*, s.v. "Christian Symbolism."

things in and of themselves, but nevertheless, all practices patterned after Greco-Roman paganism more than the practices of the earliest church. "What would Christianity look like if it didn't go down that path?" Dan asked.

"It would be highly organic—in other words, more natural than programmatic or institutional," someone said.

"It would be more of a movement integrated within society, not an organized religion over it or apart from it," Gina said. "And perhaps professional clergy and separate religious seminaries would never have developed."

"Women would be co-leaders and true equals with men in the church," a woman added.

"Churches today would be all house churches," another said, "because that is the original model."

"All be house churches?" someone challenged. "I look at the gatherings in homes like in the New Testament as a convenient place to meet, but I don't think it should be mandatory we meet in homes."

"Granted, not all, but house churches would probably be much more common," the person conceded.

"I think the whole concept of church would be so radically different, it would have adapted to societal institutions," I said. "Like, maybe followers would naturally join service organizations and nonprofits focused on practicing the love ethic of Jesus and not see the need to form a Christian religious organization at all."

"You mean like the charitable or social-justice ministries there are today?" Dan asked.

"Yeah, but with more inclusive membership than modern Christian churches," I answered. "So, one's Christian service could be done through joining a local Rotary Club or volunteering at a homeless shelter, or even through their job or vocation; like working at a hospital or in another service career, and their fellowship would be met through informally meeting other believers for support and discussion. The need for an organized church the way we know it would be minimized."

"Or for some people, eliminated," someone said.

Our study of church in *The Timeline* had opened our minds to think outside the box when it comes to how to form a community of people following Jesus' way of love. We would continue to ruminate over the historical facts around the communities of the Way and how they should impact how we view and form "church" or gatherings for fellowship today. In time, we would come to further conclusions.

Now, it was time to address other theological questions in light of history. Things like, how did the Eastern part of Christendom develop compared to the West? How is Eastern Orthodox theology different than Western theology? How do Eastern Christians view things like *original sin* and the *atonement*? What have our Catholic and Protestant traditions not told us about Christian history? It was a trip to a monastery that started us down this part of our journey.

Chapter Nine

A Visit to Eastern Orthodoxy

I WILL NEVER FORGET the time I learned another theological paradigm stemmed from the Eastern Orthodox tradition and contrary to my own evangelical roots. While we were going through *The Timeline*, one of our group's members suggested we visit a local Orthodox monastery to open our eyes to a new perspective. So, one afternoon, a group of us toured the All Merciful Savior Monastery on evergreen Vashon Island, Washington. We were led by an informative and most gracious Father Igumen Tryphon, the monastery's abbot. Donning a black robe, cap, and sporting a long gray beard, Abbot Tryphon walked us through the lush grounds and ornate chapel. He explained both the liturgy and theology of the Eastern Orthodox faith and many of the ways it differs from Western theology.

He also told us an illuminating story of how he evolved from a Buddhist student radical from Berkeley, California, to Orthodox monk and how one time he confronted corporate greed in a Starbucks trademark dispute. Starbucks owns the trademark "Christmas Blend," he explained. In 1998, they began enforcing it and taking legal action for trademark infringement against companies that used the name, including the monastery's coffee enterprise. A public outcry ensued, spearheaded by Abbot Tryphon. When he met with Starbucks officials, he confronted them on their greed of pursuing a financial settlement for the use of this name. "Every coffee company has the right to have a Christmas Blend if they choose," he said. Starbucks relented and returned the trademark to the public domain.[1]

1. Moriwaki, "Starbucks Ends Fight."

Theology of the Eastern Orthodox Faith

For most of us, Abbot Tryphon was our first exposure to Eastern Orthodox spirituality. Later, while perusing the monastery's book store, I found two books on Eastern Orthodoxy, and later still, on the campus of Montana State University, a set of articles on Orthodoxy, that helped us put Abbot Tryphon's and the Eastern church's fresh, more historically-grounded theology into sharp focus. We were reminded that this theology is traced by the Eastern Orthodox Church to the original gospel (good news) message expounded by the apostles of Jesus and the earliest church. The Orthodox Church was claiming their faith is rooted in verifiable history and that the Western church, through people like Augustine, Anselm, Calvin, and others, warped the message to produce an erroneous theology. We were about to learn how this transpired.

Original Sin

Our first revelation found in these resources concerned the theology of sin. Eastern Orthodoxy paints a vastly different picture of *original sin* than the West. In evangelicalism, we were taught that Adam was created in a state of perfection but then "fell from grace" by his sinful action of disobeying God. Moreover, all of Adam's progeny bear the consequence of his "original sin" so that a guilty sinful nature is now inborn in every human being at birth. The epitome of this view is Augustine's warped contention (we evangelicals never got the memo on this one) that even infants, until they are baptized, are by nature doomed to eternal damnation upon entering our world because they carry the guilt of Adam's sin. Astounding. Babies going to hell. We were starting to see why some Eastern orthodox theologians said Augustine had a "dark imagination."

This legal, ancestral view of original sin led to the belief by some reformers, such as Calvin, that the divine image of God in which humankind was originally created has been marred beyond recognition. Therefore, every human being is totally depraved and incapable of choosing goodness or salvation without God's sovereign intervention. Eastern Orthodox theologians often stipulate the erroneous source of this dreadful doctrine: "This doctrine of 'original sin' is a hideous one and found its way into the Western theological construct through the flawed Latin text of St. Paul's Epistle to the Romans having passed through the dark imagination of Augustine."[2]

The Orthodox view, on the other hand, is that Adam was not created perfectly holy but rather spiritually immature. The consequence of his "original sin" was that physical death was introduced into creation; but also that humans experience spiritual and physical death as a consequence of their own individual sin, not Adam's. (This stems from a more accurate translation of the Greek in Rom 5:12.) To the Orthodox, the image of God in humankind may have been damaged by transgression but it has never been destroyed. We are not totally depraved individuals without God. We still retain God's beautiful image within us and are capable of drawing on that image to heal whatever damaged connection there is.[3] One Orthodox theologian explains this using a metaphor of a damaged eye.

> The total depravity model views the Fall as having destroyed man's spiritual eye so that he is no longer capable of having any spiritual sight whatsoever. His only hope is to be given a completely new eye from God. . . . In contrast, in the original biblical Orthodox view, the Fall damaged the spiritual eye but did not totally destroy it. We are not totally blind. Why? Because having been created in the image and likeness of God, we still retain free will and some degree of desire for God.[4]

We also learned that these fresh but historical perspectives on sin were not entirely overlooked by Western Christians. Particularly, the voices of some mystics echoed these Eastern viewpoints. In the 1370s CE, Julian of Norwich (at the time the largest city in England), a laywoman or nun (historians disagree) who lived a monastic life, wrote a short book called *Revelations of Divine Love*. It chronicles sixteen revelations of Jesus she had during a serious illness. It is thought to be the earliest surviving book written by a woman in the English language. In it, and in a later book, she expounds on an optimistic, joyful view of a loving God, even in the midst of the circumstances of her day, known for peasant revolts and plague epidemics. Contrary to the prevailing theology of the day, she believed suffering was not a punishment from God, that humans sin because they are naïve [immature], not because they are evil, and that God loves all and desires to rescue all to the point of her having a passionate hope for universal

2. Arnold, *Orthodoxy Revisited*, 112.
3. Bernstein, *Original Christian Gospel*.
4. Ibid., 11.

salvation.[5] Her merciful theology and experiences with the presence of a comforting God with intense love for all of humanity inspired the Anglican and Lutheran churches to venerate her to this day. Norwich, England, still celebrates an annual week in her honor citing her book as "a creative response to a stunning revelation of human and divine compassion that has resonated strongly with creative artists, writers, and thinkers throughout the centuries."[6]

The Atonement

Two common questions that arise among younger converts to evangelicalism are: Why did God have to make Jesus die on the cross in order to forgive us? And why can't God just forgive us outright without the need for the crucifixion?

We already knew the typical evangelical or Western theological answer to that question. It's a description of what is called the "penal substitutionary atonement" theory, widely accepted among fundamentalists and evangelicals today. "God's holiness and justice demands our sins be punished," the standard answer is. "We actually deserve to die and go to hell because of our sin. Because we are sinful by nature, we can't pay this debt we owe God. But Jesus, because he is sinless, can pay our debt. He did it by dying on the cross to take the punishment for our sins. Now, anyone who believes in Christ's atonement can receive God's mercy and forgiveness."

The argument continues: "Divine justice demands a sacrifice for sins. Christ's sacrifice on the cross placates God's anger toward sin. When we receive Christ, God looks at us as no longer needing to be punished. But without Christ dying on the cross, or without us accepting him and his work of salvation, we would still be under God's wrath."

We soon discovered the Eastern view of salvation and certain historical facts uncovered the fallacy of this theory. The Western view is trying to solve problems that don't exist. First, as stated above, we are not totally depraved sinners who deserve to be eternally punished in hell. Eastern theology says we are image bearers of God who have temporarily lost connection with our Maker.

Second, according to Western theology, humankind has a legal problem that needs to be rectified; God is an angry Judge who is obligated to

5. *Wikipedia*, s.v. "Julian of Norwich."

6. Julian Week 2015, "About," http://julianweek.org/about-2.

mete out divine punishment to sinful man. The only way to pay the legal debt without us suffering punishment is to have a sinless Jesus pay the price for us through his death on the cross.

In Eastern theology, the problem is not judicial or legal in nature. It is relational. We don't need someone to appease an angry God or pay a debt to a system of divine justice; we need to be healed of a disconnection with our Creator. God is not obligated to some divine justice system. That would create a God above God—as God then *must* follow some imaginary Necessity to sentence sinners and *cannot* simply forgive them; a divine judicial rule that strips God of his sovereignty[7] and makes him out to be a vindictive God. This image of God can be very damaging.

> If salvation is primarily about the Father punishing the Incarnate Son in our stead, then as a judicial necessity, our failure to believe in Jesus compels God to punish us. Such theologies see the Cross as saving us from the punitive, legally determined wrath of God—God the Son saving us from God the Father. Viewing God as vindictive can cause us great damage, particularly if we believe that the physical and spiritual harm we inflict on ourselves through sin comes from God (when it actuality, it comes from us). Confusing our guilt with God's anger can cause us to fear and flee from Him, which only weakens us further.[8]

The view of the mystics, like Julian of Norwich, was very similar to this. There is no place for a wrathful God. History teaches us the Western view of atonement did not derive from the earliest first-century traditions. In its full form, the substitutional atonement theory did not originate until the eleventh century when the Archbishop of Canterbury, Anselm, wrote a treatise on the atonement. In it, he corrected a popular, erroneous view that Jesus' sacrifice freed humanity from the devil's claim over humans (considered the "Ransom Theory," in that Christ was the ransom God paid to the devil). Anselm rightly rejected that Christ's death was God's way of paying the devil. However, he wrongly argued that Jesus' death was a payment to appease an angry God. He was the first to introduce the idea of atonement through substitution—Christ paying the debt on our behalf that was owed God. Later, Protestant Reformers built on Anselm's theory emphasizing a

7. Bernstein, *Original Christian Gospel*, 13.

8. Ibid., 14.

penal component that introduced the idea that Jesus took the punishment we deserve.[9]

The Western view of atonement, when critically examined, is frankly, abhorrent: God is a fierce, vindictive Judge, pouring out his wrath on humankind because of deserved eternal punishment, but showing his "love" by transferring that wrath onto a crucified and bloodied Jesus—a Savior who had to be tortured on a cross in order for humankind to be forgiven. This view of God can cause ongoing guilt feelings in some Christians as Jesus had to endure untold suffering because of their wickedness. "The Western Church has through a long process of theological convolution over the course of many hundreds of years finally succeeded in transforming the biblical God of love into little more than a petty tyrant."[10]

The Eastern view, on the other hand, lines up with the loving character of God as found in the teachings of Jesus.[11] Atonement is incarnational, based on unconditional love. It is not a legal, judicial concept. Being "saved" is therapeutic and transformative; something that heals us and makes us whole individuals, no longer disconnected with God. God is incarnated in Jesus, not to pay a debt, nor to be a substitutionary offering, but to rescue us from the disconnected state we are in. It wasn't the death of Jesus that solely or primarily rescues us, but the incarnational nature of his life as a whole. Part of that was his nonviolent confrontation of evil that inevitably ends in his Roman execution, in which he demonstrates forgiveness in the face of hatred, providing a moral example, not only for us to emulate, but that transforms us when we contemplate his pure love in action in the face of evil. Whatever evil to which humans succumb, God's incarnational love responds like Jesus, warning of impending judgment (which, as we learned, brings restoration not retribution), as in his lament over Jerusalem, but interceding on people's behalf, as in, "Father forgive them, for they know not what they do," not "Father forgive them, now that I have taken the tortuous punishment they deserve."

Western views of atonement have done much harm in our world. They have pushed people away from genuine spirituality toward materialism, agnosticism, or atheism. "The view of God as a fierce Judge—angry, vindictive, pouring out His divine wrath upon His Son Jesus because of 'love' for us sinners—appears ludicrous to many non-Christians. It explains in

9. Ibid., 12–14.

10. Arnold, *Orthodoxy Revisited*, 121.

11. Bernstein, *Original Christian Gospel*, 17–19.

part why so many are repulsed by institutional churches and only admit to admiring Jesus on a strictly private and non-institutional level."[12]

The Bible

As we learned in a previous chapter, the Eastern Church looks at the Bible altogether differently than popular Western concepts, particularly evangelicalism. For example, on the question of inerrancy. "Nowhere in the New Testament itself can there be found any appeal for the believer to recognize the Bible as the single, infallible source of divine revelation and authority."[13] For Eastern Christians, the "Logos" or Word of God, as incarnated in Jesus—both human and Divine—is paralleled in the view of the written Word, the Bible. The Bible is both human and Divine. It is wrong to consider it as self-sufficient and self-interpreting. It never claims to be such.[14] Eastern Christians point out that the oral traditions of the earliest followers of Christ (traditions that communicated the Logos of God) came first, before the New Testament. So, they must be taken into account. And these traditions are partly determined through a careful study of history. However, they are not doctrinal statements or simply historical writings. They, along with the New Testament, are seen as *a way of life* that followers of Jesus lived.

Eastern theology differentiates between Scripture and the Word of God.[15] The Word of God must be determined through a combination of disciplines, not simply by reading an English Bible. We were reminded that, strictly speaking, Jesus alone is the Word of God, not the Bible, according to the New Testament (John 1:1) and Eastern theology. The Word or "Logos" (rationality) of God is a Person who can be known and experienced. Modern Western Christianity has made the Word of God into a set of writings to be read, studied, memorized, and obeyed, not a personality to know and love. This is why fundamentalist/evangelical churches seem to worship the Bible above God and Christ.

Moreover, the New Testament itself was not dropped from the sky, but slowly emerged in a certain historical and cultural context that must be understood or else it will be misinterpreted. Therefore, although he is not an

12. Ibid., 15.

13. Arnold, *Orthodoxy Revisited*, 38.

14. Bajis, *Common Ground*, 56.

15. Ibid., 39.

Orthodox believer, what John Dominic Crossan says is extremely relevant: "The presumption that you can pick up a 2,000-year-old text that happens to be in English and know what it's talking about is silly. You have to do your homework. You have to prod it with questions."[16] As Jordan Bajis aptly concludes, "To declare, 'I just believe what the Bible says' as a justification for ignoring any truth outside of the text is neither wise nor godly."[17]

We learned how this relates to the concept of *sola Scriptura*, a popular belief originally developed by the Reformers and promoted by modern conservative Christians who claim the Bible is the sole authority for the church. Orthodox teaching showed us that this was not the original definition of *sola Scriptura*. Later Reformers twisted the original meaning. Initially, the concept of *sola Scriptura* did not preclude historical tradition interpreting the Bible. It was "not a call to see the Bible as the authority of the Church, but a call for the Church to once again interpret the Scriptures in accord with the [earliest church Fathers]," as opposed to the ruling Roman Catholic Church. In other words, one can't just read the Bible individually or in isolation of history, but must know what the great voices of church history have said is the Bible's meaning.[18] As we have discovered in an earlier chapter, although there is much those earliest voices agree on, they are not necessarily uniform when it comes to interpreting Scripture. Again, it was a call to not grip the Bible so tightly.

Finally, a long-standing mystery in my mind was solved through reading about the Eastern Orthodox view of the Bible. Why are there so many fundamentalist and evangelical churches today that end up spiritually abusing their members? I had experienced and read about this abuse myself many times. In the first chapter, I mentioned some examples, e.g., the shepherding movement of the 1980s, the proliferation of ex-member websites that have painstakingly documented cases of spiritual abuse in churches like Sovereign Grace Ministries (SGM), Calvary Chapel, Mars Hill, and many more. There is also the patriarchy teaching in many fundamentalist churches that put women in submission to men to the nth degree.

This spiritual abuse stems from these churches' view that the Bible is their sole authority, I concluded. When the Bible is your sole authority, when you can declare in isolation from sound historical, cultural, literary, and linguistic context something is "scriptural," then you open the door

16. Simmons, "Biblical Alternatives."

17. Bajis, *Common Ground*, 57.

18. Ibid., 42.

to abuse the Bible, misinterpret it, and misuse it by imposing it on others. When church leaders do this to members, particularly ones that love to be in control, they can easily commit spiritual abuse. It leads to "a perverse kind of authoritarianism, in which a leader, claiming to have no guide but the Bible rigidly imposes his form of Scriptural interpretation on followers who likewise profess to be heeding no guide but the Bible."[19]

People are manipulated to blindly obey church leaders, to not question them, to tithe their income to the church, to control their children by spanking them, to refrain from sharing hurts in the name of squelching gossip, to not call the authorities when sexual abuse occurs in the church, to submit to "church discipline," and a host of other impositions that are products of a faulty view of the Bible that endorses private interpretation absent context. They are often merely justifications to control people or protect the reputation of the church. A non-holistic interpretation of the Bible, without historical and cultural context and early church tradition and history, etc., can come from an individual, a leader, a church, or whole denomination, or even a whole movement. Its imposition in the name of being "scriptural" or "biblical" strips away an individual's and community's freedom and responsibility to interpret the meaning of the Bible according to what they perceive to be sound principles and practices.

These facts led us to conclude that distilling the message and meaning of Christ's life, interpreting the New Testament for example, is not a perfect science. Interpretation and application must be weighed through the use of sound exegetical and hermeneutical principles and practices.[20] We determined at least five of these. To soundly interpret the message of the Path of Christ, (1) study the New Testament with an understanding of its original language and historical setting; (2) consider early oral traditions and other sacred texts of the early church; (3) use our God-given sense of logic and reason; (4) try to discern the Spirit's illumination in concert with a community of believers; and (5) compare what we discover to our personal experience. Lastly, where we have disagreement with others, let the principle of "love one another" rule the day. Oh, and one more thing. If you still seem to be in conflict with someone after all this, sit down and

19. Ibid., 58.

20. Exegetical is referring to "exegesis," the practice of determining the original meaning of the biblical text (what it meant back then to the original audience). Hermeneutical is from "hermeneutics," the practice of determining the contemporary application or modern interpretation of the biblical text (what it means for us today).

have a microbrew or two together. It's amazing what a little craft beer can do to iron out our differences.

Eastern Orthodox Reflection

"I think the sitting-down-and-having-a-beer-together principle should be number one," a woman said, laughing, after we had discussed some of the lessons we had learned from Eastern Orthodoxy and the five principles of Bible interpretation. Our familiar group of "pub theologians" were gathered at Tizzley's Europub in my current stomping grounds of Poulsbo, a divine little venue with an incredible selection of local, regional, and European beers.

"Ha!" another said. "I'll drink to that." It was getting late and, for some of us, a beer buzz had kicked in big time.

"Okay, all this talk about Eastern Orthodox theology has got me wondering," someone said. "If they supposedly have the right theology, why don't you join their church?"

"I might, if I found a good one," I said.

"But aren't they just another church institution that can be controlling?"

"Sure," I said. "I like to say that churches are only as bad as the theology behind them. I won't consider a church unless they have a historically-grounded theology and an open mind."

"I'd only join one that doesn't demand allegiance and recognizes people's freedom to pursue God and fellowship outside church," Dan said.

"And some Orthodox churches are like that, I believe," the first woman said. "Author Frank Schaeffer goes to one and talks about how their attitude is like that."

"What's amazing to me," Gina interjected, "is how Eastern Orthodox theology on original sin and the atonement makes so much more sense. And, how it clears up so much confusion over the Western view of having to appease an angry God."

"Agreed," someone else said. "It fits the compassionate nature of Jesus. It really needs to be taught more. Most people don't know there's another way at looking at salvation."

"And, it's not just pulled from the sky," I added. "It's grounded in the history of the Eastern church."

"Yeah," another added. "It's like conservative believers are trapped in an Augustinian way of looking at salvation and they're unaware there's historical grounds that it's flawed."

Most of us had had little or no exposure to Eastern Orthodox theology until we began our study. The discoveries were refreshing. My comment about "grounded in history" reminded me of another area we needed to learn—the history of the Church in the East. We had heard there were vibrant communities of Jesus followers throughout the Middle East and Asia in the first several centuries after Christ; ones that rivaled or exceeded the West in terms of academics, peaceful coexistence with other cultures, historic theology, and resisting the temptation to set up a church state. After our spirited discussion ended and we all made our way home that night, it wasn't long before we began another historical journey into that world.

Chapter Ten

The Unknown Church of the East

FOR SOME OF US, the history of Christianity is a gradual progression to thrones of European power and colonialism. From humble origins in Palestine, it ultimately aligned with European culture, forged a political church state, and isolated itself from other religions and worldviews. The result was the modern "Christian" nations in Catholic Southern Europe and Latin America in one world, and Protestant Northern Europe and North America in another. Only recently, we think, did Christianity spread to Asia and Africa through modern missionary movements that began with Catholic explorers and Protestant missionaries after the Reformation. Our study of the history of the Jesus Movement in Asia and North Africa and my own research revealed how skewed this view is. In our often arrogant attitude of Western superiority, we have ignored a vibrant swath of the Christian story. Here is some of what we learned.

Eastern Christian Traditions

One example that people conveniently forget or were never taught is the rich history of the Eastern Churches—the Eastern Orthodox Church, the Coptics of Egypt, the Ethiopian Tewahedo Church, the Nubia Church (northern Sudan), the ancient Armenian Apostolic Church, the Syriac Orthodox Church, and the Malabar "Thomas" Church of Southwest India. These communities of followers of Jesus were founded early in Christian history. Eastern Orthodoxy has roots in Antioch, mentioned predominantly in the book of Acts. Tradition states that the Coptic Orthodox Church of Alexandria, Egypt, was established in 42 CE by the Apostle Mark. Even today, 10 percent of Egyptians are Coptics. The Malabar Church in India (modern Kerala) is said to have been established by the Apostle Thomas, one of Jesus' original Twelve. It still survives today. Armenia made Christianity its official faith in 300 CE and to this day its church is strong. Nubia in modern-day Sudan was a Christian kingdom from the sixth to the fifteenth century. Ethiopia, known as Abyssinia, became a Christian land before the time of Constantine. When Europeans discovered it in the seventeenth century they marveled at the depth and breadth of people's faith. In 1982–84, as a young evangelical missionary in refugee camps in neighboring Somalia, I became close friends with many Ethiopian Christians who could probably trace their faith's historical roots to the fourth century.

Even more obscure are the lost, other Christian worlds of Asia—known by historians as the Church of the East—mostly made up of two great transnational churches: the Nestorians and Jacobites, strongholds of the faith that once stretched throughout Iraq (including Basra, Mosul, and even Tikrit, the hometown of one Saddam Hussein) to Syria, Arabia, Yemen, Turkestan, Turkmenistan, Afghanistan, Sri Lanka, India, and China.[1] Among these centers of Christian faith were legendary hubs of learning that taught the culture and science of the ancient world, including the Greco-Romans and Persians. "In their scholarship, their access to classical learning and science, the Eastern churches of 800 were at a level that Latin Europe would not reach at least until the thirteenth century."[2] Indeed, while European Christendom was enduring "the dark ages," this lost Church of the East was flourishing in growth, classical scholarship, studies of biblical and other ancient sacred texts, peaceful coexistence with other religions, and theological diversity, without the specter of doctrinal control and heresy hanging over their head.

The Glory of the East

One of the greatest Christian leaders of all time is ironically one of the most obscure. He was a Nestorian bishop named Timothy, who in 780 CE became the patriarch of the Church of the East. He was the most significant spiritual leader of his day, more powerful than the Roman pope and equal to the patriarch of Orthodox Constantinople. Christian communities of his realm, in Iraq, Syria, Iran, Turkestan, Armenia, Arabia, Yemen, and India, spoke Syriac and a wide variety of local Asian languages, enculturated their

1. Jenkins, *Lost History of Christianity*, 1–44.
2. Ibid., 6.

message and liturgy into indigenous forms, and still retained a Semitic style of Christian faith. Even to the thirteenth century they called themselves *Nasraye*, "Nazarenes," a retained Aramaic term, and spoke of Jesus as *Yeshua*. Their ranks included impressive scholars who studied both biblical and apocryphal ancient manuscripts. Philip Jenkins calls Timothy's Syriac Churches of the East "the ultimate lost Christianity" that rivaled churches of Europe. Timothy presided over nineteen metropolitans (regions) and eighty-five bishops (heads of groups of congregations). Moreover, these communities of Jesus followers were not part of some church state system. They were mostly minorities engaging with adherents of Islam, Judaism, Zoroastrianism, Buddhism, and Taoism.

By the eighth century, Timothy's culturally and spiritually Christian world was infiltrated by Islam, as many of the Eastern Christians lived under Muslim political power. Surprisingly for modern hearers, Timothy's and other generations' Eastern church lived at peace with their Muslim neighbors. As non-Muslim subjects, they would have paid tax or "tribute" to the ruling power, but also enjoyed remarkable respect. Timothy was a key figure at the court of the Muslim caliph. Historical documents record moving interactions between him and the caliph al-Mahdi, "a precious monument of civilized, intelligent religious exchange." The Muslim leader speaks to the Christian one "not in a harsh and haughty tone . . . but in a sweet and benevolent way." In one setting, Timothy acknowledges the virtues of the Prophet Muhammad, saying "he walked in the path of the prophets." This was no watered-down appeasement, but respect for a prominent religion and the heart of its founder. In the public presence of Muslims, Timothy profoundly articulated and defended the Christian faith.[3]

In Timothy's day, Eastern Christians played a critical role inside their kingdoms as diplomats, advisors, and scholars, due to their wide linguistic abilities and cultural knowledge. They helped build Muslim architecture, politics, and culture. Historians trace much of the heralded Arab scholarship in science, philosophy, and medicine to Nestorians, Jacobites, and some Eastern Orthodox, who were the ones that preserved and translated such ancient knowledge, for example the works of Aristotle, and brought it to places like Baghdad and Damascus.

One reason Timothy, the Nestorians, and the Jacobites are obscure in history, is because they weren't the winners. They were considered unorthodox by the reigning church in Rome and Constantinople and eventually

3. Ibid., 1.

were overcome in the fourteenth century by the religious victors of Central Asia, the Muslims and Buddhists. Yet, incredibly, not before thriving throughout Asia for one thousand years! As historian Jenkins asserts about one major Nestorian region, "In terms of the number and splendor of its churches and monasteries, its vast scholarship and dazzling spirituality, Iraq was through the late Middle Ages at least as much a cultural and spiritual heartland of Christianity as was France or Germany, or indeed Ireland."[4] Their story is remarkable and sheds much light on one of the early non-Western movements of followers of Jesus' path.

Nestorian and Jacobite Roots

Nestorianism came from the man Nestorius, the patriarch of Constantinople from 428–431. He studied under Theodore of Mopsuestia at the School of Antioch. Theodore was highly esteemed in the ancient church and a biblical universalist who introduced universal restoration into the liturgy of the Nestorians, believing that "the wicked who have committed evil the whole period of their lives shall be punished till they learn that, by continuing in sin, they only continue in misery. And when, by this means, they shall have been brought to fear God, and to regard him with good will, they shall obtain the enjoyment of his grace."[5] Although it was named after his pupil, Nestorius, Theodore was technically the founder of Nestorianism. Like Theodore, Nestorius taught that Christ existed in two persons, divine and human, not one mixed person in two natures. His critics thought his position was too close to the heresy of Adoptionism, the view that Jesus was born a man and later was adopted by God as his son. Nestorius, however, was not an adoptionist and always insisted his views were orthodox.

Both Theodore and Nestorius did not hold an interpretation that God's judgment is everlasting for those who resist his call for restoration. In other words, they were universalists. "The creed of the Nestorians never did, and does not in modern times, contain any recognition of endless punishment. Mosheim says: 'It is to the honor of this sect that, of all the Christian residents of the East, they have preserved themselves free from

4. Ibid., 6.

5. "Theodore of Mopsuestia, Universalist," http://www.tentmaker.org/biographies/theodore.htm.

the numberless superstitions which have found their way into the Greek and Latin churches.'"[6]

Nestorius also refused to call Mary the *Mother of God*, but regarded her as the Mother of Christ. For this (including his view that the divine and human persons of Christ were intact), the reigning Orthodox Church, which some historians say had become corrupted by heathenism, condemned both Theodore and Nestorius as heretics at the First Council of Ephesus in 431 CE.[7] However, some churches, for example those associated with the School of Edessa, supported Nestorius. By the way, it's important to note that both Nestorius and Theodore were not condemned for their universalism, but for their Christology.[8]

Jacobites also came into being as a result of these types of Christological controversies that were prevalent in the fourth and fifth centuries. Named after Jacobus Baradaaeus, a monk who lived in a monastery near Edessa (present day Urfa in Turkey), Jacobites believed in Monophysitism, the position that after the union of the human and divine at the incarnation, Jesus had a single nature, his human nature being absorbed into his divinity. Monophysitism was declared a heresy by Emperor Justinian I, but briefly rescinded by his wife, Empress Theodora, and then reinstated as heretical by Justin II. As a result, Jacobus created a clandestine church, in which he ultimately ordained eighty-nine bishops (heads of groups of congregations).[9]

The Nestorians and Jacobites became two alternative churches that were powerful rivals to the Orthodoxy that held sway in Constantinople. Today, their "heresy" would be considered largely irrelevant, as modern Christological orthodoxy is concerned mostly with believing in the deity of Christ, a position both movements held. Moreover, when examining these controversies today in light of what the New Testament actually states, they appear like minor philosophical arguments about the nature of Christ and the Trinity, which, whatever view one holds, is still a mystery. The New Testament does not spell out a specific Christology with terms like human, divine, nature, and trinity.

6. Ibid.

7. Ibid.

8. Ibid.

9. Jenkins, *Lost History of Christianity*, 57.

Peaceful Dialogue in the Spread to the East

Before long, both churches established patriarchs and monasteries throughout Asia. By the seventh century, Nestorian missionaries were reaching the peoples of Central Asia—the Turks, Uygurs, Mongols, and Tatars. When Islam appeared, for a long period of time, as attested by Timothy's story above, they lived peaceably among Muslim kingdoms, "who accepted their Christian subjects as tributaries and taxpayers if not as full equals."[10]

In fact, as the Nestorian church spread, it actively engaged in dialogue with several world religions in Asia—not only Islam, but Judaism, Buddhism, Taoism, and Zoroastrianism. Its main rival was Buddhism, but the relationship was far from tenuous. "For many Mongol and Turkish peoples, Buddhism and [Eastern] Christianity were familiar parts of the cultural landscape, and existed comfortably alongside older primal and shamanic traditions."[11] In this part of the world in this era, Christianity not only influenced and affected other faiths but was in turn influenced by them. In fact, it appeared on the scene in some cases at the same time Buddhism was being spread by its own missionaries.

In 600 CE, when Eastern Christianity was established in Tibet, it was about the same time that Tibetans first embraced Buddhism. In 780 CE, a community of Nestorians built a monument with a summary of the good news of Jesus in Buddhist and Taoist terms: "The illustrious and honorable [Anointed One], veiling his true dignity, appeared in the world as a man; . . . he fixed the extent of the eight boundaries, thus completing the truth and freeing it from dross; he opened the gate of the three constant principles, introducing life and destroying death; he suspended the bright sun to invade the chambers of darkness . . . he set in motion the vessel of mercy by which to ascend to the bright mansions, whereupon rational beings were then released."[12] In China and in southern India, some Nestorians took on a symbol that would have been strange to Western Christians—a cross joined to a lotus, representative of Buddhist enlightenment.

Nestorian missionaries reached the imperial capital of China, Chang'an, in 635 CE and remained for two hundred years. The emperor in power, Taizong, was open to foreign ideas, including both Buddhism and Christianity. Within his kingdom, Christianity was described as

10. Ibid., 58.

11. Ibid., 14.

12. Ibid., 15.

"mysterious, wonderful, spontaneous, producing perception, establishing essentials, for the salvation of creatures and the benefit of man."[13] Monasteries, built in indigenous architectural styles, became common. By the eighth century, the Christian community was led by Nestorian Bishop Adam, who became a strong ally of Buddhism.

In 782 CE, a Buddhist missionary named Prajna came to Chang'an, China with the goal of translating Sanskrit sutras (sacred text) into a local language. He enlisted the help of Bishop Adam, who had experience translating parts of the Bible into Chinese. Adam wholeheartedly welcomed the assignment probably to foster goodwill and out of intellectual curiosity. "Together, Buddhist and Nestorian scholars worked amiably together for some years to translate seven copious volumes of Buddhist wisdom."[14] Some historians speculate whether Adam, consciously or unconsciously, inserted Christian concepts into some of these translated Buddhist texts. Japanese monks took these texts back with them to Japan, where they became the foundational works of the Buddhist schools of Shingon and Tenda. All well-known Buddhist traditions in Japan today can be traced back to these two schools, including Zen. What was happening in Christian Europe at this time when Buddhists and Christians were collaborating on a Buddhist translation project in China? In 782 CE, newly crowned Christian Emperor Charlemagne had 4,500 Saxons beheaded because they resisted a campaign of forced conversion to Catholicism.

Nestorians continued to prosper in China until the mid-ninth century, when the then Taoist emperor expelled all foreign religions from China, including Buddhism, Zoroastrian, and the Nestorians. For three hundred years there was no recorded Christian history in China. But Nestorians returned after Mongols conquered the land in the Yaun dynasty of 1271–1368 CE. Mongol rulers tolerated Christians and Buddhists and even Marco Polo reported finding Christian communities in his travels during that time. Roman Catholic missionaries did not arrive in China until the end of the thirteenth century.

Nestorians also made successful inroads in India. In the second century, perhaps earlier, Christian communities arose in southern India. Some Christian communities today in Kerala, claim ties to these earliest Christians and a succession dating back to the Apostle Thomas. Nestorians followed these early efforts with their own missions and monasteries.

13. Ibid., 65.

14. Ibid., 15.

There is evidence that in 425 CE, Indian Christians were translating parts of the New Testament from Greek into Syriac, the language of the Nestorians. Nestorian crosses were also discovered. In 1420, an Italian explorer reported Nestorians scattered all over India. As a European, he thought it odd they were living spread out among other religious groups as minorities, compared to the church-state system of Europe that dominated all inhabitants. In 1500, a Nestorian reported about thirty thousand families of "Thomas Christians" as "co-religionists" as "prosperous in every respect and living in peace and security."[15]

Finally, Jacobites also enjoyed a wide presence throughout Asia over the centuries, although not as much as the Nestorians. It was reported in 1280 that the Jacobite "patriarch" oversaw twenty "metropolitans" and one hundred bishops in Syria, Lower Mesopotamia (Iraq, Kuwait), and Persia (Iran). At the same time in England, there were only twenty-five bishops.

Although Nestorians never won over whole peoples to create a powerful Christian state as was done in the West, they came close. They gained a strong foothold among the Uygurs and Onggud Turks. Around 1000, their influence converted the king of the Kerait Turks (just north of present-day Mongolia), who won over two hundred thousand of his subjects. Kerait's Christian presence lasted four hundred years. On the other hand, there was nothing to lead us to believe the Nestorians were trying to create a Christian state. Their goal appeared to be living a way of life and shining a light amid the people they lived, not converting masses of people under a Christian institution.

When comparing these churches of the East to the expansion of Christianity in Europe, it's fascinating to note that growth in the East was relatively fast. By contrast, in Europe, it took a long time for Christianity to move beyond the Mediterranean world. Some European nations weren't converted (or more accurately, the political elites, who would drag their nominal subjects wherever they went) until close to 1000 CE or beyond, as were Russia, Poland, Norway, and Sweden. That is remarkable compared to the strong presence of Nestorian Christians in China by the seventh century. Jenkins estimates by the year 1000 CE, there were up to twenty million Christ followers in Asia and another five million in Africa. This compared to Europe's twenty-five to thirty million believers, "whose faith was very notional indeed compared with the ancient churches of Asia and

15. Ibid., 67.

Africa."[16] Many European Christians were in early generations of the faith, whereas Eastern believers could trace back their Christian heritage up to thirty generations.

Lessons from Eastern Christians

Despite the fact that most of the Church of the East—Nestorians and Jacobites, with the exception of the "Thomas Christians"—never survived later Muslim conquests and the eventual spread of Buddhism, there is much we can learn from them.

First, as Jenkins points out, it would be wrong to assume that any branch of Christianity that died out like the Church of the East must have done so because it was not valid. In other words, in evaluating church history, we shouldn't assume the winning church is the true one and the losing church isn't. Certainly, the Reformers never had that view, or else they would have never sought to reform the corrupt medieval Catholic Church, which had fallen far from its ancient roots. If they thought the winning church is always the right church, they wouldn't have tried to restore it to what at that time would have been a dead branch. No, we cannot subscribe to the dictum, "survival validates theological beliefs." If conservatives did so, they would have to accept churches they deem heretical today, such as the Mormons and Jehovah Witnesses. If liberals did so, they would have to accept those of todays' popular mega churches, of which many are steeped in narrow conservative theology and the modern heresy of the "health and wealth" doctrine.

Second, Nestorians and Jacobites may have been deemed heretics by the church councils of the fifth century, but they were far from it in modern terms. Their distinctions on the incarnation today would be considered minor. Your average modern churchgoer among conservative Christian streams, evangelicals and fundamentalists, would scarcely recognize their theological "errors."

It can't be ignored that the Church of the East was an influential, thoroughly Christian movement that remained vibrant for over eight hundred years, a far longer time span than the entire history of Protestantism. The main real reason it died was because it had not built a powerful church state like Catholic Europe to withstand Muslim incursions and Chinese expulsions. Moreover, it could be argued, through its influence on Arab

16. Ibid., 70.

scholarship, which in turn influenced medieval Europe of the dark ages, a part of it did survive.

Jenkins states, "If matters had developed differently, perhaps Christianity today would be thoroughly and 'naturally' Asian and Nestorian, just as obviously and traditionally as we think of it as Euro-American."[17] If that were true, would modern Christianity today have the stain of power and corruption from its sordid history? If the Nestorian way of peaceful coexistence with other religions, including Islam, of cooperation, allying with, and influencing Buddhism, of incarnational witness in the local language and within cultural forms, of resisting empire building in the name of God; if these Nestorian practices prevailed in Christian history, how different would Christianity look today?

Our study on the Church of the East taught us how much we have to learn from movements like the Nestorians, Jacobites, and other Eastern Christian streams. As "Euro-Americans," we inherited a thoroughly Western way of looking at our faith. We needed to recover Eastern concepts to help us know how to engage the world. For example, perhaps it's best to build bridges with adherents of other world religions, rather than focus on conversion or our theological differences. Perhaps we can recover "a precious monument of civilized, intelligent religious exchange." And learn from such examples as the Christians and Buddhists who collaborated on a Buddhist translation project in China to publicize Buddhist wisdom. Perhaps we can ally with other faiths that are progressive enough to ally with us and be an example to the whole world. We had much food for thought to contemplate how to implement these and other lessons from the history of the Church of the East and tap into a lost spirituality.

We had come to a crossroads in our long march through *The Timeline* of lost Christian history. Later, we would continue on and examine historical events like the Crusades, the Reformation, and modern church history. But, now, we needed to step back and process what we had learned and go deeper into how to apply it today. We needed to begin to envision a new spirituality in light of all of what we learned, from the purity map of the Jews of the first century to the Church of the East. As we integrated it altogether, we highlighted eleven areas we felt were important angles to a new spiritual paradigm.

17. Ibid., 28.

Chapter Eleven

Envisioning a New Spirituality

As I WRITE THIS, it is exactly one hundred years to the day from the start of the infamous Christmas Truce of 1914 between mostly British and German, and some French and Belgian soldiers on the Western Front during World War I.[1] Locked in static trench warfare five months into the war, the practice of occasional ceasefires and fraternization among enemy soldiers in "No Man's Land" had already developed due to the close proximity of enemy lines. For short periods of time, soldiers would engage in conversation, barter for cigarettes, or recover wounded and dead comrades. On December 7, 1914, Pope Benedict XV suggested an official cessation of warfare during Christmas. Political and military leaders refused to initiate a formal ceasefire. Nevertheless, reports say up to one hundred thousand troops took part in an unofficial Christmas truce that lasted at the very least through Christmas Eve and Day and in some cases up until New Year's Day. The scale of this truce went way beyond earlier ones.

In some cases, troops made a formal agreement for a truce for a specified period of time. In other locations, it was more informal. For many, it started on Christmas Eve when German soldiers began singing Christmas Carols and songs and lit candles on top of the trenches. German tradition celebrated more on the eve of Christmas, rather than the day itself. Soon, British troops, and apparently some French and Belgian troops, entered into a time of fraternization with the Germans. Each side sang their favorite Christmas songs, both secular and religious oriented. They allowed each other to bury their dead in No Man's Land and said prayers over them. They met together and exchanged things like cigarettes, cigars, bottles of wine, food, and souvenirs. They swapped jokes

1. Story told in the 2005 movie "Joyeux Noelle."

and information about the war. Some accounts say some of them even played one or more football (soccer) matches.

Unfortunately, this widespread cessation of war for Christmas over several days was never repeated in the following years during the war, although it was attempted. Afterward, all holiday ceasefires in World War I were quashed by threats of disciplinary action.[2]

In the midst of the horrors of trench warfare, thousands of troops spontaneously followed their hearts. They discovered a light within that led them to submit to Christ's command to love their enemies. That light won out over the military command to fight. Could this be an excellent example of how important it is for those of us "in the trenches" of our spiritual journeys and not part of the religious elite and leadership, to follow our hearts in forging a new spirituality? To rethink what it means to follow Christ and his way of love? As our group wrestled with the new information we discovered in *The Timeline*, we came up with the following points that we thought were worth pursuing in the "No Man's Land" of our modern religious landscape. Perhaps you might join us in a little spiritual fraternization around these themes and add to or refine these suggestions for what a new spirituality might look like for you.

Christ over Christianity

If there was one thing our historical study taught us, it was that Christianity (the way we in the West think of it) is miles, sometimes light years, apart from the original Path of Christ. There have been many throughout history who have recognized this and attempted to bring reform. But the problem, as we saw it, was that a call to reform Christianity is not the solution. We don't need to reform Christianity. We need to redefine it. And, redefine it in a way that fits what Jesus meant and his earliest followers did. The purpose of this is not to institute a new, more pure model of Christianity or the church. That is a fruitless exercise, we learned, that only perpetuates new forms of fundamentalism. What is needed is to put Christ—the Anointed One who taught and modeled the Way of love absent religion—over Christianity. We must remember that, historically speaking, Jesus did not found a new religion called Christianity. He was not a Christian. He was and is a profound historical picture of God's love in action.

2. "Christmas Truce of 1914," *History.com*.

Evangelicals are fond of saying that true Christianity is not a religion, but a *relationship* with Christ. This has much truth to it. The problem is that the evangelical claim that their movement only promotes personal connection to God through Christ and not a religion is hollow. Corporate, institutional religion (sacred people, places, rituals, doctrines, and schools esteemed higher than loving people) permeates all fundamentalist and evangelical streams, and even many progressive or liberal ones. If you don't believe us, while you're inside the evangelical/fundamentalist world, just quit attending church or start writing books questioning the traditional view of the Bible, church authority, homosexuality, or hell and you'll quickly see why it is a religion with pharisaical gatekeepers at every turn. People lose their jobs, ministries, and reputations over such things. Not because they harmed other people, but because they questioned the status quo. That's religion.

Christ over Christianity means one can follow the Way of Jesus—his love ethic—without being recognizably Christian. One is free, of course, to choose to be a member of an institutional church and identify with the Christian faith, but that is not a prerequisite for simply having Christ and his teaching as one's anchor and guide. One can be a "none" and choose to be in Christ. One can be Jewish and in the spirit of the first-century "Anointed One" and rabbi who turned his people back to the Way of love and freedom. One can be Muslim or Buddhist or Hindu and recognize the genius of Jesus and follow his Way. Gandhi did and was more of a "Christian" than most Christians. Look at the dedication, courage, and love that Pakistani and Muslim education activist Malala Yousafzai exemplifies. She is not on the road to hell because she is not a "born again" Christian, as fundamentalists claim. She is following the Way of Christ whether she realizes it or not. She is helping the "least of these" of whom Jesus spoke. It's not one's religious identification that counts. It's one's life pattern and attitude of their heart. Love for fellow humanity and inner purity are what God desires.

In fact, one can be an atheist and still be in the spirit of Jesus. It's not a religious "faith" in a specific "god" that counts, as Frank Schaeffer affirms in his book *Why I Am an Atheist Who Believes in God*. One can doubt, be uncertain, embrace mystery, and live in paradox while still walking in connection with a Way that "gives love, creates beauty, and finds peace." That, too, is the Way of Christ.

Granted, we all will need to "repent" or turn to the Way of love. To follow Christ's radical way of love a Hindu must reject the caste system, a terrorist who claims to be Muslim must reject terror, a "none" must reject interior selfishness, a Christian must reject harmful fundamentalism, and anyone who hurts their fellow human beings by their actions or supports systemic evil needs to turn. We all must change. We must become a new kind of Jew, Hindu, Muslim, "none," Christian, or atheist. Or, perhaps we realize in some ways we already have done so. Regardless, it's not to a religion we turn. It's to a new Way of life grounded in the ethical teachings of Jesus. Or, perhaps grounded in other traditions that echo Jesus' way of love and compassion over religion and over the conventional wisdom on power in the world.

Jesus called people to physically follow him to learn a new way of life of love. He never insisted a Gentile convert to Judaism or a Jew be anything but a Jew who saw past the legalism of the Purity Code and loved God and loved his neighbor. He insisted there be no sacred people, places, and performance codes except the code to love one another and cultivate interior righteousness. We learned that Paul and the earliest gatherings, despite later Christian claims, did the same. People were converts to the Way of Jesus not to a Christian institution. They remained Gentile or Jewish. They changed their hearts and minds to love their fellow human beings like they never did before and stopped idolizing man-made gods and religious practices. But they never converted to Christianity as a religion. They never formed a religious institution. That didn't happen until hundreds of years later.

Trust over "Faith"

Another thing we learned is that true "faith" is not having certain belief in a Christian creed or doctrine or sacred book, but rather trusting there is a Mind or a God in the universe with the essence of Love. Robin Meyer calls *faith* "the most misunderstood word in our religious vocabulary."[3] Its original Greek word is *pistos*, which means *trustworthy action*. It is not absolute certainty. It is not merely having belief that something is true. "Faith in contrast, is an *orientation* toward the mystery of God, best understood by many as unconditional love, not a list of claims that one can know with

3. Meyers, *Underground Church*, 115.

certainty what that mystery is or wants, or even whether it exists! . . . It is a form of *trust*, the ultimate form of *trust* in fact."[4]

In my conservative Christian background, I was taught that true "believers" must adhere to a "statement of faith." Almost every evangelical church, denomination, or ministry had its own *statement of faith* that members must accept to become a member of the church. Or, it was used to show their organizational peers they were true to Scripture or the gospel. The true meaning of faith, as *trust* in the mystery of God's love, however, requires no absolute certainty about things like the infallibility of the Bible or the deity of Christ or the virgin birth or the resurrection or even the historicity of Jesus, let alone a general belief in them. One may believe those things, but that is not true faith. True faith is trust in or dependence on the mystery of God's love and can happen even in the midst of doubt. A new spirituality would need to embrace this; a more accurate view that God desires *trust*, not religious certainty. The outcome is we don't have to all come to the same doctrinal conclusions to be people of true faith. And, according to one of the themes of the New Testament, this simple *trust*, not good works, is all God requires to connect with us.

Bear in mind this doesn't mean a new spirituality must accept, like some liberals might, a philosophy of relativism that all ideas and religions are valid. True faith may not be certain about specific religious dogma or may differ from others on such dogma, but it does have convictions. It trusts that love is better than hate, forgiveness is better than revenge, peace is better than war, and hope is better than despair, to name only a few.

Love over Law

One of the simplest concepts we had learned was that it's better for us to lighten our grip on the Bible and stop looking at it as an internally-consistent, self-sufficient, universally applicable Rulebook. Why? Because history teaches us that is the way that Jesus and his earliest followers used Scripture.[5] Jesus is our model for applying love over law and narrowly defined biblical imperatives. He interpreted the Torah and the prophets this way. He stood up to the scriptural legalists of his day, the Pharisees and teachers of the law. What conservative Christianity has done is to make the New Testament into a new, legalistic law and have largely abandoned the prin-

4. Ibid., 118.

5. See Flood, *Disarming Scripture.*

ciple that choosing the loving thing to do over obeying the letter of the law is what God wants.

Moreover, we learned the Bible as a finalized canon of Scripture containing the Word of God for all humanity to obey was not how the earliest Jesus Movement viewed the Bible. They weren't concerned with getting the exact message, doctrines, and commands down on parchment. They focused on living a new way of life based on sacrificial love that emulated Jesus. It wasn't that an accurate story of Christ's life and teachings wasn't important. Eventually it was. But it was secondary to the principle of love.

Finally, Paul is our model for the principle that in the new spirituality of Jesus, people are released from the law and a law-focused way of looking at God. Our only real "law" under the "new covenant" is the law of love. Love does no harm to its neighbor and love is the new fulfillment of the law, as Paul taught (Rom 13:10), "for whoever loves others has fulfilled the law" (Rom 13:8).

Of course, we also learned how this didn't mean we should toss the Bible out as altogether nonhistorical. That is the way of the other fundamentalists, staunch materialists, who also practice a narrow form of religion and are blind to how good history matters. We can treat the Bible like any other historical document and use our minds, common sense, coupled with historical and biblical scholarship to determine what is historical and inspired. We can then draw out the hopeful message of "God with us" and Jesus' Way of Love from its pages. We are under no obligation to accept everything we read in the Bible—hook, line, and sinker. When in doubt, we should check for mistranslations, study historical context to shed light on more authentic interpretations, and accept that, although generally much of it was, not everything in the Bible was properly transcribed or universally accepted by the early church. Even people who believe the Bible is inerrant end up consciously or unconsciously selecting what to apply literally and what not to. We learned that some of what we read, we have good historical and linguistic reasons to reject. Yet it was obvious to us, that much, if not most of it, especially the core of the New Testament (the four gospels and the seven letters of Paul deemed authentic by the overwhelming majority of historians, when interpreted in their historical and cultural context), along with other historical writings on the Jesus Movement, contained a key to a new, refreshing spirituality. Notwithstanding some problematic exceptions (based on historical and biblical scholarship and common sense), the Bible contains a wonderful, life-changing message for humanity. Ironically, much of the New Testament teaches us not to make the New Testament into a book of laws, because "we have been released from the law so that we serve in the new way of the Spirit, and not in the old way of the written code" (Rom 7:6).

We don't scrap the Bible, we change our way of viewing it. From a Rulebook to a historical document with God's fingerprints on it when we find its pearls of wisdom. Paul admonished a few first-century churches about specific local issues. Not everything he said is the Word of God to all humankind. Not everything recorded by the gospel writers is spot-on historical fact. But there are themes, principles, and pearls in the Bible that teach us profoundly how to live and what is the heart of God. Like the New Testament theme that love is the answer. It trumps law and religion. Love for God, love for neighbor, love for ourselves, love for enemies, and inner purity is the heart of God. God is love. When unbelievers or atheists love, they are closer to God than a believer who does not. Even when there are warnings of judgment, it is for the purpose of loving restoration. Love trumps everything.

We don't toss the Bible. We stop idolizing it. We start using it more responsibly with a view of the history it claims to cite within its Jewish and time-referenced cultural context.

The Reign of God over Religion

Not many of us realized how much we and the religious movements we were a part of had misunderstood and misused the phrase "kingdom of God" and "kingdom of heaven." It is neither a political or religious system nor an angelic destination in the afterlife. It is the reign of a loving God in the here and now. It is already in our midst (Luke 17:21) and still emerging in the world. It has nothing to do with religion or its institutions. By Jesus' criteria, nonreligious people often enter into the reign of God before religious people do as first-century tax collectors and prostitutes did ahead of the temple elites. They didn't enter through the doors of the church or by accepting a doctrine that states Jesus took the punishment that they deserved. The tax collector changed and became a more loving person, no longer ripping people off by squeezing out more taxes than were required (which was how it became a lucrative profession). The prostitute changed by leaving bitterness behind and trusting God was on her side; as he sides with all marginalized women who are abandoned by husbands leaving them no certificate of divorce (without which they could never remarry) and with no immediate family to which to return. This would have been the situation of most, if not all, first-century Jewish prostitutes.

We learned a new spirituality recognizes the reign of God has nothing to do with religion. Religious people can access it, but not because they are religious, but rather in spite of it. The reign of God works in the world outside the walls of the church and religious edifices. It welcomes anyone who feeds the hungry, gives drink to the thirsty, welcomes the stranger, clothes the naked, cares for the sick, and visits the prisoners (Matt 25:34–36).

Inner Purity over Codes of Conduct

A new spirituality recognizes what really counts is interior purity of the heart, not outward religious practices or codes of conduct. A person with a loving, humble heart who never prays or goes to church or reads the Bible is as close or closer to God than the most religious person in the world. A person who drinks beer, smokes pot, and doesn't follow the traditional view of proper sexual conduct to the tee can be more "righteous" than the religiously arrogant. What counts is whether someone is living in a loving way, as to not harm others. When controlled substances or sex cross the line into harming oneself or others, they become "sin." When they don't, they are inconsequential. Inner purity doesn't require strict morality or a "religious" life.

In fact, it's possible that the more religious you are, the farther away you are from what God desires. Think Pharisees and the teachers of the law in Jesus' day. Their religion harmed others, as does the religion of much of fundamentalism and evangelicalism today (barring exceptions, of course). We were reminded of myriad cases of *spiritual abuse* by church leaders and members, no matter how well meaning, who focus more on obeying Scripture than loving people. This doesn't mean one must abandon prayer or church or studying the Bible, but rather put them in proper perspective. They are secondary. Jesus taught interior righteousness (a heart on the side of love, restoring relationships, and social justice) is what counts, not niggling legalism or moralism.

Orthopraxy over Orthodoxy

Orthopraxy is correct ethical conduct. *Orthodoxy* is what a church or movement considers correct belief or doctrine. We learned the former is worlds more important. A new spirituality places ethical conduct, which is different from religious conduct, as paramount. It may be interested in what is orthodox or right doctrine, but it doesn't marginalize people if they don't hold the same doctrine or creed. In this brand of spirituality, there is no room for calling people *heretics*. The greatest concern is over whether someone harms another human being in their conduct, not over what their doctrine or belief is. Again, this was the Way of Jesus and the earliest church before a rising institutional church began to call out people as *heretics* in the second century and before it became a full-blown paranoid occupation under Constantine, Augustine, and the later Western church. Even reformers like Calvin practiced a despicable form of heresy hunting.

A new spirituality focuses on conduct that loves our local and global neighbors. It does not need to be under the umbrella of a church or religious institution. One of the most revolutionary service organizations in the world, Rotary International, has this simple mandate: Service over Self. It is a purely secular organization with no religious or political affiliation. Its thirty-four thousand-plus clubs all over the world provide humanitarian services and help build goodwill and global peace while encouraging high ethical standards. I am honored to be a Rotarian and assist on some of the most cutting-edge, world community service projects conceived. Rotary International exemplifies a focus on ethical, humanitarian conduct. There is no need for orthodox, religious "doctrine." Ironically, its mandate of selfless service is the very core of Jesus' teaching.

There are countless other organizations like Rotary International that emulate ethical conduct and do things like fight poverty and injustice. A new spirituality, with an open mind, can embrace such organizations from the secular Amnesty International and the Bill and Melinda Gates Foundation to the faith-based World Vision and countless others in between. They strive to make a difference in the world by doing things that the historical Jesus Movement did, whether they hold to a formal faith or not.

Organic Community over Institutional "Church"

We learned that the roots of our modern Protestant churches and denominations and the Catholic Church did not stem from the earliest first-century gatherings of followers of Jesus but rather from pagan Greco-Roman practices and its hierarchal society. We realized that didn't make all modern churches necessarily bad, but it did make them *optional* for a new spirituality. It also showed us how problematic the modern church model is with a clergy/laity distinction, a professional class of religious leaders, suppression of women, and focus on church "authority" to keep people in line. Studying the history of the church and gaining knowledge of the widespread problem of church-related spiritual abuse taught us how easy it is for religious institutions to attract egomaniacal leaders, foster unquestioning members who enable those leaders, and protect their own reputation over caring for people.

It was clear that small-scale organic communities of spiritually like-minded people, although not mandatory, were a safer choice compared to church institutions. A new spirituality must rethink how best to form "Christian" community. For now, our informal discussion group, gatherings at pubs to talk about faith, and/or involvement in a service organization or project (whether secular or faith-based) where we could join others in *orthopraxy* seemed a wonderful alternative to church. Again, church is a legitimate choice for many people if it's not spiritually abusive. There is freedom to structure a spiritual community as a modern church institution. However, if one is honest about their historical roots, there needs to be acknowledgement that modern churches are not the only way to form Christian community and arguably not the ideal way. We need to welcome new models of Christian community like the one we discovered called The Refuge.

Dianne Butler Bass agrees that the pursuit of a new spirituality, or a new global awakening as she calls it, naturally occurs outside church walls. "The awakening is being performed in the networked world, where the border between sacred and secular has eroded and where the love of God and neighbor . . . is being staged far beyond conventional religious communities. Although churches seem the most natural space to perform spiritual awakening, the disconcerting reality is that many people in Western society see churches more as museums of religion than a sacred stage that dramatize the movement of God's spirit."[6]

6. Bass, *Christianity After Religion*, 258.

Common Grace over Individual Salvation

As evangelicals, we were taught that we were called to "evangelize"—to share the gospel of Jesus with the lost in hopes of them "accepting" Christ, believing in his "atonement," repenting from their sin, making him "Lord" of their life, and thereby getting "saved." To an evangelical, salvation may be a free gift in theory, but in practice it must be "received" and one must consciously follow and obey Christ to be in right standing with God. Otherwise, because of "original sin" and the lack of Christ's "substitutionary atonement" covering that sin, we are destined for judgment and eternal separation from God in hell. The "good news" becomes a fire insurance policy to keep us out of the flames.

It was also generally taught, in order to follow and obey Christ, one must be an active member or participant in a local evangelical "Bible-believing" church. So, for most, salvation was dependent on entering into some type of institutional church model that had the right doctrines. A Calvinistic model of salvation would be the same, but have the additional belief that God chooses who will ultimately be saved so that no one really has free will to choose salvation themselves. God does all the work leading someone to get "saved," so it is a true gift. At least for the ones he selects. The others are hopelessly lost.

Despite a few caveats like the notion that only God knows a person's heart and whether they have correctly responded to God's "gift" of salvation (which the theory says is possible right up until the time of death but not afterward), our *Timeline* study taught us how incredibly problematic these views of salvation are. First, are the moral dilemmas that make God out to be a masochistic monster (not a God of unconditional love), who creates humankind as depraved people (after the first generation) steeped in "original sin" destined to eternal conscious torment unless his sinless son is tortured on a Roman cross and each individual "repents" and "accepts" the "atonement" this brings. Moreover, they must continue in obedience to a Sacred Text and stay in good standing in an institutional church. This leaves the majority of the human race going to hell in a hand basket. Moreover, if you're a Calvinist, you're left with a God who consciously sends them to hell while claiming to be a God of love. Defenders of these views will say we don't understand the holiness and justice of God. Well, yeah! Which is why the problematic nature of traditional salvation leads people to reject modern Christianity. It doesn't make sense.[7]

But our historical study also provides the remaining nails in the coffin of these nonsensical theories of salvation. These views cannot be traced back to the original Path of Christ. They were never expounded until people like Augustine, Anselm, and Calvin formulated them. The Eastern Orthodox Church rejects them on both historical and theological grounds. These views are not derived from a fair, exegetical reading of the New Testament, its original language, and good history, but rather are read into the texts by people already steeped in them.

So, how does a new spirituality view salvation? It is not exclusivist. Jesus turned the world upside down; he didn't condemn the majority of it to an everlasting hell. Salvation is for the whole community and the world, not just select individuals. Prostitutes and tax collectors enter the reign of God before the religious Pharisees (Matt 21:31). But notice the Pharisees still enter. They just enter last while the prostitutes enter first. Judgment corrects and rehabilitates; it never gives up on people. The "day of judgment," whatever it is literally for any of us, does not last forever. It purifies and restores as fire purifies and refines. Salvation is the destiny of all of us. That is why we can extend love and forgiveness to everyone. This is common grace.

It's not that there's no such thing as individual experiences that feel like a spiritual rebirth, it's that those experiences are not necessary for ultimate connection with a loving God.

Restoration over Retribution

We had learned that judgment in the teaching of Jesus had a specific purpose in the here and now. He was not referring to the afterlife when he warned the religious elites and those who rejected his message of love and forgiveness for all, even enemies, that a time of "punishment" and "tribulation" was coming. It was not everlasting hell he was referring but the coming of Roman legions upon Jerusalem and the temple. He was a prophet, in this regard, in the spirit of the Old Testament prophets who predicted catastrophe if the people of Israel did not repent.

We were also reminded the purpose for judgment in the Old Testament and in Jesus' and Paul's teaching was restoration. "I will not accuse them forever, nor will I always be angry, for then they would faint away

7. A good case for this is Jersak, *A More Christlike God*.

because of me—the very people I have created," Isaiah had said (57:16–18). Paul said, "For God has bound everyone over to disobedience so that he may have mercy on them all" (Rom 11:32). Our study of the history of the theology known as Universal Reconciliation had revealed how the New Testament, most of the early church fathers, and many others throughout history had taught that ultimately, in the end, all of humankind would be reconnected with a God of love, who doesn't judge people for the purpose of eternal *retribution*, but rather for the purpose of personal *restoration*. The historical record was clear.[8]

A new spirituality based on historical reality must make restoration of relationships paramount, whether it's in our view of salvation or how to confront and punish evil and crime. We became convinced that the reason we have a need for things like prison reform and rethinking our criminal justice system—a call to focus on restoring and truly rehabilitating criminals rather than punishment for the sake of retribution—is because our society has bought into a retributive God who sends moral and spiritual criminals to eternal dungeons to rot away forever with no hope of future repentance, pardon, or parole. A new spirituality rejects this God of "justice" that ignores the original innocence of human beings made in the image of God, not to mention the teaching of Jesus on forgiveness that always leaves the door open for restoring relationships. Judgment has a purpose—to lead people to change and embrace the Way of love and mercy. Ironically, rescue from judgment is not possible until one changes and becomes merciful, says James, when he concludes, "mercy triumphs over judgment" (2:13). And yet the belief in the traditional view of an everlasting hell is the ultimate form of mercilessness. Residents of "hell" are not allowed, let alone encouraged, to repent of evil and receive mercy.

Personal Transformation over Religious Conformity

In the evangelical worldview, the purpose of life is to "get right with God" through faith in Christ's "work" on the cross that satisfies the legal requirement for divine punishment for being a depraved "sinner." Once right with God, our purpose is to obey God and discover some plan he has for our life which includes attempting to evangelize others to get right with God and do the same. More thoughtful versions of this include "sanctification" beyond salvation, where one becomes set apart from sin and set aside for

8. Stetson, *Christian Universalism*.

God's use, to evangelize and perhaps to care for the poor and needy in obedience to Christ.

Besides the problem with how salvation works, which we addressed above, the main problem with this view is that the typical measuring rod for whether one is truly "saved" or "sanctified" has more to do with religious conformity than having a true Christ-like nature. One's obedience to God or sanctification is measured in terms of what you believe, and too often, whether you are in good standing at a "Bible-believing" Christian church. Practicing gays and lesbians, people living together before marriage, unchurched people, sometimes divorced people, people of other religions, and anyone who doesn't believe in the infallibility of the Bible, the doctrine of hell, the deity of Christ, or other beliefs, are not considered "saved," let alone "sanctified," no matter how loving they are. In this mindset, a Jewish man can love God with all his heart, soul, and mind, and love his neighbor as himself, fulfilling Paul's admonition that "anyone who loves has fulfilled the law," but he is still condemned by fundamentalists for his lack of religious conformity to be recognizably "Christian" or a "Messianic Jew." A divorced Christian woman, who divorced her husband without "biblical basis," and hasn't "repented" of it because she sincerely believes she had good cause for divorce, e.g., ongoing attempts to address physical and/or emotional abuse, or emotional abandonment with no change—is also condemned even though she also loves God and neighbor. A lesbian couple who are committed to each other in a marriage relationship, don't attend church, consider themselves spiritual-but-not-religious, is also condemned despite their love for others and their humanitarian heart.

A new spirituality looks beyond religious conformity to encourage people in their own personal transformation with the goal of becoming a more loving person, irrespective of religious expectations. The purpose of life is to grow in love for our local and global neighbors (and ourselves), not to conform to religious codes or creeds. Since Christ is the prime example of love, the purpose of life, for those who recognize his uniqueness, is to become more like Christ. Not the Christ of modern churches or religious movements but the Jesus set in his own historical context who demonstrated a radical, nonviolent, egalitarian message of love and forgiveness, while opposing corruption and evil wherever it reared its ugly head, especially inside religion. For those who don't revere Christ in this way, a new spirituality states life's purpose as growing in a life of love. (I love the bumper sticker I saw recently, that said, "Love is our *soul* purpose.")

In our studies, we had learned that the Eastern Orthodox have a similar teaching called *theosis* or *deification* where human beings develop union with God or Christ so as to participate in the *divine nature*—in other words a nature of divine love. This is in no way a form of pantheism where people might be told to recognize their own intrinsic divinity. It is encouraging a union with God's energy rather than claiming a melding with his essence. It is a practice that recognizes the distinction between created beings and the being of God. The created human being is not equal with God. But we can have divine union with God and take on more and more of God's loving nature. Some non-Eastern Orthodox streams of Christianity teach this with different terms, like *sanctification*, as did C. S. Lewis,[9] and as do some evangelicals.

A new spirituality encourages spiritual transformation and union with God that leads to individuals participating more and more in God's or Christ's divine nature of love, forgiveness, and pursuit of social justice for all human beings. Whether one calls herself or himself a Christian or not, they can pursue union with God's loving energy, or Holy Spirit if you will, and become more like God. This union can manifest itself in many ways—by simply helping someone become a more caring, empathetic person, growing in love for partner or spouse or neighbor, or perhaps by transforming them into a courageous, human rights activist. This union also requires ongoing repentance and humility, or turning, toward a more Christ-like life when one recognizes they have fallen short (but without the excessive guilt some have over their supposed inherent, "depraved" sinful state).

A new spirituality sees Christ working beyond Christianity within people of other religions (even among ethical atheists), to bring love and restorative justice to the world. So, when Soaad Nofal, a woman Muslim schoolteacher from Syria, resisted ISIS brutality by leading hundreds of protesters in nonviolent, daily vigils outside ISIS headquarters in Raqqa, Syria[10] (that led to some anti-ISIS activists being released), she exhibited spiritual transformation or *theosis*. She became more like Christ standing up to religious corruption—just as much as a Christian might while meditating on the compassion of Christ and then reaching out to the oppressed.

9. Shuttleworth, "Theosis."

10. Stephan, "Resisting ISIS," 14.

Faith and Science over Religious or Secular Dogmatism

Theists Dr. Michael and Rhonda Jones are the hosts of an Internet show called *The Place.* I had the privilege of being on the show twice. What makes the show special is it welcomes both theists and atheists to engage in healthy, respectful conversation. It attracts anyone who is truly open-minded, whether one believes in God or not.

Religious or secular fundamentalists will struggle with this show because they are the ones who always have to try to convert another. A fundamentalist Christian sees the need to lead an atheist to Christ because they are "lost" (think "unclean") and the fundamentalist puts conversion above love for people. A fundamentalist Materialist sees the need to lead a theist to atheism[11] because theists are mentally lost (think "irrational" or "unclean") and the fundamentalist Materialist puts their own worldview above empathy for people. On *The Place*, both theists and atheists have learned to go beyond this and respect and understand one another.

Regular guest and former Christian fundamentalist Bob Greaves calls his former preaching "protected self-loathing." He understands how his former fearful fundamentalist self alienated atheists. He believes the mind-blowing Love he felt during a near-death experience extends to atheists and unbelieving scientists. Regular guest and biologist/atheist Greg Brahe understands the desire to believe "because I understand that death will come for us all, and that most of us have suffered the death of a person that we hold dear." He understands the desire for an afterlife where one "could see these people again." He would love to convince himself that these things are true, but can't, given he has not seen any compelling evidence in life and science. He admits he may be wrong, as Bob admits he was wrong in his past and hasn't arrived at absolute truth today. They both admit they really can't be 100 percent certain about their faith or lack of faith.

Together Bob and Greg represent a new understanding or *spirituality.* Where faith or lack of faith is respected and no one feels obligated to persuade others to believe the way they do. It is a place where love rules, not religion, whatever your spiritual or philosophical position. It is a place for honesty, where one is encouraged to follow where they see the evidence lead, to think for oneself, and not impose one's conclusions on another.

This is the way of a new spirituality where theists and atheists can love one another and drink beer together. Where science and faith can live

11. Harris, *Letter to a Christian Nation.*

either side by side or integrated, however one chooses, but where they are no longer at odds with each other.

As a theist who studies science, I am amazed at the gap between scientific Materialism and old-earth Creationism. These two sides of a life-origins continuum get most of the press. Many of the moderate voices in the middle are lost in the noise. Non-fundamentalist theists see science, particularly the fields of cosmology and microbiology, containing evidences that Materialism is hard pressed to explain all of life. They see pointers to a spiritual Mind behind the cosmos when they examine the extraordinary fitness for life of the universe and planet earth.[12] They read respected authors like philosopher and atheist Thomas Nagle of New York University, who argues (in his book *Mind and Cosmos*) against the neo-Darwinian view of the emergence of consciousness, thinks standard neo-Darwinism flies in the face of common sense,[13] and that the proponents of intelligent design theory and other skeptics of materialistic evolution should be taken seriously by the orthodox scientific community because they have uncovered real problems with the prevailing view. According to R. C. Henry, a physics and astronomy professor at Johns Hopkins University, the discovery of quantum mechanics logically leads to the conclusion that the universe is mental: "The stream of knowledge is heading toward a non-mechanical reality; the universe begins to look more like a great thought than like a great machine."[14] These voices are not calling for biblical Creationism or even theism, necessarily. They are calling to look where the evidence points, not force it into a predetermined religion, whether that religion is faith-based or science-based. A new spirituality is bolstered by these voices as it also recognizes that because life is still a mystery, theist and atheist need not mock each other. To disagree agreeably is enough.

A new spirituality would acknowledge that much of the theory of evolution is based on scientific evidence whereas old-earth Creationism ignores much of that evidence. On the other hand, it sees there just might be "a third way," as non-orthodox evolutionist James Shapiro argues, between Creationism and Darwinism, a process he calls "natural genetic engineering."[15] It understands that the origins of life, genetic information, and consciousness are still a mystery and that concepts like *intelligent*

12. Davies, *Goldilocks Enigma*.
13. Nagle, *Mind and Cosmos*, 5–6.
14. Henry, "Mental Universe."
15. Shapiro, "Third Way."

evolution,[16] *theistic evolution*, and other non-Darwinian explanations for the development of life (even purely naturalistic ones) are not necessarily a threat to sound, scientific inquiry nor belief in the Divine. Science has not ruled out God and the spiritual realm. A recent study indicates that most scientists are theists.[17] In fact, some scientific discoveries lend themselves to theistic explanations more than staunch materialists care to admit just as other discoveries don't fit like a glove into a theistic worldview more than staunch theists care to admit. A new spirituality sees the need for humility in the study of life origins.

Nonviolence over Militarism

Toward the end of our study of *The Timeline*, after we had delved into the Crusades, the Reformation (both not addressed in this book), and modern Christianity, we looked briefly at examples of movements that followed Jesus' ethics of nonviolent opposition in the face of evil. We were surprised how many of them there were. As we had already seen, Mahatma Gandhi and the nonviolent fight for India's independence and Martin Luther King's leadership in the civil rights movement were the most famous adherents of the last century. One night, we sat down with our food and drink to watch a DVD called *A Force More Powerful* and learned five other examples.

In 1940, Denmark stood up to Nazi occupation in a most extraordinary way. Rejecting militarism, they first used "resistance disguised as collaboration." In time, through noncooperation at factories (Nazis had taken them over to build war armaments and ships), acts of sabotage, and governmental stalling, they saved countless lives while opposing the Nazis at every turn. An underground resistance movement supplanted the Danish government that had eventually walked out on Nazi demands. Their indirect tactics and the compassion of the populace protected almost all of Denmark's seven thousand Jews from the holocaust.

In 1964, black college students in Nashville, Tennessee, organized nonviolent lunch counter sit-ins to fight racial segregation. Their tactics worked and became a model for the civil rights movement.

In 1980 in Poland, a young electrician name Lech Walesa cofounded a trade union called Solidarity and led a series of illegal workers' strikes in opposition to the reigning Communist Party. Their demands and nonviolent

16. Camp, *Confessions of a Bible Thumper*, 283.

17. Ruth, "Misconceptions of Science and Religion."

tactics prevailed as the communists eventually improved working conditions and allowed independent unions to flourish. A democracy movement grew and in 1989 Walesa was elected president of Poland in the first free election in over sixty years.

In 1983, in opposition to the military dictatorship of General Augusto Pinochet, Chilean workers began a series of nonviolent protests that eventually led to Pinochet's defeat.

Finally, in 1985, Mkhuseli Jack led a nonviolent consumer boycott that led to widespread awareness of black grievances and support for an end to apartheid. What's more, after Nelson Mandela became president of South Africa in 1994, although he rightly demanded justice for white South African crimes, he formulated a policy of reconciliation, refused to seek revenge, and paved the way for peace going forward.

These were examples of a new spirituality dealing with injustice through nonviolent means, which we saw as the hallmark of Jesus' teaching on how to confront evil. What struck us was how these strategies involve great sacrifice and the risk of imprisonment and loss of life the same way military strategies do, but how few lives were lost compared to war. Moreover, the long-term outcomes did not backfire as often happens with military solutions. Militarism, however our society decides when it is necessary, comes with the gravest risk of all—that our enemies will grow bitter over our retributive acts and collateral damage and return to fight us another day. Nonviolent opposition holds the promise of restoring enemies as new friends and not perpetuating cycles of violence and war. Today, new voices for pacifism and nonviolence among followers of Jesus, based on historical arguments, are gaining ground.[18]

Hopeful Future over End of the World

It was refreshing looking at the historical reasons for rejecting the traditional religious view of the end of our space-time world. Belief in the "end times," the return of Christ, and a final judgment that ends our physical stay on planet earth and ushers in a new age of the "kingdom of heaven" either makes people complacent to our current environmental and social challenges and/or instills fear in impressionable hearts that God is coming in judgment and we better be ready, or else. Why worry about climate change if God is going to wipe the celestial slate clean? Why work for global peace

18. John Deere, Stanley Hauerwas, Michael Hardin, Greg Boyd, and Preston Sprinkle.

if it's impossible to achieve until the final judgment weeds out evil and most of the human race?

The problem, we discovered, is the traditional view of the "end times" has no exegetical or historical basis. Not only are the extreme versions of it like the "rapture" (note the *Left Behind* books and the 2014 movie by the same name) absurd and bordering on comical (true believers are "raptured" up to heaven in an instant, resulting in unoccupied cars, boats, trains, and planes, and leaving behind unbelievers to deal with seven years of tribulation), it has absolutely no basis in reality.[19] None. Nadda. Zip. Even conservative theologians who are honest enough to look at the data have shown this,[20] whether they still hold out for some future return of Christ or not.

Our study of N. T. Wright and how the New Testament was formed confirmed our suspicions. The references to the "day of judgment" or the "wrath to come" or "the time of punishment" or the "punishment of the coming age" or "the wide gate of destruction" were not about hell or the final judgment but about Israel's looming national disaster on the horizon coming in the form of Roman legions destroying Jerusalem and the temple within one generation. The references to the "coming of the Son of Man on the clouds" and the return of Christ were Jewish cosmic imagery denoting an imminent massive socio-political change. And, it was likely a vindication that Jesus' way of peace and love for enemies (as opposed to the traditional wisdom of violent uprising and revolt) was right. N. T. Wright argues "coming on the clouds" is more accurately "going" into the presence of God in a symbolic way. The "last days" were the final days of the Old Covenant. The temple age was ending and the age of the "Anointed One," where the reign of God works mysteriously in society and transcends all religions and philosophies, including a future religion called Christianity, was about to begin. "A new heaven and new earth" was coming and the old one was passing away, not literally, but just like a good student of Jewish apocalyptic literature would interpret it, figuratively.

What's more, the controversial book of Revelation, from which most of the more dramatic and sensational end-times material comes, was rejected widely in the first centuries of the faith. Half the church ignored it. And understandingly so. As Frank Schaeffer is fond of saying, much of it reads like Jesus on acid. Today, the Eastern Orthodox Church has followed

19. Camp, *Confessions of a Bible Thumper*, 173–201.

20. See Sproul, *Last Days according to Jesus*; DeMar, *Last Days Madness*; Gentry, *Before Jerusalem Fell*; Russell, *Parousia: A Critical Inquiry*.

Martin Luther's recommendation and count it of secondary importance to the rest of Scripture (they don't use it in their liturgy).

When you strip away the sensationalism and look only at solid historical grounding and sound biblical scholarship, you're left with no "end times" at all. Shouldn't a new spirituality follow this path as well? If the Bible really doesn't teach with certitude what the future holds for planet earth, let alone that it will end in cataclysmic catastrophe, stemming from the outcome of some cosmic court room presided over by a retributive Judge, and if history confirms this, then the future of planet earth is a mystery, and for the time being, we just need to relax. Take a deep breath. Maybe drink a nice craft beer or two.

A new spirituality rejects unsubstantiated, unbiblical claims of the end of world with an angry Jesus returning to exact untold judgment and suffering on unbelievers. A new spirituality recognizes there is such a thing as judgment of evil, but for the purposes of reconciliation, not to send the guilty into oblivion at the end of the space-time world.

Given the teaching of Jesus on the reign of God and today's worldwide movement to overcome poverty and use business, social enterprise, and technology to do it, as well as to promote social justice, there is a bright, hopeful future for planet earth and humanity.[21] The reign of God is in our midst and continues to make headway in the world. Shouldn't that be what we focus on? As N. T. Wright suggests, perhaps the message is that whatever good we do here today will remain, so we can continue to work toward a better, more just, loving world with confidence it is not in vain. And, perhaps one day, heaven will come down to earth and the planet will be renewed.[22] This is what a *craft brewed Jesus*, a historically-ground one, taught his followers to pray and where a new spirituality points. I invite you to embrace it. And, answer this question: Where might a new spirituality take you?

21. Rosling, "Let My Dataset Change Your Mindset."

22. Wright, *Surprised by Hope*.

Chapter Twelve

Why Follow Jesus (Christianity Optional)

STARTING ABOUT THREE YEARS after my conversion to Christ within the evangelical movement, I started a faith shift. Over a period of twenty-plus years (very slowly for most of the time) I transformed from a typical evangelical believer to a "progressive" Christ follower. At the height of the shift, around 2005–2008, when the changes started to grow exponentially, my pendulum of faith swung very far to the left. This was the period of time that Kathy Escobar would call the "unraveling" stage.[1]

Although I never became an agnostic or atheist, I was angry and confused over two major areas: One, how the leading voices of the traditional conservative church made up of both evangelicals and fundamentalists, whether consciously or unconsciously, never tried to learn the historical facts about myriad issues; they appeared to cover up the truth about how the New Testament was compiled, how most biblical scholars approach the texts in a historical-critical manner with the historical/cultural context in mind, the many mistranslation issues, the real problems with the doctrines of inerrancy, hell, and the traditional view of sex and homosexuality, and the history of the prevalence of universalism, to name only a few.[2] It was like they lied to me. "Trust us. This is what the Scriptures teach," they said. But, anyone who looked under the hood and used a little common sense and consulted sound scholarship could tell you, "No, that's not exactly what the Scriptures teach." Most of us just didn't bother to look under the hood.

The second thing that bothered me was how so few of my evangelical friends seemed to care about these things. Who cares if "eternal punishment" is mistranslated? Or, it's impossible for that to be, so don't even consider it.

1. Escobar, *Faith Shift.*

2. Camp, *Confessions of a Bible Thumper.*

It was a don't-confuse-me-with-the-facts-I've-already-made-up-my-mind mentality. No one wanted to uncover what might be something closer to the mind of God and the original meaning of the New Testament. In other words, they appeared to care more about evangelical tradition than the truth of the historical Jesus Movement and even what the Bible really says. It was too controversial. It was too outside the box. It rocked the boat too much. When I didn't relent, I was criticized and deemed an apostate.

During this "unraveling" stage, I made many mistakes. I grew bitter. I lost patience with evangelical friends and family. I succumbed to something that much of America and its religious and secular institutions are locked into—an "us-vs.-them" mentality. But as I further evolved into a more stable and understanding "rebuilding" stage, I realized that at the end of the day, despite my philosophical and theological differences with evangelicals, we really are on the same team.

I believe my story represents one of the hallmarks of Jesus' teachings and the good news of the loving reign of God—that all of humanity, despite our cultural, economic, and religious differences, is really on the same team, whether people realize it or not. There is no "us vs. them." The sooner we recognize this and leave behind our us-vs.-them, fundamentalist ways, whether it's a conservative, progressive, liberal, New Age, or secular brand of fundamentalism, the sooner we can get on with the business of making the world a better place through the vehicle of love. Of course, many people will continue to treat others as "them fundamentalists," "them evangelicals," "them progressives," "them liberals," or "them heretics," but we don't have to share that attitude. (It's also prevalent in politics as we talk about "them Republicans" or "them Democrats.") We can uncover and challenge fundamentalist extreme views that harm others without looking down on or disparaging or hating people who hold such views. Frankly, I still struggle with this. It's easier to divide my world into neat boxes and demonize people who disagree or who I consider closed minded. But I'm convinced the former is the preferable way. At worst, "the other" is misguided. Extremists are brainwashed. We are all on a journey to find meaning and make sense of life and some of us lose our way. Although, we should challenge and confront anyone or any action that hurts other human beings, we need to do it with a dose of empathy and compassion.

This is one of the reasons I believe we should follow Jesus and his Path. The way of life he points us to leads to breaking down barriers and restoring estranged people. It comes with a price—the risk of persecution, danger, sacrifice, and even death when evil is confronted with the force of love (think Jesus, the apostles, Luther, Gandhi, Martin Luther King Jr., and Malala Yousafzai)—but it is well worth it.

And here's the rub. As we learned in *The Timeline*, following Jesus doesn't require one be a Christian the way we think of it. In other words, Christianity is optional.

In 1978, the late psychiatrist M. Scott Peck wrote a book that became widely popular, called *The Road Less Traveled*. Combining lessons learned in psychiatry and spirituality, Peck described four major attributes necessary to become a fulfilled human being. (1) Spiritual discipline (delayed gratification, personal responsibility, and pursuing and balancing "Truth"); (2) Actionable love for others and oneself; (3) Abandoning dysfunctional religion (not personal faith); and (4) Common grace (including the miracle of serendipity), a force that Peck believed originates outside human consciousness, that is, through God. The book became a best seller in 1984.

Because all four of these attributes are powerful "Christian" themes, some people thought Peck was hiding his Christianity in the book in order to subtly communicate a Christian message to readers. But Peck was not a Christian when he wrote that book. "I came to God through Zen Buddhism,"[3] he writes. It was a combination of his experiences with Zen, Islamic mysticism, and his study of psychiatry that led him to embrace these "Christian" themes. Peck believes, as I do, that people can come to God through a variety of ways and religions. That's because "God, unlike some organized religions, does not discriminate."[4] A loving God is not concerned with what institution or movement or medium is tapped. He or She works outside any religious boxes humans construct.[5] Peck discovered the essence of the path of Christ through Zen Buddhism and his own experience with modern psychology.

But Peck's Zen Buddhism was "just the first stretch of the road." Many people don't remember he later formally became a Christian (not the evangelical variety) after he wrote the book. He didn't think he could have come to Christ without his experience with Zen, he said, because Zen taught him about paradox, and he sees the way of Jesus as a path of embracing paradox. But why Christ? Because Peck came to believe that Jesus' life and love ethic (he calls it "Christian doctrine," but he's really talking about a spiritual path,

3. Peck, *Further Along*, 156.
4. Ibid., 155.
5. See Bass, *Grounded*.

not dogma) best approaches the reality of God and reality in general.[6] In other words, the path Jesus paved makes sense. He cites the genius of Jesus as one reason. He cites Jesus' understanding of the nature of sin as another. He's not talking about the doctrine of original sin or human depravity, but simply the truth that Christ pinpoints all humanity as missing the mark. We obviously don't always hit the bull's eye in our actions and behaviors. We're not perfect. In that sense, we are "sinners." But here's the paradox. In our God-image-bearing state, when we embrace humility and contrition when we've hurt others, we are also forgiven for missing the mark and given a clean slate. When we draw from within ourselves the attributes of that image-bearing state, we do hit the mark. We are also saints.

When Peck read the gospels for the first time he said he "discovered a man so incredibly real that no one could have made Him up."[7] Like many of us, Peck uncovered the pearls of wisdom in the New Testament that point us toward a new way to live. A way of life that shows us since we aren't perfect we need humility. That since others aren't perfect we need to learn to forgive them. That since the world isn't perfect, we need to correct it, but only after we correct ourselves. That since God is perfect love (unbiased, consistent, and sincere), we need to receive his love and then pass it on. And, that this way of living life can be pursued outside organized religion, even outside Christianity. Or pursued within any spiritual path or faith that has outgrown fundamentalism. Since Christ wasn't a Christian, we don't have to be.

Yet perhaps the world really would become a better place if people followed Jesus' way, if we recognized and embraced his genius. As Peck believed, when stripped of fundamentalist misinterpretations and misreadings, Jesus was arguably the wisest person who ever lived. (According to Peck, the second wisest is the twelfth-century Muslim mystic Jalalu'l-Din Rumi. And according to Marcus Borg, Buddha's wisdom was often on par with Jesus'.) And just like many of us might pay attention to wise people like Rumi and Buddha, whatever our religion or lack thereof, we should probably pay closer attention to Jesus—the Jesus of history. Not revisionist history. Not tainted history. But a craft brewed history that taps a truer-to-life *craft brewed Jesus.*

6. Ibid., 166.

7. Ibid., 160.

Bibliography

Alexander, Eben. *The Map of Heaven: How Science, Religion, and Ordinary People Are Proving the Afterlife*. New York: Simon & Schuster, 2014.

———. *Proof of Heaven: A Neurosurgeon's Journey into the Afterlife*. New York: Simon & Schuster, 2012.

Armstrong, Karen. *Fields of Blood: Religion and the History of Violence*. New York: Anchor, 2015.

Arnold, Robert Lloyd. *Orthodoxy Revisited: Contrasting the Faith and Practice of the Eastern Orthodox Church with Evangelical Doctrine*. Salisbury, MA: Regina Orthodox, 2005.

Bailey, Sarah Puliam. "How the 'Cussin' Pastor' Got into Megatrouble." *Wall Street Journal*, November 13, 2014. http://www.wsj.com/articles/sarah-pulliam-bailey-how-the-cussin-pastor-got-into-megatrouble-1415924941.

Bajis, Jordan. *Common Ground: An Introduction to Eastern Christianity for the American Christian*. Minneapolis: Light & Life, 2006.

Bakke, O. M. *When Children Became People*. Translated by Brian McNeil. Minneapolis: Fortress, 2005.

Barnes, Christopher. "The Brewing Monks: A Brief History of the Trappist Order and Monastic Brewing." *I Think about Belgian Beer* (blog). May 9, 2013. http://ithinkaboutbeer.com/2013/05/09/the-brewing-monks-a-brief-history-of-the-trappist-order-and-monastic-brewing.

Barnes, Ed. "Baptism: A Pre-Christian History." October 2005. http://www.bible.ca/ef/topical-baptism-a-prechristian-history.htm.

Bass, Diane Butler. *Christianity After Religion: The End of Church and the Birth of a New Spiritual Awakening*. New York: HarperOne, 2012.

———. *Grounded: Finding God in the World—A Spiritual Revolution*. New York: HarperOne, 2015.

———. *A People's History of Christianity: The Other Side of the Story*. New York: HarperOne, 2009.

Berghoef, Bryan. *Pub Theology: Beer, Conversation, and God*. Eugene, OR: Cascade, 2012.

Bernstein, James. *Which Came First: The Church or the New Testament?* Ben Lomond, CA: Conciliar, 1994.

Borg, Marcus. "Context: Social/Cultural World of Jesus." http://www.aportraitofjesus.org/social.shtml.

———. *Meeting Jesus Again for the First Time*. New York: HarperCollins, 1999.

Borg, Marcus, and N. T. Wright. *The Meaning of Jesus: Two Visions*. New York: HarperCollins, 1999.

Boyd, Greg A. *The Myth of a Christian Nation*. Grand Rapids: Zondervan, 2005.

Brodersen, Brian. "The Case for Big Change at Calvary Chapel." Interview by Timothy C. Morgan. *Christianity Today*, February 26, 2014. http://www.christianitytoday.com/ct/2014/february-web-only/change-calvary-chapel-chuck-smith.html.

Bromiley, Geoffrey W. *Theological Dictionary of the New Testament*. Abridged in 1 vol. Edited by Gerhard Kittel and Gerhard Friedrich. Grand Rapids: Eerdmans, 1985.

Bunge, Marcia J., and Terence E. Fretheim, eds. *The Child in the Bible*. Grand Rapids: Eerdmans, 2008.

Callison, Walter. *Divorce: A Gift of God's Love*. Leawood, KS: Leathers, 2002.

Camp, Michael. *Confessions of a Bible Thumper: My Homebrewed Quest for a Reasoned Faith*. Seattle: Engage Faith, 2012.

"Christmas Truce of 1914." *History.com*. http://www.history.com/topics/world-war-i/christmas-truce-of-1914.

Collins, Francis S. *The Language of God: A Scientist Presents Evidence for Belief*. New York: Free Press, 2006.

Cox, Harvey. *The Future of Faith*. New York: HarperCollins, 2009.

Davies, Paul. *The Goldilocks Enigma: Why Is the Universe Just Fit for Life?* New York: Mariner, 2006.

Dawkins, Richard. *The God Delusion*. Boston: Houghton Mifflin, 2006.

DeMar, Gary. *Last Days Madness: Obsession of the Modern Church*. Atlanta: American Vision, 1999.

Ehrman, Bart D. *Did Jesus Exist? The Historical Argument for Jesus of Nazareth*. New York: HarperOne, 2013.

———. *Jesus Interrupted: Revealing the Hidden Contradictions in the Bible (and Why We Don't Know about Them)*. New York: HarperOne, 2009.

———. *Lost Christianities: The Battles for Scripture and the Faiths We Never Knew*. New York: Oxford University Press, 2003.

———. *Misquoting Jesus: The Story behind Who Changed the Bible and Why*. New York: HarperOne, 2005.

Enns, Peter. *The Bible Tells Me So: Why Defending Scripture Has Made Us Unable to Read It*. New York: HarperOne, 2014.

Escobar, Kathy. *Faith Shift*. New York: Convergent, 2014.

Evans, Rachel Held. *Faith Unraveled: How a Girl Who Knew All the Answers Learned to Ask Questions*. Grand Rapids: Zondervan, 2010.

"Exodus International Shuts Down." *Huffington Post*, June 20, 2013. http://www.huffingtonpost.com/2013/06/20/exodus-international-shuts-down_n_3470911.html.

Fee, Gordon D. *The First Epistle to the Corinthians*. Rev. ed. Grand Rapids: Eerdmans, 2014.

Flew, Antony, and Roy Abraham Varghese. *There Is a God: How the World's Most Notorious Atheist Changed His Mind*. New York: HarperCollins, 2007.

Flood, Derek. *Disarming Scripture: Cherry-Picking Liberals, Violence-Loving Conservatives, and Why We All Need to Learn to Read the Bible Like Jesus Did*. San Francisco: Metanoia, 2014.

Francisco, Wendy. "Does God Really Hate Divorce?" *God's Word to Women* (website). http://www.godswordtowomen.org/francisco1.htm#Does_God_Really_Hate_Divorce.

Friedman, Richard Elliot. *Who Wrote the Bible?* New York: HarperCollins, 1987.

Gentry, Kenneth L., Jr. *Before Jerusalem Fell: Dating the Book of Revelation*. Powder Springs, GA: American Vision, 1998.

Grossman, Kathy Lynn. "Richard Dawkins to Atheist Rally: 'Show Contempt' for Faith." *USAToday*, March 24, 2012. http://content.usatoday.com/communities/Religion/post/2012/03/-atheists-richard-dawkins-reason-rally/1#.VG4Vm_nF_Po.

Gushee, David P. "Disputable Matters: Five Books That Are Changing the Evangelical Discussion about LGBT Christians and the Church." *Sojourners* 44 (2015) 23–25.

———. "Tackling the Hard Questions." *Sojourners* 44 (2015) 16–21.

Hadas-Lebel, Mireille. *Flavius Josephus: Eyewitness to Rome's First Century Conquest of Judea*. Translated by Richard Miller. New York: Macmillan, 1993.

Hanson, J. W. *Universalism: The Prevailing Doctrine of the Christian Church During Its First 500 Years*. Boston: Universalist, 1899.

Hanson, K. C. "The Galilean Fishing Economy and the Jesus Tradition." Originally published in *Biblical Theology Bulletin* 27 (1997) 99–111. http://www.kchanson.com/ARTICLES/fishing.html.

Hardin, Michael, and Lorri Hardin. *The Jesus Driven Life: Reconnecting Humanity with Jesus*. Lancaster, PA: JDL, 2013.

Harris, Sam. *Letter to a Christian Nation*. New York: Vintage, 2008.

Henry, R. C. "The Mental Universe" Nature 436:29 (2005).

Homan, Michael M. "Did the Ancient Israelites Drink Beer?" Biblical Archaeology Review 36:05 (2010) 49–51.

Instone-Brewer, David. *Divorce and Remarriage in the Church: Biblical Solutions for Pastoral Realities*. Downers Grove: InterVarsity, 2003.

Jenkins, Phillip. *Lost History of Christianity: The Thousand-Year Golden Age of the Church in the Middle East, Africa, and Asia—and How It Died*. New York: HarperOne, 2009.

Jersak, Bradley. *A More Christlike God: A More Beautiful Gospel*. Pasadena, CA: Plain Truth, 2015.

Josephus, Flavius. *The Jewish War*. Rev. ed. Translated by G. A. Williamson. New York: Penguin, 1970.

Kinnaman, David, and Gabe Lyons. *UnChristian: What a New Generation Really Thinks about Christianity . . . and Why It Matters*. Grand Rapids: Baker, 2007.

Lieuwen, Daniel F. "The Emergence of the New Testament Canon." http://www.orthodox.net/faq/canon.htm.

MacDonald, Gregory. *The Evangelical Universalist*. Eugene, OR: Cascade, 2006.

Melancon, Darla Hannah. *The Things I Learned After Being Kicked Out of Church*. Bloomington, IN: Author House, 2010.

Meyers, Robin. *The Underground Church: Reclaiming the Subversive Way of Jesus*. San Francisco: Jossey-Bass, 2012.

Monton, Bradley. *Seeking God in Science: An Atheist Defends Intelligent Design*. New York: Broadview, 2009.

Moriwaki, Lee. "Starbucks Ends Fight Over Name." *Seattle Times*, February 3, 1998. http://community.seattletimes.nwsource.com/archive/?date=19980203&slug=2732309.

Mykytiuk, Lawrence. "Archeology Confirms 50 Real People in the Bible." *Biblical Archaeology Review* 40 (2014) 42–50.

———. "Did Jesus Exist? Searching for Evidence beyond the Bible." *Biblical Archaeology Review* 41 (2015) 44–51.

Nagle, Thomas. *Mind and Cosmos: Why the Materialist Neo-Darwinian Conception of Nature Is Almost Certainly False*. New York: Oxford University Press, 2012.

Noll, Mark A. *The Scandal of the Evangelical Mind*. Grand Rapids: Eerdmans, 1994.

Noll, Mark A., et al. *In Search for Christian America*. Colorado Springs: Helmers & Howard, 1989.

Nyland, Ann. *The Source New Testament: With Extensive Notes on Greek Word Meaning*. Translation and notes by Dr. A. Nyland. Australia: Smith & Stirling, 2004.

Pagels, Elaine. "The Gospel of Thomas." In *Beyond Belief: The Secret Gospel of Thomas*, 401–30. Large print ed. New York: Random House, 2003.

Peck, M. Scott. *Further Along the Road Less Traveled. The Unending Journey toward Spiritual Growth*. New York: Simon & Schuster, 1993.

Porterfield, Jason. "40 Early Church Quotes on Violence, Enemy Love, and Patriotism." *Enemy Love* (website). http://enemylove.com/40-early-church-quotes-on-violence-enemy-love-patriotism.

Rosling, Hans. "Let My Dataset Change Your Mindset." TED Talk, June 2009. Video, 19:56. https://www.ted.com/talks/hans_rosling_at_state.

Ross, Allen. "The Priests: The High Priest." *Bible.org*, April 21, 2006. https://bible.org/seriespage/priests.

Russell, J. Stuart. *The Parousia: The New Testament Doctrine of Our Lord's Second Coming*. Grand Rapids: Baker, 1999. Originally published 1887.

Ruth, David. "Misconceptions of Science and Religion Found in New Study." Rice University News and Media. February 16, 2014. http://news.rice.edu/2014/02/16/misconceptions-of-science-and-religion-found-in-new-study.

Shanks, Hershel. Review of *Zealot*, by Reza Aslan. *Biblical Archeological Review* 39 (2013) 18.

Shapiro, James. "The Third Way: Evolution in the Era of Genomics and Epigenomics." http://www.thethirdwayofevolution.com.

Shore, John. "Betraying the Spirit: How the Christian Right Gets the Bible Wrong." *Huffington Post*, June 13, 2013. http://www.huffingtonpost.com/john-shore/betraying-the-spirit-bible_b_3430290.html.

Shuttleworth, Mark. "Theosis: Partaking of the Divine Nature." http://www.antiochian.org/content/theosis-partaking-divine-nature.

Simmons, Tracy. "Biblical Alternatives." *Spokesman-Review*, September 28, 2013. http://www.spokesman.com/stories/2013/sep/28/biblical-alternatives.

Smith, Christian. *The Bible Made Impossible: Why Biblicism Is Not a Truly Evangelical Reading of Scripture*. Grand Rapids: Brazos, 2012.

Sprinkle, Preston M. *Fight: A Christian Case for Non-Violence*. Colorado Springs: David C. Cook, 2013.

Sproul, R. C. *Last Days according to Jesus: When Did Jesus Say He Would Return?* Grand Rapids: Baker, 1998.

Stark, Rodney. *Cities of God: The Real Story of How Christianity Became an Urban Movement and Conquered Rome*. New York: HarperSanFrancisco 2006.

Stephan, Maria J. "Resisting ISIS." *Sojourners* 44 (2015) 14–16.

Stetson, Eric. *Christian Universalism: God's Good News for All People*. [Mobile, AL]: Sparkling Bay Books, 2008.

Symons, Barbara. *Escaping Christianity—Finding Christ*. Barbara Symons, 2014.

Talbott, Thomas B. *The Inescapable Love of God*. Eugene, OR: Cascade, 2014.

———. "The Theological Justification for Terror." http://www.thomastalbott.com/terror.php.

Throckmorton, Warren. "Mark Driscoll—Currently Unfit for Any Pulpit." http://wp.production.patheos.com/blogs/warrenthrockmorton/files/2015/05/HandoutGoldCreek.pdf.

Tippett, Krista. *Einstein's God: Conversations about Science and the Human Spirit*. New York: Penguin, 2010.

Todhunter, Andrew. "In the Footsteps of the Apostles." *National Geographic*, March 2012.

Vincent, Ken R. "The Salvation Conspiracy: How Hell Became Eternal." Article appeared in the July/August 2006 issue of the *Universalist Herald*. http://www.christianuniversalist.org/resources/articles/salvation-conspiracy.

Viola, Frank. "The Myth of Christian Leadership." July 17, 2012. http://frankviola.org/2012/07/17/christianleadership.

Viola, Frank, and George Barna. *Pagan Christianity? Exploring the Roots of Our Church Practices*. Ventura, CA: Barna, 2008.

Watanabe, Teresa. "No Doomsday Rapture for S. Korea Sect." *Los Angeles Times*, October 29, 1992. http://articles.latimes.com/1992-10-29/news/mn-925_1_south-korea.

White, Michael L. "The Essenes and the Dead Sea Scrolls." *PBS.org*. http://www.pbs.org/wgbh/pages/frontline/shows/religion/portrait/essenes.html.

———. "Jews and the Roman Empire: The First Revolt." *PBS.org*. http://www.pbs.org/wgbh/pages/frontline/shows/religion/portrait/jews.html.

Wills, Garry. *What Jesus Meant*. New York: Penguin, 2006.

———. *What the Gospels Meant*. New York: Penguin, 2009.

Wright, Bradley. "How Many Americans Are Evangelical Christians?" *Patheos*, March 28, 2013. http://www.patheos.com/blogs/blackwhiteandgray/2013/03/how-many-americans-are-evangelical-christians-born-again-christians.

Wright, N. T. *Jesus and the Victory of God*. Minneapolis: Fortress, 1996.

———. *The New Testament and the People of God*. Minneapolis: Fortress, 1992.

———. *Simply Good News*. New York: HarperOne, 2015.

———. *Surprised by Hope: Rethinking Heaven, the Resurrection, and the Mission of the Church*. New York: HarperOne, 2008.